Crisis Counsel

Navigating Legal and Communication Conflict

by Tony Jaques, PhD

Print – ISBN: 978-1-944480-65-3
EPUB – 978-1-944480-66-0
WEB PDF – 978-1-944480-67-7

ROTHSTEIN
PUBLISHING
A Division of Rothstein Associates Inc.

www.rothsteinpublishing.com

Print – ISBN: 978-1-944480-65-3
EPUB – 978-1-944480-66-0
WEB PDF – 978-1-944480-67-7
Library of Congress Control Number: 2020938672

ROTHSTEIN
PUBLISHING
A Division of Rothstein Associates Inc.

4 Arapaho Road
Brookfield, Connecticut 06804 USA
203.740.7400
info@rothstein.com
www.rothsteinpublishing.com

WHAT YOUR COLLEAGUES ARE SAYING ABOUT *CRISIS COUNSEL*

A must read for every enlightened CEO, Communication Specialist and Corporate Lawyer... should also be mandatory reading for every lawyer who advises on risk and liability, and every legal or communications student who has an eye on their future. **– Jeni Coutts LLB, Corporate Affairs Specialist, Australia**

Extremely useful to legal and communication professionals. Both will gain a better understanding of the other's viewpoint during a crisis. Senior executives will also benefit tremendously... Numerous cases of crises from around the world, interviews of global experts in crisis communication and senior legal practitioners... I highly recommend this book. **– Daniel Laufer, PhD, MBA, Associate Professor of Marketing, Victoria University of Wellington, New Zealand**

...Should be required reading for all the communications professionals who now add "crisis" to their websites, lawyers who venture into crisis advice, and quite frankly, anyone who wondered what it would be like to have to be a decision maker in a crisis rather than a critic. **– Richard Levick, Esq., Chairman & CEO, LEVICK, USA**

Inspiring from beginning to end. Exceptionally well written and very logically structured... everything is put so nicely into context. **– Esben Hostager, CEO, Hostager Solo, Denmark**

...Should be mandatory reading for senior managers who find themselves in the C-suite for the first time. Such specific legal and communications provocations are not covered in university management courses... replete with illuminating case studies and key takeaways... sage advice for Chief Executives who must ultimately make a decision based upon what they think is the right thing to do, often under pressure. Crisis team leaders and members will find this book equally of value. **– Jim Truscott, Director, Jim Truscott & Associates Pty Ltd, Australia**

A valuable resource for those responsible for risk, reputation, and organisational culture and strategy... provides insights and examples that will be greatly appreciated by CEOs, communication and legal professionals alike. – **Neil Green, Chief Executive, SenateSHJ New Zealand**

A wonderful book for legal and communication practitioners... rich with useful case studies and the thoughts of lawyers from around the world. A big strength is how it deals not just in process but also in relationships. A timely book, a must read for lawyers, communicators, executives, boards and others. – **Darren Behar, Managing Partner, Australia, SenateSHJ**

A critical resource for effective incident or issue communication. Pertinent case studies, provocative questions and clear guidance combine in this rich resource for communicators. A commitment to effective, accurate and timely communication shines through every page... Buy three copies of this book: one for you, one for your corporate attorney one for your CEO. – **Marc Mullen, President, Marc Mullen Crisis Communication Consulting, USA**

...The role of lawyers in crisis management has been neglected. If discussed at all, it is often in negative terms. Tony Jaques adjusts this picture in masterly, yet eminently readable terms. His comprehensive discussion of apology in crisis management is likely to be a go-to source for years to come... A welcome book for anyone interested in how crisis-confronted corporations (and other organizations) can navigate the tricky legal waters of communicating under fire... A rich source of well-researched case studies. A gem! – **Chris Galloway, PhD, Head of Public Relations, Massey University of New Zealand**

Provides riveting case studies and practical advice... highlights the financial and reputational risks of not effectively integrating communication and legal counsel... should be on every communication practitioner's reading list and companies should insist their legal counsellors read it. – **Noel Turnbull, Former Chair, Turnbull Porter Novelli, Australia**

I recommend that a leader facing major issues and crises read this book. You'll make better decisions if you do. – **Tony Langham, CEO, Lansons**

DEDICATION

Dedicated to the memory of my father Pat Jaques
1903-1980.

ACKNOWLEDGEMENTS

For data collection for Chapter Two, thanks to SenateSHJ and its PROI network partners, Lansons in the UK, The Vandiver Group in the US, and Brown & Cohen in Canada. Thanks also to the lawyers who contributed their expertise and insights.

FOREWORD by

DR. ROBERT HEATH

Tony Jaques is the right person to provide *Crisis Counsel: Navigating Legal and Communication Conflict*. The first evidence to support that claim comes early in the book when he compares the assessment provided by General Counsel and by the Communications Director following an explosion and chemical release at a manufacturing facility. Experienced readers will find the contrasting advice of these two archetypical individuals to be familiar. Readers who are novices in crisis response must mark that dramatic moment. It is a tug-of-war between two disciplines whose training and experience confront management with a difficult choice. Whose advice to follow?

Is the best advice to cautiously say little and challenge others to force the company to defend itself, a litigation model? Or should the company speak out to demonstrate that it cares and to protect its reputation, a mitigation model? Which advice should the management team adopt?

Readers will appreciate Jaques' selection of cases. Crisis communication is one of the most researched aspects of the public relations discipline today. A veteran quickly realizes that what a lot of research uses as its basis is at best a bad news day that will be gone tomorrow, leaving no tracks in the sand. Jaques makes the point that a true crisis can have lasting reputational and financial damage. It can pose response choices, none of which lead to optimal answers. Now, this is a serious topic!

Jaques' valued advice draws on his years of work with issues management. It helps him cut to the heart of threats. It helps him point out that crises are unsettled matters. How legal counsel and communication can work together to help such matters be settled to the satisfaction of various contexts, courts of law or public scrutiny.

His perspective on this topic evolves slowly, methodically. That helps readers to understand the fair-minded teamwork required for examining and addressing the many aspects of a crisis. Listing the array of crises which he features also allows other voices at the management table to come through. He notes that discipline specialists such as environmental engineers or technology experts provide insights and substance which move each crisis beyond being merely a "legal" crisis.

It takes a team to manage a company's response to a crisis. The challenge is to make the most of the expertise needed and available. Also, it is important to understand the presumptions that underpin professionals' training. Thus, team management needs to recognize collective expertise rather than presuming that a lawyer should lead crisis management.

A benefit of this book, (especially for junior practitioners, legal counsel, or students,) is the presentation of the roles communicators play in a crisis. The more the crisis team members know about each other's specialization, the better collaboration can occur. It can reduce stereotyped comments, such as telling the communications director "to make it go away." "Communication" is *not* a magic bullet.

Jaques emphasizes how both general counsel and communications directors need to know each other's roles, procedures and expertise. The cases featured do an excellent job of providing concrete illustration of Jaques' advice. Each offers ample information about timeframe differences between a "communication" response and a "legal" response to crisis. The public communication phase can last a few days and might recur as legal events recur. In fact, it is often the case that communication about a legal event, a trial or ruling, may require the presentation of historical detail so that individuals who have not monitored or even known about the crisis can put a trial or ruling into context.

The cases emphasize the need for "leadership," which includes helping to set agendas of various kinds. Leaders help set the tone of crisis response, often more inadvertent and less strategic than they might wish. Tone can be conciliating or provocative. Tone has legal as well as reputational implications. Tone can be street friendly or laden with legal jargon; both suggest the character of the company and its leaders.

Chapter 4 takes up the timeless topic of apology. Sorry, did I state that well? People in general, and some cultures more so than others, use apology routinely, ritualistically, even indifferently. As a rhetorical device, it is as ancient as the Golden Age of Greece, rhetorical apologia. Today, in social media, it can be expressed by emoji. Jaques poses both a reputational cost argument as well as common decency theme to guide the use of apology. I recommend the reader look at his "reasons for your organization to apologize" and ponder them until they become top of mind. Apology is best when it is mindful. It may be one element of crisis response, not the "only" element. But other elements may fail without a heartfelt and appropriate apology.

Jaques reasons that leaders need to know when and how to apologize. To that end, he recognizes the strategic advantage of critically, reflectively observing mistakes, but also notes the importance of recognizing "what was done well."

Throughout this book, and especially relevant to crisis, the topic of perception is persistent. Lots of do's and don'ts of media relations come down to strategies for influencing perception. It has a legal angle, as well as a communication one. Jaques' core advice is this: "perception of an organization during a crisis often has a far greater impact on reputation and recovery than the crisis itself." Reading that statement on a hot June day in Central Texas, I was reminded of a senior practitioner at a major utility company who contracted a misting company to cool down customers who were patiently waiting outside for rebates. The resulting headline was: "Utility company hoses customers."

Jaques emphasizes that what is said, how it is said, and where it is said counts, for better or worse. It may require, he adds, that spokespersons need the "capacity to communicate empathy as well as authority." On this matter, and many more, Jaques' rich reservoir of cases, lines, examples, and illustrations help fix key points into readers' minds. However good a spokesperson is, the total effort requires teamwork.

This book offers sound information and advice which can be consumed quickly. But, it also can be consumed slowly. It is provocative. Quick reading can help bring a novice up to speed, but slow reading with a fair amount of pondering involved gives the wisdom of years in the trenches time to penetrate the reader's judgment. Developing informed and ethical commonsense can be a slow and thoughtful process.

Chapter 8 brings the discussion of the previous chapters into focus and sets the scope and purpose of the chapters that follow by emphasizing the leadership need to do what's right: the balance of liability versus responsibility. Cases, quotations, best practices, and commonsense blossom into a coherent philosophy for responding to crisis in a collaborative manner. Jaques likes to provoke insightful pondering by asking questions such as "did the company do the right thing?"

I have known Tony Jaques for nearly two decades. I read his online commentary and have read other of his publications. I can hear his voice, and even know when his wit is adding an edge to his commentary or it is softening the blow. Reading his book reminds me of what I read not too long ago about aging: Young people remember names, dates, and myriad other facts; older people have to rely on wisdom gained by experience. Wisdom is more than knowing; it is recognizing the value of what one knows, and why it makes a difference.

This book impresses upon novices and reminds "experts" that crisis response demands preparation, planning, and collaborative response. Given the multidimensionality of crisis, response also needs to be multidimensional. Apropos to the theme of the book, and foretelling a successful career, Tony Jaques emphasizes the need for leadership navigation: *"lawyers and communicators need to respect each other's expertise and need to work better together in the interests of the whole organization."*

Dr. Robert Heath

Emeritus Professor of Communication
University of Houston
Jack J. Valenti School of Communication
Houston, Texas USA
July, 2020

FOREWORD by

HELIO FRED GARCIA

I have been a crisis advisor for more than 35 years and have taught crisis management and crisis communication in graduate business and professional schools for more than 30 years. I have advised lawyers and been hired through lawyers to advise our mutual clients. I have taught lawyers through bar associations and have trained individual lawyers in crisis management. And I have fought with lawyers; sometimes I have won those fights. And I have learned from lawyers.

A typical interaction is this: In the CEO's office the lawyer will give all the legal reasons to say as little as possible in the early phases of a crisis. The CEO will then look at me.

My reply, "I believe you have received excellent legal advice. And you should take it seriously. But please recognize that you don't have a legal problem, at least not yet. You have a business problem. And you need to make a business decision. You need to consider the risk of legal liability seriously. But not exclusively. You should also consider the consequences of the loss of trust of those who matter to you: your employees, customers, investors, regulators, and others. You can protect yourself from legal liability that will play out years from now but lose the company in the process. Or you can attend to the immediate needs and concerns of your stakeholders now, in ways that manage future legal liability."

It's very hard for the lawyers to object to that. I then offer, "Between self-defeating silence and self-destructive blabbering, there's lots of room to maneuver." I then ask the lawyer about categories of possible communication:

- Acknowledge: Can we acknowledge awareness of what has happened? The answer is usually Yes.
- Can we express empathy toward those who are affected? The lawyers usually say, Yes, but we need to be careful not to admit blame. My reply, Great. Let's do it carefully.
- Can we declare our values? We typically have them published on our website.
- Can we describe the overall approach we will take to address the crisis and resolve it? The lawyers usually say we need to be very careful. I again reply, Great. Let's do it carefully.
- Can we make some kind of commitment? How about a procedural commitment: We'll update you when we know more. Or a substantive commitment: We'll get to the bottom of this and fix it.

This often leads to the lawyers and communicators collaborating early in the crisis to find the balance. It doesn't need to be adversarial or either-or.

Tony Jaques has written a masterful guide to managing the natural tension between lawyers and communicators. *Crisis Counsel: Navigating Legal and Communication Conflict* is a highly readable guide to effective and respectful interaction among lawyers, communicators, and business leaders. He helps us understand the mindset of lawyers and the mindset of communicators, and how leaders can exercise good decision skills. He includes a wealth of real-world examples of well and poorly handled crises from around the world and across forms of organization. It contains both wisdom and practical tools for responding effectively in a crisis. And he quotes a wide range of crisis experts (full disclosure: including me).

This is an important contribution to our understanding of crises, leadership, and decision-making. It's the kind of book I wish I had been able to read when I was just starting in crisis decades ago. And it is a valuable book for lawyers, communicators, and leaders in all sectors.

Helio Fred Garcia

New York City

July, 2020

Helio Fred Garcia is the president of the crisis firm Logos Consulting Group. He teaches crisis, leadership, ethics, and communication at New York University and Columbia University. He is the author of five books, including The Agony of Decision: Mental Readiness and Leadership in a Crisis.

FOREWORD by

Tony Langham

As the world has grappled with coronavirus and the resulting economic crisis, reputation has been the key word in the board rooms of major corporations and the inner circles of government. We're discovering if people trust their Government enough to do what it asks them to. We're going to find out which major brands emerge from the crisis with their reputations intact and which leave a bad taste in the mouth.

In March 2020 Warren Buffet called on American Express, in which his company is the largest shareholder, to protect its reputation during the pandemic because "the brand is special."

At a shareholder meeting in May, Amazon boss Jeff Bezos was asked if the increased scrutiny the business was under would harm its reputation with customers, to which he replied that the increased scrutiny would enhance its reputation with customers.

Reputation is, according to American academic and author John Doorley, an assessment of performance, behaviour and communication, underpinned by an assessment of an organisation's authenticity. Most of us working in consultancy and advising on reputation believe that having a clear purpose and real values – and living by those values – is vital to long-term success.

Yet in 2020, we see unresolved reputational crises all over the world. Insurers are arguing over paying business interruption claims to small businesses. Travel operators are fighting to not give back money for cancelled holidays. Major corporations are being challenged over the honesty and fairness of major redundancy programmes.

Across the world, senior leadership teams are having to balance doing the right thing for their customers and staff with limiting legal liability and maximising shareholder returns. The issues at the heart of this excellent book are being played out in board rooms all over the world. CEOs are being faced with sometimes conflicting advice from legal counsel and communication counsel.

I was introduced to Tony Jaques by our friends at SenateSHJ and Lansons was delighted to help with the interviews with lawyers for chapter two of this book. As Tony highlights, the relationships between communication specialists and lawyers are rarely confrontational and are rarely straightforward. Even the words we use cross over. Reputation management is a term used equally by law firms and communications consultancies. In my work, I describe myself as a specialist in managing reputations and will often work alongside a lawyer who says the same thing – but the skills we bring and the advice we give can be very different.

The key to success for the modern CEO in times of crisis is to blend different expertise, which in turn makes it easier to get the big calls right. Tony's book uses real examples and his own experience to help this process. I would recommend that a leader facing major issues and crises read this book. You'll make better decisions if you do.

Tony Langham

London, United Kingdom

July, 2020

Tony Langham is Chief Executive of Lansons, based in London and New York and the author of Reputation Management: The Future of Corporate Communications and Public Relations.

CONTENTS

Introduction

Managing Conflicting Advice, and Why It's Important

A decision is the action an executive must take when he has information so incomplete that the answer does not suggest itself.

US Admiral Arthur W. Radford

It's 2.00 am on a very cold morning and the telephone wakes me up. Working as an issue and crisis manager in the chemical industry, late night calls are never good news, and this is no exception.

There has been an explosion and chemical release at the plant and two night-shift operators were exposed to some toxic material.

I am only half-awake and start to get back into bed when my wife jerks me back to reality: "Hey, what was that all about." So I get dressed and drive off through the eerily-empty streets.

I arrive at the plant 20 minutes later to a worrying scene. The two operators are sitting in the control room shivering from shock and from having stood in the cold under the industrial decontamination showers. They are huddling under blankets to keep warm and are giving their explanation of what happened.

The fire brigade are on hand because they were automatically called when the deluge system was activated to knock down the release. Tons of firewater is flooding across the site and pouring into stormwater retention ponds. We know the local media monitor the police and emergency radio, so it won't be long before reporters and TV cameras are on the scene.

The engineer says production will be shut down for months and might never reopen. He predicts – correctly as it turns out – that the government will instigate a full-scale inquiry into the incident.

It has all the makings of a major financial and reputational crisis, and it's a somber group of managers who gather in the Board Room at 3.00 am to decide what to do.

How this crisis was managed, and its long-term aftermath, is a story for another occasion. The two operators were ok and there was no lasting environmental impact. But I did not realize at the time this would become the most complex crisis issue I would ever deal with.

While the crisis circumstances may differ for you, the urgent meeting in the Board Room is a familiar scenario played out in organizations everywhere.

The Crisis Management Team has assembled, and your CEO asks each person to present their assessment.

The Operations Director, Sales Manager, Chief Accountant, HR Manager, Production Manager and others chime in with their thoughts. All goes smoothly until it comes to the General Counsel and Communications Director.

The corporate lawyer recommends saying as little as possible and waiting until the full facts are known to avoid compromising any future litigation. The communicator wants to proactively speak out to demonstrate that the company cares and to protect reputation.

Now the CEO and executive must weigh the legal and communications positions along with other inputs, and your concern is to make an urgent decision at a time of great risk and uncertainty.

This book is about the factors which drive that disparity of advice and how you can help to develop a response – in the pressure-cooker environment of a crisis – which assesses competing counsel and navigates between what's legally right and what's right in the long-term interests of your organization and its stakeholders, and ultimately your reputation

My objective is not to favor one type of professional counsel over the other, but to support a workable and sustainable balance between legitimate differences, and to help you make the right decisions.

The book will help you to:

- Balance reputation protection and legal obligation during a crisis.
- Know why and how to apologize without increasing liability.
- Weigh legal and communications advice when a crisis strikes.
- Learn from original research which lets lawyers and communicators speak in their own words.
- Draw practical, everyday lessons from real-world examples of conflict between lawyers and communicators.
- Navigate the legal and communication challenges of dealing with the media in a crisis.
- Motivate lawyers and communicators to work better together.
- Identify and avoid crucial areas of potential conflict from selected crisis case studies.
- Understand the essential difference between corporate responsibility and legal liability.
- Make decisions and do the right thing to protect your organization.

If you haven't lived through a genuine organizational crisis it's not easy to appreciate the intensity of the situation. In one crisis where I was the communications focal point during a national transport strike, I was at my desk almost continuously for a week with only brief breaks to go home for a shower and a change of clothes, plus a snatch of sleep. That experience helped me understand how physical and mental exhaustion can threaten the effectiveness of the executive group. Add to that the modern expectation of being on-call 24/7 and you can imagine the pressure.

Furthermore, being personally involved in managing a genuine crisis helps you really appreciate what might be at stake. A serious crisis – either well or badly managed – can create reputational or financial damage from which your organization might never recover. One study of crises across a ten-year period in Australia found that more than a quarter saw direct costs associated with the crisis exceed AUD$100 million. One in four of the organizations concerned went out of business or ceased to exist in their previous form.[1] A one in four chance you won't survive surely is reason enough to get it right!

The potential impact of a crisis

The *Economist Magazine* examined the impact of crises which struck eight major corporations (worth over $15 billion) from 2010 to 2018 and the median share price fell by 33 percent. While most clawed back their absolute losses, compared with a basket of industry peers over the same time period the median firm was worth 30 per cent less in 2018 than it would have been without the crisis, a total deficit of $300 billion across the eight companies.[2]

A survey of 685 business leaders from Fortune 1000 firms found they believed it would take

[1] Coleman, L. (2004). The Frequency and Cost of Corporate Crises. *Journal of Contingencies and Crisis Management, 12*(1), 2-13.
[2] Getting a handle on a scandal (2018, March 28). *The Economist.* https://www.economist.com/business/2018/03/28/getting-a-handle-on-a-scandal

> more than four years to recover from a crisis which damaged an organization's reputation, and three years for a crisis to fade from the memory of most stakeholders.[3]
>
> And an international law firm analyzed major reputational crises around the world and found that in companies unable to recover pre-crisis share value, 15 per cent of senior executives left within a year, compared with a departure rate of just four per cent in companies where share value did recover.[4]

The wider impacts of a crisis were neatly captured by American communications practitioner David Weiner:

> *"Few circumstances test a company's reputation or competency as severely as a crisis. Whether the impact is immediate or sustained over months and years, a crisis affects stakeholders within and outside of the company. Customers cancel orders. Employees raise questions. Directors are questioned. Shareholders get antsy. Competitors sense opportunity. Governments and regulators come knocking. Interest groups smell blood. Lawyers are not far behind."* [5]

---

[3] Burson Marsteller study cited in Burke, R. J. (2016). Corporate reputations: Development, Maintenance, change and repair, in R. J. Burke, G. Martin & C. L. Cooper (Eds) *Corporate Reputations: Managing opportunities and threats* (pp 3-44) London: Routledge.

[4] *Rogue employees and company misconduct spook markets most* (2012, December 3). London:, Freshfields Bruckhaus Deringer. http://news.freshfields.com/en/Global/r/2492/rogue_employees_and_company_misconduct_spook_markets_most

[5] Weiner, D. (2006). Crisis communications: Managing corporation reputation in the court of public opinion. *Ivey Business Journal, 70*(4), 1–6.

In the face of such pressure, my experience is that some organizations appear to have a default position to defer to legal counsel. That way, they argue, management can always claim to have pursued "good governance," irrespective of the outcome and irrespective of the values of the organization.

Yet at the same time it's become almost a cliché that a controversial legal decision may allow you to "win in the court of law and still lose disastrously in the court of public opinion."

That statement's true, but it's not very helpful or constructive. Plus, it doesn't really lead anywhere.

I think it's much more useful to consider *why* you can win in the court of law yet still lose in the court of public opinion; *what* that means in real-life situations; and, *how* you can address this important challenge.

While commentators and experts often *talk* about the contrast between the court of law and the court of public opinion, in this book we will honestly examine that paradox and provide case studies and practical advice on how to protect what may be your most valuable uninsured asset – your reputation.

Do you know what's at risk?

Nothing destroys reputation faster or deeper than a crisis or an issue mismanaged. And the value of reputation can be enormous.

The latest research as of 2019 across the world's top 15 stock market indices, shows corporate reputation accounted for 35.3 per cent of total capitalization, representing $16.77 trillion in shareholder value. Out in front was the UK's FTSE 100, which saw reputational factors contribute 47 per cent to overall market capitalization.[6]

---

[6] Cole, S. (2019). What price reputation: Corporate Reputation value drivers. AMO Strategic Advisors.
http://www.reputationdividend.com/files/6415/6215/6989/RD_AMO_GLOBAL_REP_VALUE_030719.pdf

> Some major global corporations, such as Unilever, BP and Shell, run at well over 50 percent.[7] In fact 40 to 60 percent, depending on business sector, is a commonly accepted range for reputation as a share of market value. That's what may be at risk.

Remember that reputation reflects the cumulative opinion of stakeholders about your organization's products and services and how you behave – not lay-people's opinions about how your organization may have interpreted the technical niceties of the law in the heat of a crisis. In other words, just because you can take a legalistic position doesn't mean you should.

There can in fact be a massive chasm between what's legally correct and what's accepted as morally or ethically right.

A stark example is what happened following the death of four people on a malfunctioning Water Rapids ride at the Dreamworld theme park on Australia's Gold Coast in October 2016. Just two days later, at the Annual General Meeting AGM of the parent company, Ardent Leisure, the Board approved a short-term cash bonus of $AUD167,500 for the Dreamworld CEO (equivalent to about US$100,000). In the face of massive public outcry, the Chairman said the CEO was entitled to the bonus, and that he wouldn't discuss it further as it was a commercial matter.[8]

It might have been legal, and it may well have been related to the previous year's financial performance as the Chairman emphasized, but it was reputational poison. The CEO herself recognized the difference and donated her entire bonus

---

[7] Cole, S. (2020). The UK 2020 Reputation Dividend Report. Reputation Dividend. http://reputationdividend.com/files/7515/8263/1192/UK_2020_RD_report_FINAL.pdf

[8] Pash, C. (2018, October 28). The CEO, her bonus and the Dreamworld tragedy. *Business Insider.* https://www.businessinsider.com.au/the-ceo-her-bonus-and-the-dreamworld-tragedy-2016-10

to the Red Cross to support the families affected by the tragedy. Eight months after the accident she left the company with a payment of a full year's salary.[9]

It was publicly reported that at a fiery meeting with the Board, the company's external communication consultants had fiercely disagreed with the legalistic response to the crisis and threatened to resign the account, but were over-ruled.[10] (In February 2020 a coronial inquiry into the disaster found there had been a "systemic failure by Dreamworld in relation to all aspects of safety" and the parent company was referred for possible prosecution.[11])

Such examples highlight the gap between a purely legal strategy and a strategy to address prevailing community standards.

Courts apply the law and it's up to politicians to make the law reflect what is perceived as community standards – what people think is right or how people believe organizations *should* behave. Similarly, legal counsel in a crisis can advise management on what the law provides, and the communications professional can advise on likely stakeholder response and the impact on reputation. Between them they should provide management with accurate information and sound advice to make a proper decision.

Consider this hypothetical scenario:

A bank's General Counsel has been asked to advise on the proposed foreclosure of a mortgaged property. The mortgage-holder has not made a payment in more than ten months and all discretionary periods have expired.

---

[9] Kruger, C. (2017, June 12). Ardent Leisure CEO Deborah Thomas to exit with a $731,000 payout. *Sydney Morning Herald*. https://www.smh.com.au/business/ardent-leisure-chief-ceo-deborah-thomas-to-exit-with-a-731000-payout-20170607-gwmclp.html

[10] Markson, S. (2016, October 28). Crisis of confidence in Dreamworld board. *The Australian*. https://www.theaustralian.com.au/news/nation/crisis-of-confidence-in-dreamworld-board/news-story/b5ace6efc84b7190b07e22df361cc432

[11] McKenna, K. (2020, February 24). Dreamworld Thunder River Rapids accident inquest findings handed down by coroner. *ABC News*. https://www.abc.net.au/news/2020-02-24/dreamworld-accident-inquest-coroner-findings/11993742

> *"I have reviewed all the processes and formal notifications and the bank has fully complied with our legal requirements and correctly applied the hardship provisions. In my legal opinion we should proceed to foreclose on the property."*

However, the bank's Communications Director has also been asked to review the same situation.

> *"The mortgage-holder is an Iraq war veteran who lost a leg and was partly blinded by an improvised roadside bomb. He is the sole support for his autistic daughter after his wife left him, and he can't get paid work. We know from regular media monitoring that his story has already been taken up by the Association of Iraq and Afghan War Veterans and has generated sympathetic support. Unless we want to feature in the news throwing this man and his daughter out on the street, in my opinion we need to find a way to negotiate a better outcome."*

Over to you Mr. or Ms. Senior Executive. It's your call!

Or take a real-life case, when Nestlé, the world's largest food company, launched legal proceedings in the early 2000s to recover £3.7 million (about US$4.5 million) from the Government of Ethiopia during a terrible famine. [12] The claim was compensation for assets seized 25 years earlier, and Ethiopia offered £926,000, (US$1.1million) which Nestlé declined "as a matter of principle" (although the company said any money received would be channeled into famine relief in Ethiopia). Threatened by a coordinated international campaign of protest, Nestlé eventually announced it would drop the claim.

A leading British finance journal reported at the time:

> *"There may well have been strong legal arguments for suing the Ethiopian Government, but this course*

---

[12] Denny, C. (2003, January 23). Nestlé U-turn on Ethiopia debt. *The Guardian.* https://www.theguardian.com/world/2003/jan/24/debtrelief.development

of action is obviously going to have a negative PR aspect once it becomes public knowledge. Too often companies are dominated by lawyers and accountants who, while happy to stick to the letter of the law, seem oblivious of the complex human issues involved in situations like these."[13]

My hypothetical mortgage foreclosure scenario, and the real-life cases involving Nestlé and Dreamworld, have one critical element in common, namely that in the end someone needs to assess conflicting priorities and make a decision. And sometimes you will also need to publicly explain or justify the position your organization takes. In the Nestlé case the Swiss food giant claimed it was "taken by surprise" and said the original decision to pursue compensation was made by an external lawyer hired by a small subsidiary in Germany. Unfortunately, justification often turns out to be finding someone else to blame. In Chapter Three you'll read about some other high-profile brand crises and how legal action can sometimes inadvertently damage brand reputation.

The difficulty of reaching a decision over contradictory advice and conflicting demands is hardly new. It's an issue identified over 200 years ago by the British statesman and philosopher Edmund Burke: "It's not what a lawyer tells me I may do, but what humanity, reason and justice tell me I ought to do."

In modern times this purpose is reflected in the well-established discipline of Enterprise Risk Management, which concerns the need to consider and balance all risks and not allow one to take unwarranted priority over the others. Or the more recent disciplines of Corporate Social Responsibility, and the Triple Bottom Line, which both set out the need to address social and environmental impacts as well as just the business objectives. It's nothing new that balancing competing needs is often central to executive decision-making.

Exactly the same considerations apply when it comes to crisis management, as illustrated in my three reputational crisis scenarios. Most importantly, it also reflects the fundamental requirement which I identified when developing my

---

[13] Piggott, C. (2003, February 2). No point in hiding. *Foreign Direct Investment Magazine*

concept of *Crisis Proofing*.[14] That idea focuses on the need not just to respond to crises when they strike, but on the expectation that you need to identify and address potential issues and problems early in a way most likely to avoid them developing into crises.

While this book talks about how organizations respond *after* a crisis strikes, it also highlights my favorite original advice to clients: *The best possible form of crisis management is to take planned, positive steps to avoid a crisis occurring in the first place.*

It's this link – the need to identify and address issues in the best long-term interests of the organization as a whole in order to avoid crises – which forms the foundation of *Crisis Counsel: Navigating Legal and Communication Conflict,* and the task of balancing communications and legal advice.

> Whether a company survives a crisis with its reputation, operations and financial condition intact is determined less by the severity of the crisis – the underlying event – than by the timeliness and quality of its response to the crisis.
>
> John Doorley and Helio Fred Garcia[15]

Structure

The book includes chapters on the respective roles of communication and legal professionals, focusing on where they intercept, overlap and sometimes conflict; as well as the crucial difference between legal liability and corporate responsibility; the legal and communication challenges of dealing with the media in the event of a crisis; and two chapters on the highly contentious issue of why, when and how to apologize.

---

[14] Jaques, T. (2016). *Crisis Proofing: How to save your company from disaster.* Melbourne: Oxford University Press
[15] Doorley, J. & Garcia, H. F. (2007*). Reputation management: The key to successful public relations and corporate communication.* New York: Routledge.

Each chapter addresses the role of senior management and the need for a balanced approach when a crisis threatens. Chapter eleven reviews the issues and summarizes practical ways forward for you as a busy executive.

This need for balance is also addressed in two chapters which share the views of the two professions at the heart of the book – namely communicators and lawyers.

I interviewed four global experts in crisis communication – two in the United States, one in England and one in South Africa – about their experiences working with lawyers in a crisis situation and their recommendations to obtain the best possible outcomes for organizations under threat.

In addition, in partnership with SenateSHJ, a reputation and change communication consultancy based in Australia and New Zealand, along with their international partners in PROI Worldwide, we interviewed senior legal practitioners in the United States, Britain, Canada, Australia and New Zealand to understand the legal view of potential conflict with communicators and how executives can balance conflicting advice. While there is some general literature on the role of lawyers in a crisis, this unique research is the first ever study to specifically address the legal/communication interface from the perspective of practicing lawyers.

Taking the lead from lawyers, who rely so often on precedent and case law, this book frequently refers to past cases where communications and legal advice may have been in conflict.

Apart from cases scattered throughout the book – and description of lessons to be learned – I have written three chapters devoted entirely to more in-depth assessment of high-profile examples which illustrate potential conflict and sometimes the reputational damage which followed. Those three chapters explore

- **Trademark and patent cases** in defense of intangible assets where legal advice may outweigh a broader management approach.
- **Product cases** where over-zealous or misguided legal action can backfire on the brand.
- **Marathon cases** which involve prolonged proceedings where the public sometimes forget what the case was about while a steady flow of negative media continues to create long-term damage to companies and brands.

Some of the cases referenced in the book are recent and some are from earlier decades. But as every law student knows, the value of citing a case is not when it occurred, but how the case applies to the present. Let's not forget that as recently as March 2019 the Speaker of the British House of Commons made a crucial and controversial decision in the Brexit debate based on a parliamentary convention dating back over 400 years to 1604. And, of course, so much contemporary American law relies on the consensus of white men in wigs who sat down to devise the Constitution for the United States between May and September 1787. What's important is not how long ago the case emerged but the fact that every example here has been chosen to make a point or offer a perspective which is relevant to you today.

> *The value of citing a case is not when it occurred, but how the case applies to the present.*

Apart from recency and relevance, remember that while some of the case examples presented in this book may portray one or the other side in a negative light, we usually don't know what happened behind the closed doors of the board room. Accordingly, we can only infer conclusions from what has appeared in the media or in open court, in other words, what was done, said or reported publicly.

There is a generous catalogue of T-shirt slogans, memes and inspirational posters warning against judging people by their actions without understanding their motivations. But when it comes to assessing corporate responses to a crisis or potential crisis, we most often don't know – and have no way of knowing – what prior discussion took place.

Sigmund Freud said, "The thought is father to the deed," so you can reasonably assume that corporate decisions in a crisis, as they appear in public, ought to reflect conscious decision-making by rational executives. But of course rational doesn't necessarily mean smart.

Was good legal advice provided and then overruled? Did the executive go along with recommendations which proved to be damaging? Did bad communications advice reflect information or circumstances which never became public? Did the executive simply ignore advice from all quarters? In most cases we'll never know for sure.

The other key point about such cases is that my commentary should not in any way be construed as a blanket criticism of lawyers or communicators or any other group. The purpose of all the cases discussed is not to blindly judge those who may have provided counsel, but to illustrate how crises can turn out well or turn out badly, and hopefully help you and your organization to learn from what's happened before. My intention is not to needlessly criticize any particular profession or any directly named organization, but to help you and professionals everywhere to understand the issues and make better decisions.

Throughout this book I have used the term communicator, or communications professional, to refer to the full range of professionals working in organizational communication. This includes public relations, public affairs, issue management, crisis management, corporate affairs, community relations, stakeholder engagement, government affairs, media management and the host of other terms which have become common.

Similarly, the generic term lawyer is taken to include attorneys, barristers, solicitors, advocates, counsel and all other legal advisers.

Neither term should be taken as exclusive. The principles and challenges remain the same regardless of job title.

Key Takeaways

- There can be a big gap between what's legally correct and what's morally or ethically right.
- Reputation may be your most valuable uninsured asset.
- In the face of a crisis you need practical methods to weigh potentially conflicting advice.
- Uncertainty and stress in a crisis make decision-making more difficult.
- Past crisis case examples involving legal and communications elements provide valuable insights for you today.
- The best possible form of crisis management is to take planned, positive steps to avoid a crisis occurring in the first place.

Disclaimer: **The author is not a lawyer and nothing written in this book should be interpreted as legal advice.**

Chapter One

Roles and Responsibilities: Who Does What in a Crisis?

"The person who knows HOW will always have a job. The person who knows WHY will always be his boss."

Alanis Morissette

Despite what some commentators assert, it is simply not true that lawyers and corporate communicators are natural enemies. Nor are they inherently in conflict, destined to always disagree.

The reality is they are two groups of professionals, working on the same team and trying to do what they believe is in its best interests.

But as President Lyndon Johnson is reported to have said: "When you're the leader of the free world it's not difficult to do the right thing. The difficulty is knowing what *is* the right thing to do."

Nor is this an issue of who is "in charge." If that was the response then it's the wrong question. My concern here is *not* about who is "in charge." It's about how lawyers and communicators can manage their differences and provide the best possible advice to decision-makers.

This chapter will help you to:

- Differentiate between the roles of lawyers and communicators.
- Identify and manage situations where legal and communications advice may come into conflict.
- Recognize genuine crises and potential crises as opposed to other management problems.
- Develop and implement workable protocols to minimize disagreements and deliver optimal solutions.
- Value differing viewpoints and secure the greatest benefits from those differences.
- Develop the skills to assess competing advice in a crisis and make informed decisions in the best interests of the organization as a whole.

It would be foolish and naïve to think that lawyers and communicators don't frequently have different opinions about any given situation – especially when a crisis threatens. That's no surprise. They typically have a different approach to what should be done and said, yet the idea that they can't work together is just plain unhelpful.

Indeed, one large study of American communications practitioners concluded that, while there was considerable discussion about this supposed turf war, lawyers and communicators do in fact enjoy "relatively harmonious and collaborative relationships."[16]

Which may be true. But in the heat of a crisis – when the stakes are high and may actually involve the survival of the organization – even the most harmonious and collaborative relationships can come under intense stress.

Over my professional career in communication I have worked with many lawyers, mainly in a corporate environment and most often in relation to high-profile issues and potential crises. And I have to say that generally I have found them to be cooperative, supportive and respectful.

The focus of this book is on crisis and potential crisis situations, and I have included scores of real-life examples where lawyers and communicators have worked well together as well as examples of where apparently conflicting advice led to dire consequences.

In a public relations journal article provocatively titled "In defence of lawyers," crisis consultant Steve Frankel wrote: "Lawyers and public relations counsellors have not always had a romantic relationship."[17]

I really like this comment, not just because it was a masterly understatement, but because I think it goes to the heart of what this book is about.

It's true that the relationship between lawyers and communicators has not always been a fond one, though I hope to show you that the relationship is improving.

---

[16] Fitzpatrick, K. R. (1996). Public relations and the law: A survey of practitioners. *Public Relations Review*, 22(1), 1–8.
[17] Frankel, S. (1995). In defence of Lawyers. *Public Relations Strategist, 1*(4), 24-27.

However, continued improvement is not without challenges, and won't happen by itself. It demands genuine commitment from lawyers and communicators to work better together and to recognize what they each contribute to effective crisis management. It also demands a willingness to change. But before discussing specific roles and responsibilities I need to briefly clarify the true nature of crises.

The Nature of Crises

A good place to start is a strong definition, and one of the most descriptive and widely quoted definitions of a crisis was developed by the Americans Christine Pearson and Judith Clair:

> *"An organizational crisis is a high impact event that threatens the viability of the organization and is characterized by ambiguity of cause, effect and means of resolution, as well as by a belief that decisions must be made swiftly."*[18]

British public relations expert Professor Anne Gregory later went even further:

> *"Crises are high consequence, low probability, overlaid with risk and uncertainty, conducted under time-pressure, disruptive of normal business and potentially lethal to organizational reputation."*[19]

Strong words. And in the face of such stress, ambiguity and uncertainty, the need to do and say the right thing and the risk of doing or saying the wrong thing is greater than perhaps at any other time. This means there is no other occasion when the executive depends more on strong, consistent advice from legal and communication professionals.

I like both of these definitions because they emphasize the seriousness of a genuine crisis. Within business and society these days, the word "crisis" has been

---

[18] Pearson, C. M. & Clair, J. A. (1998). Reframing crisis management. *The Academy of Management Review* (23)1, 59-76

[19] Gregory, A. (2005). Communication dimensions of the UK foot and mouth disease crisis 2001. *Journal of Public Affairs* 5(3/4), 312–328.

badly devalued by overuse, until it is now sometimes used to describe just about any embarrassment or minor problem. When the keynote speaker fails to turn up at your conference it is embarrassing and awkward, but it is not a crisis. When the CEO inadvertently utters a profanity during a national television interview, he or she might be revealing something about themselves, but it isn't a crisis.

And, contrary to a report I read in an IT magazine, when someone misplaces the piece of paper with the computer admin access passwords, it isn't a crisis (unless maybe the passwords fall into the hands of a hacker determined to destroy your entire database).

Furthermore, some individuals within management choose to label their particular problem a crisis or a potential crisis as a means to increase attention and perhaps spring some additional funding for their budget.

This is certainly not what I am talking about here, and it's important that you understand the true nature of a crisis. Every expert has their own crisis categories, but to make sure there's no misapprehension about what constitutes a real crisis, I have constructed my own list.

Categories of Organizational Crises	
Operational crises	Arise from workplace incidents such as spills, leaks, fire or explosions, or from sabotage, onsite shooting, social unrest or even terrorism.
Environmental crises	When society is exposed to pollution, or release of toxic substances into the environment, such as lakes, waterways, groundwater or into the air.
Management or employee misconduct crises	Moral or ethical lapses, such as corruption, bribery, scandal, industrial espionage, theft or other criminal activity.

Categories of Organizational Crises	
Management/legal crises	Such as layoffs or shutdowns, or alleged business wrongdoing including price-fixing, tax evasion, trademark or patent infringement, or unfair competition.
Technological crises	Technology failure or breakdown including computer systems crashing, breaches of privacy, hacking or loss of data.
Product crises	Product tampering or product failure, such as contamination, manufacturing error, or design fault causing illness, injury or even death.
Labor relations crises	Industrial disputes or employee allegations such as racial or sexual discrimination, bullying, wrongful dismissal, or dangerous working conditions.
Social concerns	Arise from concerns such as animal testing, genetically modified organisms, unsustainable packaging or suppliers who use exploited labor.
Natural disasters	When external events like floods, earthquakes, cyclones and wildfires trigger organizational crises by threatening facilities, raw material or markets.

It should go without saying that not all of these examples will necessarily develop into full-scale crises. That's why crisis prevention is such an important part of crisis management. However, my list should give you a clear idea of the range and breadth of possible crises.

Avoiding the Legal Response Syndrome

Regardless of the category of crisis, there's a good reason why legal advice is important in crisis management, namely that just about every crisis or potential crisis has a distinct legal component. But at the same time just about no crisis or potential crisis is ever *solely* about legal matters. I need to say that again because it pervades this entire book: *Just about no crisis or potential crisis is ever solely about legal matters.*

Failure to understand that leads to what I call the Legal Response Syndrome, where your organization treats every crisis as if legal considerations override all others. Of course, it's important that all legal angles are appropriately addressed. And of course, you need to seek and listen to legal advice. No responsible executive should proceed without fully appreciating the legal position. Moreover, executives and boards have a statutory obligation to act in the best interests of shareholders. That's spelled out by law.

Given that framework it's perfectly understandable that you tend to listen to lawyers. After all CEOs and the Boards they report to must be well versed in all legal responsibilities and requirements of compliance and fiduciary duty (not to mention that they may be paying very handsomely for legal advice).

The Legal Response Syndrome arises when legal counsel is allowed to trump all other advice, be it operational, business, marketing, human resources, financial or communications. But that's no reason to just default to "Let's go with what the lawyers say."

The lawyer can be acting as a litigator dispensing caution or as a counsellor helping to find team solutions. At the same time you need to fully understand the difference between legal advice and business advice.

As American attorney David Bernick has written:

> *"Good litigators are not necessarily good counsellors, particularly where the company's reputation may be destroyed long before the first trial is completed."[20]*

His Californian fellow-lawyer Adam Treiger was even more blunt:

> *"When your client has a crisis that could put it out of business, call the crisis manager first, think about legal issues later. If you do it the other way around your client might not survive to utilise your keen legal analysis."[21]*

Put another way, if you eventually appear in court as a result of the crisis, those legal proceedings will most likely be years in the future. But the court of public opinion is already in session and the jury is already assessing the fate of your reputation. So it's often the difference between an imminent crisis versus the uncertain possibility of litigation some time down the road.

The bottom line here is that when you're facing a crisis or potential crisis the impact is immediate, and it's not a question of which function is "in charge" or who has the greatest seniority, or the most qualifications. The real question is *what is the best strategic response in the interests of your organization and the interests of your stakeholders?*

You will probably have a small group of people who act in a crisis to determine what's in your best interests and how to get there. That might be a formal Crisis Management Team which also includes HR, Accounting, Operations, Logistics, IT, Sales, Manufacturing and so on.

I am not in any way diminishing the importance of these other areas of responsibility. But I am focusing here on two key management functions – communication and legal – as well as the third important activity, which is the decision-maker.

---

[20] Bernick, D.M. (2000, October 16). Corporate Crisis: The attorney's role. *The International Law Journal.*

[21] Reprinted with permission

A key problem is the common mischaracterization of what lawyers and communicators actually do. Although it should be obvious, lawyers don't just deal with matters in court and communication professionals don't just deal with the news media.

Many lawyers never appear in court for their client, and many communicators rarely, if ever, deal directly with the media. This lack of clarity about roles becomes especially important when it comes to crisis response.

What's the Right Decision?

You are the Vice Chancellor of a technical university which runs an undergraduate course in aircraft maintenance, catering mainly to international students working for overseas airlines.

A senior lecturer has just been fired for taking bribes from students in relation to revealing exam questions in advance and the university is facing a potential reputational crisis threatening the credibility of the course. At the moment there has been only one brief news report.

Your in-house legal counsel recommends you say as little as possible – only that the individual is no longer on staff and that you have initiated a full review of student exam results. The lawyer and HR suggest you do not comment on whether the lecturer was fired or was allowed to resign.

Your Communications Director recommends that you use this as a learning moment to restate the university's commitment to academic integrity; to remind staff and students throughout the whole institution that cheating will not be tolerated. The Communications

Director also recommends that you arrange a formal briefing and Q&A session for all staff and students involved with the aircraft maintenance course and an online briefing for the overseas airlines involved.

How would you proceed?

The Role of Lawyers

In a world where Hollywood's box office is dominated by superheroes, it's not so easy to identify the individual heroes we really admire.

As part of the AFI 100 series, the American Film Institute compiled its list of the 50 greatest heroes and villains of American cinema.[22] They began with a list of 400 characters, and 1,500 artists and leaders in the film industry voted on the list.

And who came put as the "top movie hero?" Atticus Finch, in the 1962 classic *To Kill a Mockingbird.*

This honest, small-town lawyer who defended a black man accused of raping a white woman, outranked Indiana Jones in *Raiders of the Lost Ark*; James Bond in *Doctor No*; Rick Blaine in *Casablanca*; and Ellen Ripley in *Alien.*

Law Professor and film scholar Michael Asimow has described Atticus Finch as the "patron saint" of all lawyers who rise above exclusive concern with the bottom line. "He is a mythic character. He is everything we lawyers wish we were and hope we will become."[23]

"But more often," Asimow added, "lawyers today are presented in courtroom movies as money-hungry, boozed-out, burned-out, incompetent, unethical sleazebags."

---

[22] AFI's 100 years . . . 100 heroes and villains (2003). *American Film Institute.* https://www.afi.com/afis-100-years-100-heroes-villians/

[23] Asimow, M. (1996). When Lawyers were heroes. *University of San Francisco Law Review*. Summer. 30(4), 1131-1138.

One of the ironies of western society is we are proud that democracy is built on the rule of law, yet this negative image of lawyers themselves remains so prevalent. Look no further than the catalogue of dishonest lawyers in the legal novels of John Grisham.

Indeed, Law Professor Emeritus Marc Galanter, in his entertaining book on lawyer jokes and legal culture,[24] makes the point that from Ancient Greece and the New Testament to our own day, lawyers have long been what he calls objects of derision. "Animosity towards lawyers," he concludes, "is perennial."

At the same time the presence of lawyers as a proportion of the working population has grown substantially.

So why is this important to crisis management? Because litigation by businesses has increased more rapidly than litigation by individuals; legal expenditure by businesses and government has increased more rapidly than expenditure by individuals; and the large-firm sector of the legal profession which provides services for corporations and large organizations has generally grown and prospered more than the small-firm sector which services individuals.[25]

There is also the rapid growth of reputational crises arising from allegations of sexual and racial discrimination, executive misbehavior, the #MeToo movement, workplace harassment and wrongful dismissal, all of which are more likely to involve larger organizations with deep pockets.

Given these trends, it's little wonder that lawyers are playing – and expect to play – an increasingly significant role in how businesses and large organizations prepare for and respond to crises and potential crises.

In fact, a survey of communicators and lawyers in large American corporations [26] revealed that the one area where legal encroachment into communication is most likely to occur is crisis-related activities.

---

[24] Galanter, M. (2005). *Lowering the Bar: lawyer jokes and legal culture.* Madison, WI. University of Wisconsin Press.
[25] Galanter ibid
[26] Lee, J., Jares, S. M. and Heath, R. L. (1999). Decision-making encroachment and cooperative relationships between Public relations and Legal Counsellors in

That early study found that legal counsel predominantly influenced top management's decision making before the crisis, such as identification of potential crises, creation of a plan, selection and training of the crisis response team and testing the plan. But it also found legal influence during and after crises regarding such matters as communicating with employees and media and conducting evaluation, and that has been reinforced over recent years.

Which reverts to my previous point: hardly any crisis or potential crisis is ever solely about legal matters, but just about every crisis or potential crisis has a distinct legal component.

> "Lawyers are generally trained to avoid, or at least minimize, legal risks and exposure to the greatest extent possible and typically tend to look to long-term consequences. However, in a crisis situation, adopting a legalistic approach may only serve to worsen the outcome."
>
> Keith Ruddock. Former in-house counsel for Shell.[27]

The Role of Lawyers in a Crisis

- Protect the organization from criminal or civil prosecution.
- Advise on the law specifically in relation to the crisis as well as broader legal matters, such as privilege, discovery, confidentiality, disclosure, defamation.
- Ensure compliance with governance issues, including statutory reporting to regulators, stock exchange announcements, statements to shareholders, insurance obligations, Directors' and Officers' liability.
- Present and recommend possible legal strategies in response to the crisis or potential crisis.

---

the management of Organisational Crisis. *Journal of Public Relations Research, 11*(3), 243-270.

[27] Ruddock, K. (2018, July 23). The challenging role of lawyers in crisis response. *Law Society UK*. https://communities.lawsociety.org.uk/july-2018/the-long-read-the-challenging-role-of-lawyers-in-crisis-response/5065498.article

- Identify legal ramifications of different management strategies including future liability.
- Review written and verbal communication for possible legal consequences.
- Manage any consequent litigation or potential litigation.
- Prepare legal documents such as injunctions, notices to desist, settlements, agreements.
- Oversee the audit trail to record decisions made and documents shared with external stakeholders.
- Work with communicators to ensure alignment of legal and communication strategies.
- Act as spokesperson, if agreed, or provide legal support to the designated spokesperson.
- Support the executive in making informed decisions.

In addition to this list there is one further role for the lawyer in a crisis – which also applies to the communicator and in fact everyone on the Crisis Management Team – namely that each team member not only brings their professional skills, but also has a responsibility to bring their broader experience and knowledge to help the team make the best decisions. Responding to a crisis truly is an occasion for teamwork, not silo-thinking or turf-protection. There is no Most Valuable Player award in a crisis.

You may have noticed that my list does *not* include the lawyer chairing or leading the crisis response team. While lawyers typically have a wide range of skills to contribute beyond the purely legal – which may be why some are called General Counsel – the lawyer is often viewed as an adviser rather than as an integral team member, even when in-house. Moreover, having the lawyer lead the crisis response invariably gives it a legal focus.

My firm recommendation is that the lawyer should *not* lead the crisis response team. It's not a reflection on their leadership capacity, but on their role and training. And it's a view supported by Professor Daniel Diermeier, formerly of the Kellogg School of Business at Northwestern University.

> *"Good crisis management teams have a strong, opinionated General Counsel, while poor crisis management teams are run by the General Counsel."[28]*

Or as crisis Attorney Richard Levick has put it:

> *"Lawyers don't drive the bus. They're only sitting near the front."* [29]

I should add here that I don't think the communicator should lead the team either. Usually it should be the CEO or another top executive with authority and knowledge of the field.

While it is relatively easy to identify what lawyers *should do* before and during a crisis, it is much more difficult to assess what contribution legal advice actually made in any specific crisis.

As I explained in the Introduction – and reiterate throughout this book – in most crises we don't know, and likely will never know, what specific legal advice was given. There are rare instances where the organization openly disclosed what legal advice was given and why that advice was or was not followed. You'll read about some examples of this in Chapter Five. But such discussion mostly takes place behind closed doors and we can draw conclusions only from what appeared in the media or in open court – in other words, what was done or said or reported publicly.

This is crucial in any discussion of the role of the lawyer because, in some cases, the lawyer may have given good advice which was ignored or overridden. The result is that the outside observer – and that's us – may incorrectly assume the lawyers were to blame for what we judge was an undesirable outcome.

Take for example the gas explosion which killed 29 coal miners at the Massey Energy mine in Whitesville, West Virginia, in April 2010.

---

[28] Diermeier, D. (2011). *Reputation Rules: Strategies for Building Your Company's Most Valuable Asset.* New York: McGraw Hill.
[29] Levick, R. S. & Slack, C. (2010). *The Communicators: Leadership in the Age of Crisis.* Washington DC: Watershed Press.

It was an undoubted crisis, made even worse by the revelation that the explosion was entirely preventable, and that over the previous five years the company had been issued with 1,342 safety violations, totaling $1.89 million in fines.

What makes this crisis important here is that it was claimed at the time that, instead of improving safety, the company chose to contest the citations and keep the cases tied up in court through legal argument about regulations and procedures.[30] The appeals process reportedly kept the mine from being placed on a pattern of violations which would have triggered tougher enforcement.

This example takes us to the heart of the fact that the role of the lawyer in a crisis is seldom known outside the organization. For instance, we don't know in this case who made the decision to fight the safety violations through the courts, and we don't know why or how seventeen Massey executives refused to be interviewed by the state inquiry into the disaster.

What we do know is that the official report found the company operated its mines "in a profoundly reckless manner" and that a "pattern of negligence" ultimately led to the worst American mining disaster in 40 years. [31]

We also know that six years later, in April 2016, former Massey Energy CEO Don Blankenship was sentenced to 12 months in prison for conspiring to violate Federal mine safety laws.[32]

The Massey Energy mine disaster was not the first time a company failed to heed crisis warnings, and sadly won't be the last. But I hope it helps you appreciate the importance of caution when it comes to making assumptions about what role the lawyer may or may not have played in the legal strategy of a real-life crisis.

---

[30] Smith, S. (2010). A "Massey"ive catastrophe. *EHS Today,* 3(5) 8-9.
[31] Tavernise, S. (2011, May 19). Report faults mine owner for explosion that killed 29. *New York Times.* https://www.nytimes.com/2011/05/20/us/20mine.html
[32] Maher, K. (2016 April 6). Former Massey Energy CEO Sentenced to 12 Months in Prison. *Wall Street Journal.* https://www.wsj.com/articles/former-massey-energy-ceo-sentenced-to-12-months-in-prison-1459961064

The Role of Communicators

Despite the rise of digital communication and AI and apps for just about every activity, the core expertise of professional communicators is the ability to absorb and analyze sometimes complex situations and to produce strategic written and oral materials which are accurate, concise and easily comprehensible.

Add to that the ability to plan, to build relationships, and to communicate effectively across management functions and across the full range of stakeholders and you have the essence of the communicator's role in crisis management.

> "When companies have a crisis situation, how you communicate as a brand may end up being more important than what you do and what actually happened."
>
> Dennis Owen, Cathay Pacific[33]

The role of the communicator in a crisis is easier to understand than that of the lawyer and is typically more visible. Of course, a well-written media statement on behalf of the organization might not reflect what the writer personally thinks or originally advised, but in my experience it is rare for the professional communicator to knowingly lie on behalf of the organization (though the same might not always apply to communicators in the world of politics).

Some years ago, while working on a potential reputational crisis, I issued a media statement for my company on the basis of the facts I was given, which was accurate but turned out to be incomplete.

The result was a misleading story in the local newspaper next day. When it became clear that I had unwittingly misinformed the reporter, I explained to the Operations Manager that my personal credibility was an important asset of the company and this incident put my professional reputation and that of the company at risk.

---

[33] Cathay Pacific Searches For PR Network To Handle Global Crisis Comms (2016, October 10). *The Holmes Report*.
https://www.provokemedia.com/latest/article/cathay-pacific-searches-for-pr-network-to-handle-global-crisis-comms?utm

I told him I planned to visit the Chief Reporter and explain what had happened. After a long pause he said – to his credit – "I'll go with you."

The Chief Reporter appreciated our candor, and the Operations Manager became a trusted colleague and never again kept me in the dark with only half the story.

This possibly trivial incident has some important lessons for crisis communication.

The first is that executives need to trust their communicator and not be worried that they will "blab to their friends in the media."

The second, and perhaps even more important lesson, is that the communicator must have *all* the available facts in order to make an informed judgement about the communication plan and what should and shouldn't be said. That's their role and expertise.

For its part, the executive group need to trust the communicator as a valued member of the team and need to respect their professional contribution to the final strategy.

The Role of Communicators in a Crisis

- Bring external stakeholder viewpoints into the organization.
- Develop a communication strategy and tactical plans.
- Protect organizational reputation and brand.
- Prepare communication materials such as statements, speeches, backgrounders, Q&A.
- Manage proactive and reactive media contact.
- Act as a buffer between executives and reporters.
- Choose the most appropriate channel to reach key stakeholders.
- Provide expertise to achieve consistently simple and effective language.
- Review legal documents for clarity and lay-person comprehension.
- Advocate for stakeholder/staff interests. Play the devil's advocate.
- Help secure employee and community support for executive initiatives.
- Monitor and engage via social media where required.
- Identify post-crisis and longer-term communication needs.

- Work with lawyers to ensure alignment of legal and communication strategies.
- Act as spokesperson, if agreed, or provide support to the designated spokesperson.
- Support the executive in making informed decisions.

To expand on this list, a key *informal* role for the communicator is to bring a broader perspective to the crisis response. Some of the case studies in this book show examples of how organizations got so close to the problem that they lost sight of the possible consequences, or of stakeholder perceptions. In some of these cases I have asked what was the communicator's input when they made that decision? Or was the communicator even present when the decision was made?

Over time it has become the communicator's task – outside their written job description – to ask the difficult questions, to be not only the eyes and ears of the organization, but also its nose – to sniff out anything that doesn't seem right.

- Do we really want to take this action?
- How would your position look on the nightly TV news?
- Would you want to stand up in the staff dining-room and explain this to the workers?
- What will the neighborhood or community think?
- How would I react if I was the local activist leader?
- It may be legal but is it ethical?
- How might it affect the stock price?
- Does this align with our organizational values?
- And that ultimate show-stopping question: Who could finish up in court if it all goes wrong?

Beyond being able to write and speak well, asking the hard questions is another key element of how an experienced communicator adds value and helps manage the crisis, and at the same time protects reputation.

> "Good public relations counsellors understand that there is more involved in crisis communications than the tactical considerations of getting the message out. They deal with the reality that there are critical business and legal issues to be considered"
>
> James E. Lukaszewski[34]

While discussing the roles of the communicator in a crisis, I need to take a moment to clarify the limits of communication.

Remembering that the impact of a crisis is often related more to how it is managed than the crisis itself, it's quite common that disgruntled executives assert "it would have been OK if we had communicated better."

Unfortunately, that is sometimes just an excuse for poor management or a poor strategy. It's much easier to blame communication than to admit the executive group may have got it wrong.

Take the response of Facebook CEO Mark Zuckerberg to his company's prolonged reputational crisis.

Speaking at an analysts' briefing in February 2020, Zuckerberg flagged a shift in the company's philosophy and outlook, noting it no longer wants to be "liked," but instead wants to be "trusted."

> *"We're also focused on communicating more clearly what we stand for. One critique of our approach for much of the last decade was that because we wanted to be liked, we didn't always communicate our views as clearly because we worried about offending people... So we're going to focus more on communicating our principles."[35]*

---

[34] Cited in Fitzpatrick, K. R. (1995). Ten guidelines for reducing legal risks in crisis management. *Public Relations Quarterly,* 40(2), 33-38

[35] Gaus, A. (2020, January 29). Mark Zuckerberg: We're Not Here to Make Friends. *The Street.*
https://www.thestreet.com/investing/mark-zuckerberg-were-not-here-to-make-friends

The problem here is that the CEO may be confusing action with communication. My answer to Mr. Zuckerberg would be that you need to *live* your principles and demonstrate your commitment to them beyond just *communicating* them. Facebook's reputational crisis is based mainly on what the company does, and what they are perceived to do, rather than on what they say. Effective communication has enormous power, but no amount of communication alone can make a bad situation good. So, to paraphrase Stephen R. Covey: "You can't communicate your way out of a problem you've behaved yourself into"[36].

So What's Different?

Before we start to consider the differences between the roles of lawyers and communicators in a crisis, it is important to recognize that the two professions have quite a few roles and skills in common.

Both lawyers and communicators:

- Are good with words and can think on their feet.
- Want what's best for the organization.
- Can think beyond just their professional area.
- Respect (generally) the expertise of the other.
- Can work as part of a team.
- Research, analyze and provide advice.
- Use persuasion as part of their profession.
- Have good access to, and are trusted, by the CEO.
- Understand the need for urgency in a crisis.
- Are able to absorb complex information quickly.
- Recognize the importance of carefully choosing the right language.

At the same time they both have a role to present their client or their organization in the best possible light. Lawyers proudly call it advocacy, but when communicators do the same their critics sometimes accuse them of spin.

---

[36] Originally "You can't talk your way out of a problem you've behaved yourself into" in Covey, S. R. (1989). *The 7 Habits of Highly Effective People*. New York: Simon and Schuster.

Yet, for all these similarities, it remains the differences which color many of the perceived difficulties of lawyers and communicators working together and reaching agreement.

That's nothing new. Way back in 1969, before crisis management was even recognized as a formal discipline in the 1980s, Morton Simon wrote what is regarded as the first book about public relations and the law, and memorably described lawyers and communicators as "the oil and water team."[37] More than 50 years later many believe that tension still persists.

Typical of this combative perspective would be the American communication industry legend Frank Winston Wylie:

> *"The orientation of the lawyer and the public relations person are diametrically opposed in training, thinking and action... The lawyer is trained to take a myopic view of the world, to base conclusions on a narrow point of view of what the law will currently allow... By comparison the public relations person is trained to take the widest possible viewpoint, realizing that there are alternative solutions to every problem, and that gaining public confidence is the real goal... The lawyer is essentially a confronter, the public relations person a persuader"[38].*

Hopefully that's a view from a past era and we can now be more confident of a cooperative relationship. Yet still today there *are* genuine differences, and this is reinforced in Chapter Ten where some global crisis experts have their say. It's equally real that most of these differences arise from the demands of each profession and their views of the world rather than personal animosity or excessive hubris. Indeed, animosity or tension between them is just unprofessional.

---

[37] Simon, M. J. (1969). *Public Relations Law*. New York: Meredith Corporation.
[38] Wylie, F. W. (1995). Public relations should lead. *The Public Relations Strategist*, 1(4), 32-34.

Working together

A classic case of working together was the response by Fisher-Price to reports of children choking on their popular "Little People" toys. With a recall impractical, and facing the potential of massive lawsuits, the lawyers wanted to issue a nationwide alert to the choking threat.

But the company's communications consultants proposed focusing instead on safety rather than danger. As a result they launched the "Family Alert program" designed to warn parents about a whole range of threats to children in the home, of which choking on small toys was just one. (In addition, the toys were redesigned to be larger and not so easy to swallow.) The lawyers embraced the initiative and Fisher-Price established an enhanced reputation as advocates for product safety which has been sustained to the present day[39].

The simple fact is that communicators and lawyers think differently. Communicators are most often intuitive thinkers, based on strategies and theories they have learned over the years. By contrast lawyers are process thinkers, because the law is a process, with rules, standards and laws. Lawyers tend to look for problems to solve and risks to avoid rather than opportunities to communicate. They look at the legality of a planned response, while the communicator is thinking about public acceptability and the impact on reputation.

In general, such different approaches to the crisis or potential crisis arise from different training; from different professional language; from each having a

---

[39] Madore, T. et al (1992, August 28) "Family alert" safety program for children set by Fisher-Price. *Buffalo News.* https://buffalonews.com/1992/08/28/family-alert-safety-program-for-children-set-by-fisher-price/

different knowledge base, different professional networks; and often different ideas about objectives and tactics.

For example, it's a cliché – but true – that lawyers will generally want to say as little as possible to protect against potential liability while communicators will generally want to say more to protect reputation, meet the reasonable expectations of stakeholders, and be seen to take action

It's also true that lawyers, by their training, tend to look at what has come before, at precedent, while communicators need to be looking out at the horizon, anticipating what might happen next.

Similarly, lawyers want to keep focused on the facts, whereas communicators accept the importance of facts but also understand the critical importance of perception and that facts alone don't win an argument.

The lawyer's training is that you can win by argument and the force of logic and reasoning, which might be true in the controlled environment of the courtroom. But out in the wider world, facts and logic are frequently outweighed by emotions and feelings and social media fallacies. In essence, the law and argument and precedent are tangible while public perceptions are intangible.

Underpinning all of this is a common belief that the lawyer's role is to say what the organization "must do" to protect its legal position whereas the communicator says what the organization "should do" to protect the business, the brand and reputation.

It's not difficult to list these contrary approaches, yet the fundamental differences between the two professions in response to a crisis largely come down to just a few central issues:

(1) **Control of the flow of information** – who decides what we say and when. No issue is more important.
(2) **Confidentiality versus disclosure** – what can we say as opposed to what people want to know. Also, what do stakeholders deserve to know, have a right to know or demand to know.
(3) **Speed of communication** – waiting for all the facts or going with what we know so far. Lawyers prefer to work slowly and methodically, while the media travel at blinding speed.

(4) **Choice of language** – how to protect reputation as well as the legal position. While there are times when precise legal language is needed, fewer, simpler words which make an emotional connection often do the job.

These are the areas which are particularly prone to conflicting advice, and these are typically the areas where you need to make decisions about what to do when there is no "right answer."

The Decision Maker

While my focus in this book is on the lawyer and the communicator, there is a critical third party in any crisis, and that's the organizational decision maker.

President George W. Bush once famously said: "I am the decider." While some critics at the time scoffed at his language, we don't really have a very good alternative, and every organization has a different decision-making structure. So, for the purpose of simplicity I will be calling this role the CEO, or the most senior executive, recognizing that sometimes it is not a single individual but a team decision.

At the very basic level, when faced with a crisis or potential crisis, the CEO needs to answer three key questions:

1. What's the right thing to do?
2. Have I received and fully considered quality advice from legal and communication professionals?
3. Will my decision reflect a proper synthesis of that advice and will it align with our principles and our values?

From the advice provided – sometimes conflicting, sometimes not – the CEO then makes a decision as to how the organization will respond. Conventional wisdom seems to be that a decisive executive action will somehow accept responsibility and unilaterally resolve the crisis. For example:

- To litigate or negotiate.
- To apologize or not.
- To deny or accept liability.
- To shut down operations or continue business.
- To dismiss or support the people who made a mistake.

However, the process is seldom so black and white. Crises by definition are confusing, and the way forward often depends on a consensus emerging rather than on one definitive decision. Moreover, a single executive action may no longer be a feasible answer to increasingly complex crisis situations, despite public expectation to the contrary. There is typically no "magic bullet" or "fairy-tale ending" but an evolving strategy built on incremental decisions.

In fact, the question of how and when to apologize is so important that I have devoted two Chapters – Four and Five – to help you fully appreciate this key area of potential disagreement.

Another issue is that many crises are chronic rather than acute – arising from *ongoing* situations such as repeated product failure, a prolonged activist boycott or a price war with a competitor, rather than an immediate, short term threat – and such crises typically don't lend themselves to quick and easy solutions.

Yet, irrespective of the nature of the crisis, you can't wait to get every fact in order to devise the perfect response strategy, and you can't always hope that the lawyer and communicator will come to you with an agreed position. You have to recognize that, while the lawyer and the communicator may both be correct within the context of their respective disciplines, and while the full risks may never be neatly identified and quantified, nevertheless a decision must ultimately be made. That requires not only judgement, but balance between competing points of view.

> "The best-designed organization is unlikely to function effectively in a crisis if those guiding it have insufficient management skills and exhibit poor leadership."
>
> Alexander Kouzmin and Alan Jarman[40]

One of the reasons I have spent some time on the differences between the legal and communication approach to a crisis is that, if you have to balance competing advice, you need to understand *why* these two professional advisors have different perspectives and how it affects what they are saying.

---

[40] Kouzmin, A. & Jarman, A. M. G. (2004). Policy advice as crisis: A political redefinition of crisis management. *International Studies Review, 6*(1), 182–194.

Which leads to one other important aspect of decision-making, and that is the role of the CEO to make sure the lawyer and the communicator are working effectively together.

One thing that's always in short supply in a crisis is time, and time should not be eaten up by bickering between lawyers and communicators. It's bad enough to have a crisis at all without an in-house scrub-fire about roles and responsibilities.

The CEO should expect all of his or her lieutenants to give informed, assertive advice in their respective areas of expertise without second-guessing each other's positions. The heat of a crisis is no time to be working out petty rivalries and jealousies.

How to Get lawyers and Communicators Working Together in a Crisis

- Confirm confidentiality/disclosure agreements are in place.
- Provide a framework for lawyers and communicators to meet on a regular basis.
- Authorize them to discuss sensitive issues and agree on an approach to privileged information.
- Maintain equal access to the CEO and to senior management.
- Have both parties attend all crisis-related meetings.
- Plan crisis simulation exercises with both participating.
- Make sure the approved communication plan spells out roles and the strategic approach.
- Fully assess the legal and the reputation implications of both parties' decisions and advice.
- Demand that all advice is aligned with the purpose or values of the organization.
- Establish an approval process for communication drafts which honors all inputs.
- Arrange for both to attend media coaching for spokespersons.

- Develop a protocol on who will be spokesperson in different circumstances.
- Formulate a process for resolving any intractable disagreements.
- Ensure the lawyer has a good understanding of crisis communication and stakeholder expectations.
- Ensure the communicator has a good understanding of legal issues such as discovery and liability.

Recognizing the Crisis

As well as making key decisions, another important role for the CEO is recognizing that a crisis or potential actually exists and then mobilizing the necessary resources.

In one of the most important early books on crisis management, the American Steven Fink firmly positioned crisis management as a formal executive responsibility and warned:

> *"You should accept almost as a universal truth that when a crisis strikes it will be accompanied by a host of diversionary problems. As a manager, your task is to identify the real crisis"* [41.]

One of the challenges here is that your first step is getting information about a potential crisis – what has happened, what could go wrong and what may already be going wrong?

One early research project studied 20 corporations enmeshed in crises and concluded that the chief executives generally surrounded themselves with "yes-sayers" who voiced no criticism and who deliberately filtered out warnings from

---

[41] Fink, S. (1986). *Crisis Management: Planning for the Inevitable*. New York: American Management Association.

middle managers who correctly saw that their corporations were out of touch with the market realities.[42]

In this respect I like the pithy description by Kurt Stocker at Northwestern University, Chicago, who wrote:

> *"Keep in mind that top management, by definition, is the least informed group in the company when it comes to bad news. Nothing moves more slowly than bad news running up a hill, a very steep hill"* [43].

A chilling example of this problem was revealed following the disastrous explosion and refinery fire at BP Texas City in August 2005, which killed 15 workers, injured 180 others and severely damaged the refinery. Researcher Andrew Hopkins studied the crisis and found a culture at BP in which many top people knew of problems, but few would speak up.

> *"Only good news flowed upward. No one dared say the wrong thing or challenge the boss"*[44].

Which brings me to the final key role for decision-making in a crisis, and that's the critical need for an environment in which lawyers and communicators and other executives can challenge the boss.

In the military, rank may have its privileges, but hierarchical decision-making can create major problems in a crisis situation (I hope you enjoy the sidebar about a notorious British naval disaster). In organizational crises, "just following orders" doesn't impress the courts or the news media or stakeholders. Advisors must be willing to give advice – and the CEO must be willing to listen to that advice – even when it is unwelcome or uncomfortable.

---

[42] Dunbar, R. L. M. and Goldberg, W. H. (1978). Crisis development and strategic response in European corporations. *Journal of Business Administration* 9(2), 139-149

[43] Stocker, K. P. (1997). A strategic approach to crisis management. In C. L. Caywood (Ed.), *The Handbook of Strategic Public Relations and Integrated Communication* (pp. 189–203). New York: McGraw Hill.

[44] Cited in Hopkins, A. (2009). *Failure to Learn: The BP Texas City Refinery Disaster*. Sydney: CCH Australia

The boss is not always right

In 1893 the Royal Navy's Mediterranean Fleet Commander, **Vice Admiral Sir George Tryon**, was leading one of two parallel columns of warships on board his flagship, the battleship *Victoria*, in exercises off the North African coast. Tryon needed the fleet to reverse course and ordered the two columns to turn inwards towards each other, even though they were too close.

Officers on several ships recognized they were on a collision course, but no one dared question the order of an Admiral known for demanding unquestioning obedience. Two battleships crashed into each other and HMS Victoria sank with the loss of 358 lives, including Tryon himself.

The subsequent court-martial found that the disaster was due to an order by the Admiral and that the other officers could not be blamed for carrying out his directions.

When bad news or warnings are blocked for any reason the result can be a disaster. The need to listen to dissenting opinions in a crisis was very nicely captured by an unnamed manager in a recent report about the role of the CEO:

> *"One of the most important things is having people around you who tell you how wrong you are"*[45].

In the same vein, American academics Paul Nystrom and William Starbuck once argued that top managers should listen to and learn from "dissenters, doubters and bearers of warnings" to remind themselves that their own beliefs and perceptions

---

[45] Heidrick & Struggles (2015). The CEO Report: Embracing the paradoxes of leadership and the power of doubt. https://www.heidrick.com/knowledge-center/Publication/The-CEO-Report

may not be correct[46]. Andrew Hopkins – who I mentioned before in relation to the BP Texas City disaster – went even further and proposed that mindful leaders "…develop systems to reward the bearers of bad news"[47]. Rightly or wrongly, in many organizations the role of dissenter – or devil's advocate – falls to the communication professional.

It's a role which needs to be handled with care to avoid being labelled a troublemaker, or not a team player, but it's an essential part of deciding and implementing what's best for the organization.

A View from the Executive Suite

Before leaving the topic of roles and responsibilities I would like to refer briefly to a research project I conducted to better understand what top leaders involved in hands-on management believe are their roles in crisis management and crisis preparedness[48].

I interviewed Australian CEOs in the chemical and energy sector in 2012 to gain a view from the executive suite, and they certainly recognized that their role in crisis management is about a lot more than making key decisions and speaking on behalf of the organization.

The leadership roles they identified can be categorized under eight headings. Not surprisingly many have a strong focus on the importance of planning. I don't have space here to review the whole project, but I think you will agree that their view of their own role aligns well with this chapter:

- Encourage a proactive crisis culture.
- Establish and enforce standards and processes.
- Prioritize and set an example.
- Properly assess the full range of risks.

---

[46] Nystrom, P. C. & Starbuck, W. H. (1984). To avoid organizational crises, unlearn. *Organizational Dynamics, 12*(4), 53–65.

[47] Hopkins cit op

[48] Jaques, T. (2012). Crisis leadership: A view from the executive suite. *Journal of Public Affairs, 12*(4), 366–372.

- Promote open, upward communication.
- Build relationships before the crisis.
- Be ready to deal with the news media.
- Encourage a learning environment and share experience.

I believe that if lawyers, communicators and leaders each understand their roles and responsibilities in a crisis – and the role and responsibilities of the other parties – you can overcome any disputes and disagreements to deliver the best possible outcomes for your organization.

Key Takeaways

- There are many differences between lawyers and communicators, but there are also many similarities.
- Legal advice is important but should not trump all other considerations.
- Listening to dissenting opinions is an important part of decision-making
- It's not about who's "in charge" but about what is best for the whole organization.
- Lawyers and communicators need to establish a proper working relationship long before any crisis strikes.
- The CEO has to make decisions, but crisis management is a team task.

Questions for Discussion

1. *Why is it crucial to distinguish between a "legal opinion" and the lawyer's opinion as a member of the management team?*
2. *What really is a crisis and how do you manage an executive who misuses the word to exaggerate minor problems?*
3. *What specific actions can a communicator take to demonstrate their value to strategic decision-making?*
4. *Are there other common professional conflicts in a typical crisis situation other than the lawyer and communicator? How are they managed?*
5. *How can a communicator bring uncomfortable views to the executive without risking being branded a dissenter or troublemaker?*

Chapter Two

Lawyers' Insights

"It is unfair to believe everything we hear about lawyers. Some of it might not be true."

Gerald F. Lieberman.

In many of the examples and crisis case studies I introduce in this book, the role of lawyers is, by necessity, based on what they have said in the media or in the courtroom or on what can be interpreted or deduced from how the organization responded to a crisis.

It's pretty rare for lawyers to publicly discuss their role in how a corporate strategy was developed, and even more rare for them to talk about their relationship with communicators during a real-life crisis. By contrast communicators frequently comment and write about what they see as the challenges and difficulties of working with lawyers in a crisis. But what about the lawyers' point of view?

I knew from the start writing this book that it would be impossible to get lawyers to sit down for an interview "on the record" about how a particular high-profile crisis was managed. So I set out to achieve the next best thing, to secure interviews with senior lawyers around the world – without publishing their names – to understand how they see their role in crisis management; the difficulties they face in advising CEOs in a crisis, and what they believe are the challenges of working with professional communicators.

This chapter will help you to:

- Better understand the role of lawyers in a crisis.
- Hear the insights of lawyers in their own words.
- Avoid unnecessary conflict between lawyers and other counsellors.
- Learn how to get the best from legal advisors when a crisis strikes.
- Appreciate the constraints of legal recommendations.
- Make the lawyer a valued member of the crisis management team.

To undertake this interview project, I worked with SenateSHJ, a reputation and change communication consultancy based in Australia and New Zealand, along with their partners in PROI Worldwide, a network of leading independent public relations firms across 50 countries and 100 cities around the world.

Together we recorded and analyzed interviews with 24 lawyers in Australia, New Zealand, Canada, the United States and the United Kingdom.

The interviews revealed a considerable divergence of opinion, as well as some common attitudes across the profession and across national borders.

It's clear from the responses that lawyers recognize their own shortcomings when it comes to crisis communication. Yet they remain concerned about the lack of legal awareness among communicators. They are also concerned that communicators are too ready to disclose information which may jeopardize liability or future litigation.

> "Generally, a lawyer does not have appropriate expertise and experience in communication matters, although they might think they do."
>
> (Lawyer)

Where Advice Conflicts

Most lawyers interviewed acknowledged that conflict between legal and communication advice is an issue, but some regarded it as relatively rare. One, for example, thought it resulted from the two professions being "too trenchant and refusing to listen to one another." But he added that this conflict was not intractable.

Another even suggested that some lawyers simply don't trust communicators and added some litigators went so far as to actually think they made their living "by selling secrets to journalists to curry favor." As she added: "Oh my goodness."

The area identified as the most prone to conflict over advice in a crisis related to the classic hurdle of the lawyers wanting to say as little as possible and the communicators tending to prefer communicating openly and transparently. This was viewed by the lawyers as creating a legal risk.

The divergence of opinion reflects two separate but related concerns. First, messaging – what to say and how to say it. Second, disclosure – how much to say, how much to keep back, when to say it, and to whom to say it.

Seen as equally challenging are issues of business ethics and professional privilege, ahead of the vexed question of how and when to apologize. At the same time, disagreement and discussion about the exact choice of language and "playing with words" was not identified as a concern.

> "Explaining or saying sorry creates the potential for conflict. But from a legal point of view, liability alone should not be a bar to doing what's right. That's part of being a values-based organization."
>
> (Lawyer)

Some of the lawyers surveyed suggested conflict between legal and communication was not a problem. In large part, they argue, this is because "… there is general deference to legal, especially when the business is on the back foot."

Overall, the lawyers interviewed believe disagreement is not so much a battle, as a process to arrive at an acceptable position. Most said, given goodwill on both sides, you can work through competing concern for legal and communication in a way that doesn't leave the organization unnecessarily exposed legally or reputationally.

Litigation was identified as an area particularly prone to conflict because, as one lawyer put it: "There are certain things which will anger the judge yet may be important for your shareholders or the public."

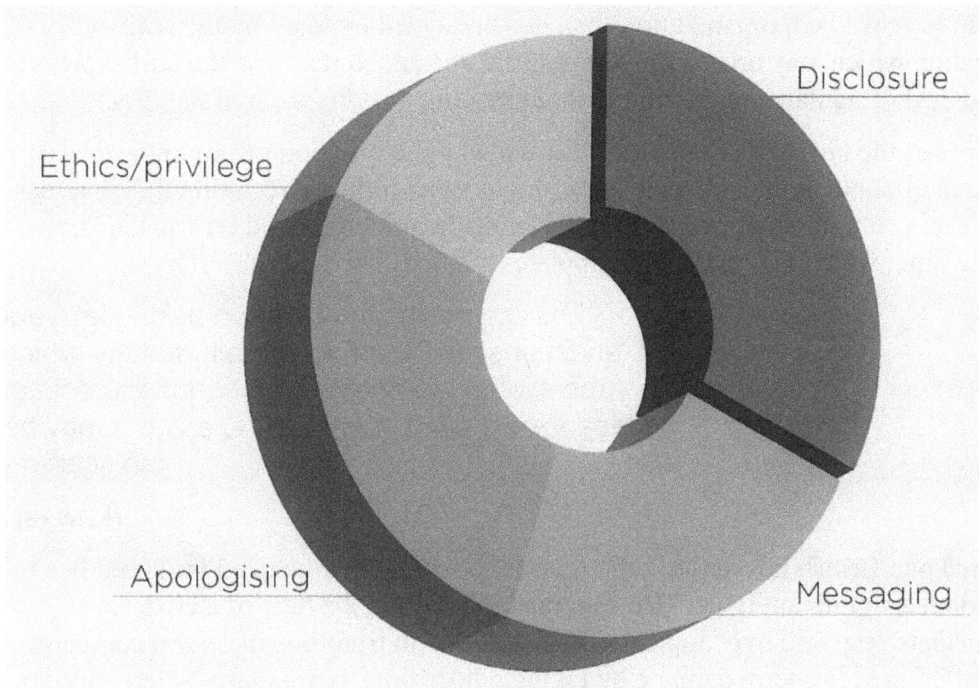

Figure 2-1 What Areas Are Most Prone To Conflicting Legal and Communication Advice?

The Risk of Speed

Another perceived area of conflict – related to process rather than each profession's roles – was how to balance speed and accuracy. Almost every lawyer in the study emphasized what they saw as the need for certainty before communicating in a crisis, and one commented that: "Lawyers are generally not good at reaching a decision too quickly."

Many spoke about the importance of a balanced, measured, proportionate approach. As one said: "The desire to respond quickly can conflict with getting the advice you want and need. The first rule is to make sure you have collected enough facts." Situations where an apology is needed were identified as particularly concerning. "The media often want the company to say sorry before it can know what's really happened."

As another warned, organizations can be "paralyzed by fear" by the scale of litigation which may arise from a crisis. But she added that you can still express a great deal of human compassion without making an admission of liability,

However, the lawyers' responses illustrate why the question of prompt action is an area of contention, and some appeared to show little appreciation that in a real crisis it is common that decisions must be made quickly, based on what is known at the time, which is typically incomplete.

> "The communication person asking lawyers questions gets them to explain matters which the clients themselves might not appreciate, because they will often want to ask but may be too scared."
>
> (Lawyer)

Indeed one British lawyer took the unusual position that the need for speed is "seldom a significant issue." He said that although in the heat of a crisis an immediate response may appear to be required, "in truth it is rare for a company to suffer any long-term damage by taking a little time, particularly where this can be justified."

Compare this with a New Zealand respondent who argued the best lawyers may welcome a little risk as opposed to seeking to control the whole scenario: "Lawyers who are legally defensive to a fault," he said, "tend to be tortured souls who agonize over every possible scenario when the risk may be real but very small, while the upside is so obvious." Another added that legal advice has to be independent and forthright, and providing advice to management should not be regarded as a popularity contest.

Who Should Be in Charge?

When asked who should take the lead in a crisis, a majority of the lawyers said it should be them. However, there were several who said it should be the communicator. Others felt it should be neither the lawyer nor the communicator, but the Client/CEO who takes the lead after weighing up the combined advice and considering the risks.

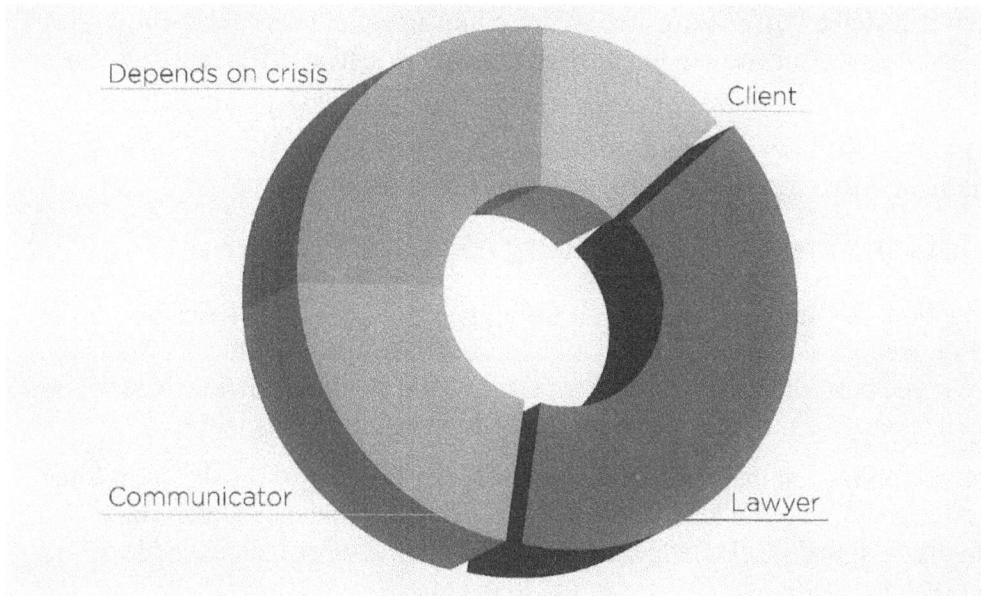

Figure 2-2 Who Lawyers Think Should Lead in a Crisis

Also emerging from this discussion was an understanding this is very much a situational decision. It might, for example, depend on where the greatest risk lies – legal or reputational – or whether the crisis is primarily about litigation, or stakeholder expectation and management.

> **"Legal is only ever one input into the way you deal with a crisis."**
>
> (Lawyer)

The lawyers were also asked whether there were crisis situations when the communicator should take the lead. Some suggested situations with significant public interest and where communication would not compromise the legal situation. Others indicated this may also be when the news media needed to be "kept at bay," or when there are human victims and the CEO needs to express compassion without making damaging legal admissions.

One American lawyer described communication as the vessel through which the legal issue travels: "If the vessel doesn't hold water or make sense, the legal issues won't come through with any veracity or practical understanding."

Another described the relationship as more like a pendulum which swings one way and then the other, with either party taking the lead at different times during a crisis.

Yet many of the lawyers remained firm in their view they could not envisage crisis situations when the communicator should take the lead.

Relationships and Working Better Together

Throughout this study – despite their differences in some areas – the lawyers broadly recognized the need to work collaboratively with communicators in a crisis in the best interests of the organization. "We just need to work together with mutual respect," said one. "After good discussion a consensus will result."

Another pointed out that lack of clarity and understanding of the different roles and what they bring can lead to confusion: "There is a balance which can normally be found – acknowledge rather than ignore, relay fact and address speculation, describe the process rather than judge."

When conflicting advice arises, several lawyers stressed the importance of what they called a "hand-in-glove" approach. One added: "It's not so much a question of conflicting advice but the need for alignment of what could, or couldn't, happen."

The lawyers were asked what specifically they think could be done to help lawyers and communicators work better together.

> The best outcomes are when the lawyer and communication person respect each other's role, there is no ego in terms of who leads, and both advisors are focused solely on their client's best interests."
>
> (Lawyer)

Collaboration and mutual respect emerged as strong themes. The most common recommendation was for both parties to respect each other's roles. This was closely followed by the need for open discussion and the importance of establishing trusting relationships before the crisis occurs.

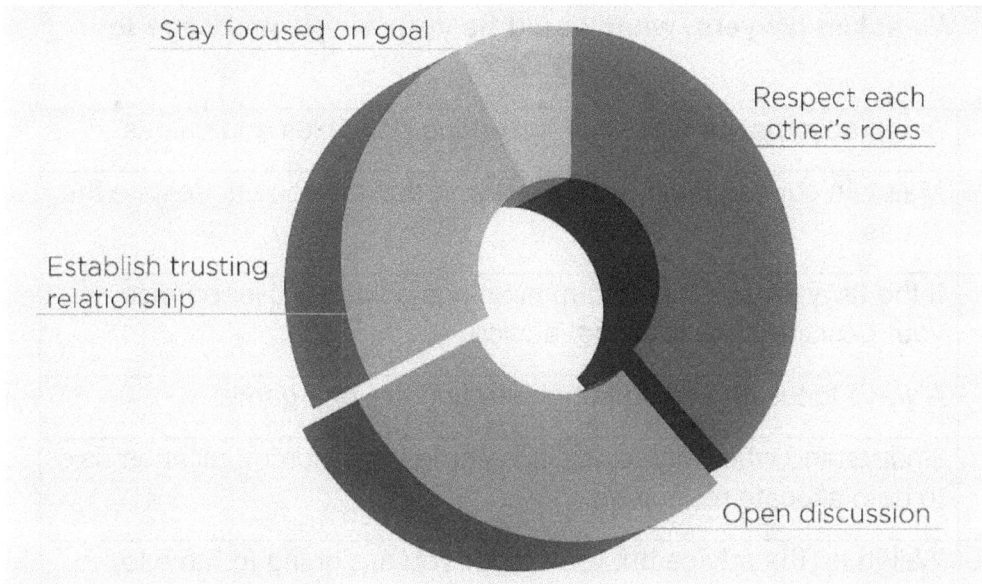

Figure 2-3 How Can Lawyers and Communicators Work Better Together?

The value of a proper working relationship was captured by one lawyer who spoke of the need for gentle diplomacy. He said it is essential that the lawyer does not erode trust by being critical of the communicator in a personal way: "In the end the lawyer simply needs to be clear about their advice and the consequences of not accepting it – and the client needs to make final decision."

"Ordinarily the value of being authentic and honest is significantly greater than the legal risk involved."

(Lawyer)

We asked lawyers, what would be your single message to CEOs?	
1	Act in accordance with your governing principles and values.
2	Maintain confidentiality in a crisis and don't breach it, despite the stress.
3	If the lawyer says the communications advice will jeopardize your position, take the legal advice.
4	Always focus on key stakeholders and the end game.
5	Understand whether there is greater legal or communication risk to help allocate resources.
6	Weigh up the advice but remember you are going to have to make tough calls.
7	Work cooperatively. Get a well-prepared team ready in advance and bring everyone to the table.
8	Get lawyers and communicators together to reach common understanding and engage with both
9	Take the advice and think about it. Your plan must be detailed, well thought through and considered.
10	Have regard for the full life cycle of risk associated with your decision, not just the short-term.
11	Don't use lawyers and communicators who don't understand you and your business.
12	Trust your instincts but think about your own people first and foremost.

We asked lawyers, what would be your single message to CEOs?	
13	Follow the advice you are given by the people you trust the most.
14	Trust your team or get new team members – but probably not mid-crisis.

Perceptions of Value

Lawyers were asked what strengths they think their profession brings to a crisis. The most frequently mentioned strength – ahead of legal expertise – was calmness and predictability.

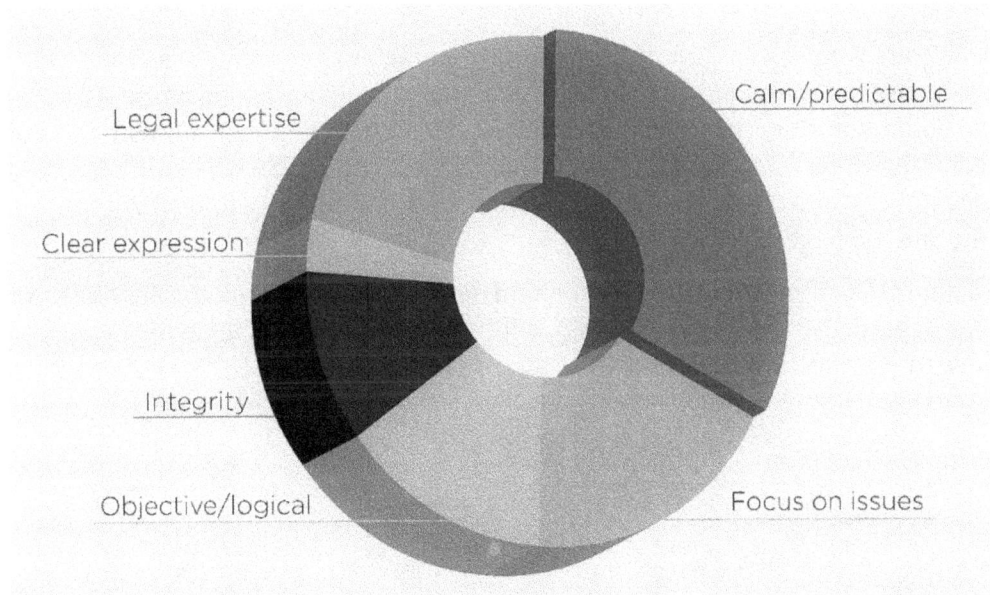

Legal expertise

Calm/predictable

Clear expression

Integrity

Objective/logical

Focus on issues

Figure 2-4 What Strengths Lawyers Think They Bring to a Crisis

One respondent said: "Lawyers bring calm, taking it step by step, knowing there is no good path and doing it carefully, monitoring all of the implications." Another added: "We are good at identifying the risk and getting people to understand the manifestation of the risk, where it's likely to go and the consequences."

Several lawyers noted they are "officers of the court" and accordingly have a duty to maintain integrity, look to the truth and honestly represent the law. A Canadian respondent identified one of their strengths as being able to see beyond the strict letter of the law: "A strength we bring is knowing what is appropriate and good judgement, not just what is legally possible."

Another participant emphasized that clients "don't want the lawyer to give legal advice." Instead they want the lawyer to solve their problem and get them out the other side. One even suggested that lawyers are never trained formally to consider the communication aspects or the commercial reality or the business consequences. He said those wider considerations are "trained out of us through law school" and had to be gradually picked up in the first few years of legal practice.

The lawyers were also asked what strengths communicators bring to a crisis. Their focus was not on tactical skills. Instead the most common response was about communicators' being able to bring an understanding of stakeholders and of all communication channels, including social media. Some lawyers conceded they tended to be over-analytical and don't have the same capability to deal with the public and the media.

"Communicators understand better than the lawyer how stakeholders are likely to receive a particular message, how they will respond, and how the company may be able to prepare for that response."

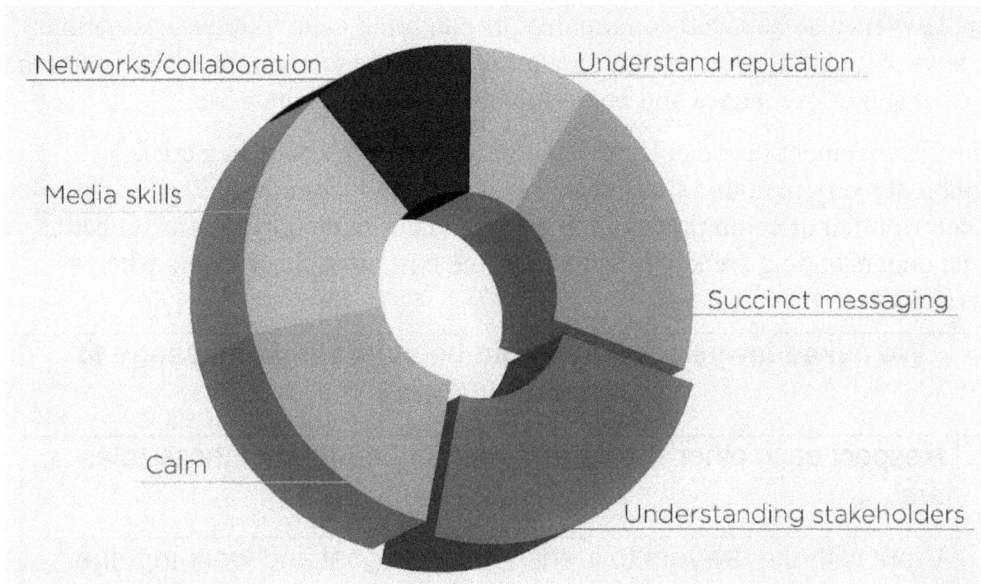

Figure 2-5 What Strengths Lawyers Think Communicators Bring to a Crisis

In that respect the lawyers also identified the communicator's ability to develop succinct messaging. The lawyers commonly noted that they are inclined to over-complicate messaging and that communicators can simplify the message – be it an offensive or defensive form of communication.

One said communicators have an ability to take the big picture and distil that into core propositions or messages that resonate with stakeholders, that sound authentic, that are factually correct and don't create other legal risks: "That is a real skill."

> "Sometimes you need to put your PR hat on, or your business hat, and let the lawyer in you just settle down."
>
> (Lawyer)

Another praised the ability of communicators to deal with things quickly and react immediately. They added: "They understand the imperfections of human nature better than lawyers. They understand the gladiatorial nature of media better than lawyers."

Many lawyers also believed communicators can bring calm to intense situations. One lawyer said: "They are calm, they bring down the temperature. They calm the nerves of senior executives and board members and collaborate well."

While disagreement between legal and communication advice in a crisis is undoubtedly very real, this study shows that lawyers recognize and value the role and contribution of communicators. It also validates that cooperation and better mutual understanding are key to delivering the best possible outcome when a crisis strikes.

	We asked lawyers, what would be your single message to communicators?
1	Respect each other's roles and work out early what those roles are.
2	Work with the lawyers to identify the end goal and work together to achieve it.
3	Stay in your lane and focus on the client. Showing off doesn't work.
4	Help me understand what you need to achieve so I can help you and you can help me.
5	Question to understand and appreciate that there are legal constraints.
6	Don't worry, we are not trying to eat your lunch. We can work together to make each other look good.
7	Listen to all perspectives, develop a communication strategy informed by assessing the legal risks.
8	Ask lots of questions, even if you know they are pretty simple. Make the lawyers explain their advice.

	We asked lawyers, what would be your single message to communicators?
9	Be patient, understand the law, the process, and the immediate and long-term risk.
10	Always challenge a legal view which is so constrained that it will damage the client's reputation.
11	Have patience. Make sure the lawyer understands the stakes and don't assume they do.
12	Respect the lawyer's advice. Don't see them as a "black hole."
13	Trust the lawyer your employer has hired to have the company's best interests in mind.
14	It isn't a battle of wills - for either of us.

Summary of findings

- Most lawyers believe that they, not communicators, should lead in a crisis.
- Lawyers are concerned about a perceived lack of legal awareness among communicators.
- The areas most prone to conflicting legal and communications advice relate to disclosure and apologizing.
- Lawyers believe communicators are too ready to disclose information and that conflict between disclosure and potential legal liability is a concern.
- Making decisions in a crisis under time pressure with inadequate facts is seen as a major challenge for lawyers.
- Lawyers strongly support face to face meetings with communicators to reduce conflict and achieve optimal crisis strategies.
- Although some lawyers believe conflict with communicators is not common, many still don't trust communicators to do the right thing when a crisis strikes.

- Lawyers believe the main strength they bring to a crisis – ahead of legal expertise – is being calm and predictable.
- Lawyers believe the main strengths communicators bring to a crisis are understanding stakeholders and the ability to develop succinct messaging.
- Better understanding and respect for each other's roles is identified as the single most important factor in working better together.

Key Takeaways

- We must listen to lawyers to hear their views beyond just the legal issues.
- There are legitimate challenges in the relationship between lawyers and communicators.
- Executives need to actively encourage all crisis counsellors to work as a team.
- The broad lawyer perspective is largely consistent across national borders.
- Lawyers genuinely want to work better with communicators and are willing to learn.

Questions for Discussion

1. *Why is external counsel better placed than an in-house lawyer to give advice in a crisis?*
2. *How would you answer the lawyer who told us: "Taking a measured approach is usually the best outcome for all"? Is that realistic in a time-critical crisis?*
3. *Is it simply a convenient argument when lawyers say they are "officers of the court"? How should non-lawyers respond?*
4. *Why are lawyers "not good at reaching a decision too quickly"? Is it training or personality?*
5. *Was one lawyer justified in asserting that it's rare for an organization to suffer long term damage by taking time to respond in a crisis? Does the evidence support this position?*

Chapter Three

Cases: Product Crises and Why They Hurt

"Lose money for the firm, and I will be understanding. Lose a shred of reputation for the firm, and I will be ruthless."

Warren Buffet.

It's no surprise that crises involving brands and products are some of the hardest fought and most emotional challenges to corporate success.

It's also no surprise that product crises so often expose seriously contested ground between lawyers and communication professionals.

Not every product problem or recall becomes a crisis and not every product crisis involves a recall. But the reality is product crises – particularly those involving serious failure or risk to consumers – typically impact nearly every management function. That helps explain why they tend to attract such intense senior executive attention, and why they often involve conflicting advice and demand difficult decision-making. Because product reputation and brand equity can represent an organization's most valuable and potentially vulnerable assets. Moreover, the impact of a major product crisis can be devastating to the bottom line and even to the survival of the business.

This is the first of three chapters devoted to in-depth review of situations where lawyers and communicators often come into conflict, in this case focusing on crises involving products.

This chapter will help you to:

- Identify the high – and sometimes fatal – cost of a brand crisis.
- Recognize how a heavy-handed legal response can turn a problem into a reputational crisis.
- Learn from companies which have faced reputational threats and which badly misread their stakeholders.
- Define and plan for the rising influence of consumers in brand crises.
- Evaluate two high-profile examples where a legal defense strategy seemed certain to damage consumer brand value.

It's worth considering the dramatic and sometimes fatal impact that a product crisis can bring, especially when it's badly managed on either the legal or the communications front. Take just a brief sample of some recent and not-so-recent devastating product crises:

- The recall of the Merck painkiller Vioxx after it was found to be responsible for increased risk of heart attack and stroke cost the pharmaceutical giant nearly $6 billion in litigation-related expenses alone.[49]

- President-elect Donald Trump tweeted his displeasure at the cost of the F-35 fighter jet, one of the key products of plane maker Lockheed Martin. The company's shares fell $4 billion in value, or $28.6 million for each character in the tweet. [50]

- The toxic chemical benzene was detected in bottles of Perrier water, leading to a global recall and a temporary shutdown of the entire production process. The crisis cost Perrier almost $263 million and the struggling French company was eventually sold to Nestlé of Switzerland.[51]

- Faulty airbags made by Japanese giant Takata led to the largest recall in history, involving tens of millions of vehicles across some of the world's biggest motorcar brands. With three executives indicted and a $1 billion criminal fine in the United States, the company was forced into bankruptcy.[52]

---

[49] Sukkar, E. (2014, September 19). Still feeling the Vioxx pain. *The Pharmaceutical Journal*. https://www.pharmaceutical-journal.com/news-and-analysis/features/still-feeling-the-vioxx-pain/20066485.article?firstPass=false

[50] Thielman, S. (2016, December 13). Trump's tweet about Lockheed-Martin cuts $4bn in value as share prices fall. *The Guardian*. https://www.theguardian.com/business/2016/dec/12/lockheed-martin-share-prices-donald-trump-tweet?utm_

[51] Kurzbard, G. & Siomkos, G. J. (1992). Crafting a damage control plan: Lessons from Perrier. *Journal of Business Strategy*, 13(2), 39–43.

[52] Mullen, J. (2017, June 26). Takata brought down by airbag crisis, files for bankruptcy. *CNN Money*.

- Young people on social media showed how to open Kryptonite bicycle locks in seconds with nothing more than a ballpoint pen. The embarrassed company was forced to exchange 380,000 locks worldwide at a cost of $10 million, almost half its annual revenue at the time.[53]

- An outbreak of listeriosis in cold meats produced by South African company Tiger Brands killed more than 200 people with another 1,000 seriously ill. The crisis cost the company 1.4 billion rand, equivalent to about US$96 million[54].

- Following a reported link between potentially blinding fungal infections and one of its contact lens solutions, US eye-care giant Bausch + Lomb lost 17 per cent of its share value in a single day. After further sustained destruction of shareholder value, the company was sold to private equity investors[55].

- Baby formula produced by Chinese dairy giant Sanlu was found to have used melamine-contaminated milk, resulting in six infant deaths and perhaps 300,000 babies becoming sick. Not only was Sanlu bankrupted, the CEO was sent to prison for life and two contractors were executed for their role in the scandal[56].

While these examples don't necessarily represent a conflict between legal and communication counsel, they do illustrate why product crises can be critical.

---

https://money.cnn.com/2017/06/25/news/companies/takata-bankruptcy/index.html

[53] Kirkpatrick, D. (2005, January 10). Why there's no escaping the blog. *Fortune.* https://money.cnn.com/magazines/fortune/fortune_archive/2005/01/10/8230982/index.htm

[54] Brown, J. (2018, November 18). Listeriosis crisis has cost Tiger Brands R1.4 bn in revenue so far. *City Press.* https://city-press.news24.com/News/listeriosis-crisis-has-cost-tiger-brands-r14bn-in-revenue-so-far-20181123

[55] Diermeier, D. (2011). *Reputation Rules: Strategies for Building Your Company's Most Valuable Asset.* New York: McGraw Hill.

[56] Barboza, D. (2009, January 22). Death sentences in Chinese milk case. *New York Times.* https://www.nytimes.com/2009/01/23/world/asia/23milk.html#

Clearly not every product crisis is so high-profile, nor has such dramatic impact. However, product crises often reveal the public's emotional investment in brands, such as when companies decide to reformulate a beloved product or change its name or even cease manufacture.

This consumer brand involvement was starkly on display in 2010 when clothing maker Gap proposed to change the design of its iconic logo. Public outcry saw the plan abandoned within a week[58]. Analysts concluded that the company had seriously misjudged the lack of public consultation and its impact on reputation. Moreover, the case highlighted an emerging concept which attempts to enshrine the role of public participation. As influential brand blogger Chris Kasper commented at the time: "Managers and investors may own the company, but a brand belongs to consumers."

While the idea that brands belong to consumers and not the company may be debatable, it has continued to gain considerable traction, accelerated by the rise of social media.

Although the now largely forgotten Gap rebranding fiasco was embarrassing, it was not a serious corporate crisis. Some argued that it may even have been a deliberate marketing stunt. Yet it was a stark illustration of the rising power of consumers, which shows no sign of slowing. And that change is very important to future crisis management.

---

[57] Smith, L. R. and Millar D. P. (2002). *Before the crisis hits: building a strategic crisis plan.* Washington DC: Community College Press
[58] Zmuda, N. (2010, October 18). Filling in the gap of a rebranding disaster. *Ad Age.* https://adage.com/article/news/branding-gap-s-logo-change-disaster/146525

Most organizational crises involve or affect the public in some way. But product crises often have a specific and direct impact on the public and sometimes individual consumers. Management executives need to recognize that this personal involvement by consumers brings particular risks to organizational reputation and also the need for special consideration when it comes to communication and legal strategy.

The Boeing 737 MAX Disasters

It would be wrong to start in-depth discussion of product crises without focusing first on one of the biggest and most-analyzed cases of recent years – the Boeing 737 MAX crisis. At the time of this writing the planes were still grounded and this case and its aftermath will likely last years. Yet analysis of the initial phases of the disaster provides some important lessons.

Aircraft crashes are, by definition, crises for the airline concerned and often the plane maker as well. But the Boeing 737 MAX crisis is distinguished by three less usual elements:

- Reports suggested very early that the crisis was caused by a specific aircraft design fault.
- Focus was almost entirely on the plane's maker rather than the airlines involved.
- There was widespread condemnation of Boeing's communication strategy and its obvious effort to reflect both legal and reputational considerations.

On its face the Boeing crisis is relatively simple – two of their fastest-selling new aircraft lost in less than five months, something unprecedented in modern aviation – in Indonesia in October 2018 and Ethiopia in March 2019, with 357 passengers and crew killed.

It is now accepted that both aircraft crashed because of the same faulty flight control system, and I expect this may eventually prove to be the most expensive product crisis in history. The crisis saw 700 aircraft grounded, 400 of them at the manufacturing plant before production was shut down, and Boeing shares shed $35 billion at one stage, with the company taking a $5 billion charge in mid-2019. Some analysts suggest the eventual cost could be $30 billion or more.

But aside from the tragic loss of life and the enormous amounts of money at risk, this particular product crisis is notable for a series of mistakes and stumbles which frankly should not happen at a major corporation.

Most importantly, some of those initial mistakes appeared to arise from the CEO at the time allowing commercial and legal considerations to outweigh Boeing's ability to communicate openly and transparently.

Indeed, one unnamed senior airline official told the *Seattle Times*:

"Lawyers shouldn't be telling the CEO what to do, and the company can't just hide and issue a 'no comment'."[59]

After the first crash, CEO Dennis Muilenburg and Boeing officials said better training and some minor software upgrades could fix the problem. After the second disaster Muilenburg told Congress that the plane was safe with additional pilot training and that it was premature to ground the aircraft until more facts about the crash were known.

As countries around the world began to ban the troubled plane from their airspace, and amid calls for it to be grounded, the CEO responded by telephoning President Trump to reiterate that the 737 MAX was a safe aircraft and urge him to keep it flying in the US[60].

But the order to ground the plane was soon issued and the CEO grudgingly said he supported the decision "out of an abundance of caution"[61]. However, you might think that the time for acting out of "abundant caution" was likely after the first crash, not the second, and certainly not after air safety regulators around the world had already made the decision.

---

[59] Gates, D. (2019, December 24). Here's why Boeing fired CEO Dennis Muilenburg, and what aviation insiders say his successor must do. *Seattle Times.* https://www.chicagotribune.com/business/ct-biz-boeing-ceo-david-calhoun-20191224-zx3t5qd3b5ay5i37hjpgqokl2m-story.html

[60] Rapier, G. (2019, March 13). Boeing's CEO reportedly asked President Trump not to ground the company's plane that has crashed twice in 5 months. *Business Insider.* https://www.businessinsider.com.au/boeing-ceo-called-president-trump-after-737-max-8-disaster-ny-times-2019-3?r=US&IR=T

[61] Baker, M. and Rosenberg, M. (2019, March 13). FAA grounds Boeing's 737 MAX, says doomed flights "behaved very similarly". *Seattle Times.* https://www.seattletimes.com/business/boeing-aerospace/after-analyzing-satellite-data-on-737-max-crash-canada-bans-the-plane-from-its-airspace/

No more "abundance of caution"... please

For Boeing to say it grounded the troubled 737 MAX aircraft "out of an abundance of caution" was a particularly poor choice of words.

What happened to simple English? When you are facing a crisis or a serious issue is exactly the time for accurate, unambiguous language, not shallow corporate jargon.

This silly phrase seemed to gain impetus in 2009 when White House senior counsel Greg Craig explained that, following a technical mistake, the then newly-inaugurated President Obama would retake his oath of office in an abundance of caution[62]. Perhaps that was understandable, but since then hundreds of organizations in trouble have hidden behind this almost meaningless phrase as some sort of linguistic smokescreen.

Maybe it's time to retire the term and focus instead on abundance of accuracy or abundance of leadership.

Facing massive financial losses, and loss of confidence by airlines and investors, the Boeing CEO kept making over-optimistic and unfulfilled statements about when the aircraft would be cleared to fly again.

Given that the company's relationship with the Federal Aviation Administration was already coming under scrutiny, FAA administrator Steve Dickson then took the unusual step of publicly rebuking Boeing for "continuing to pursue a return-to-service schedule that is not realistic."

---

[62] *Obama retakes oath of office* (2009, January 22) NBC News.
http://www.nbcnews.com/id/28780417/ns/politics-white_house/t/obama-retakes-oath-office-after-flub/#.XhrMPsgzbIU

That – and Boeing's spacecraft Starliner being launched into the wrong orbit in December 2019 because of a system failure [63] – saw the end of the Board's patience and Muilenburg was dumped as CEO, though officially he was allowed to resign... effective immediately.

Lessons Learned

While the Boeing 737 MAX crisis still has a long way to run – and lawsuits will likely last for many years – there are already some important lessons.

The most important is undoubtedly about leadership. In crisis communication the leader needs to demonstrate genuine leadership, and that doesn't just come with the job title.

Leadership means taking the lead and helping to set the agenda, but Muilenburg effectively did the opposite – allowing others to dictate the narrative. Instead of immediately grounding the planes he said that was premature until more facts about the crash were known, allowing regulators around the world to drive the issue. And his decision to call on Donald Trump to use his Presidential authority to keep the planes in the air was – at the very least – naïve and unwise.

When he did speak, Muilenburg's statements were terse and basically focused on just two key messages – the aircraft is safe and it will be back in the air soon – both of which increasingly seemed unbelievable.

And when the CEO did issue an apology after the second crash, it was via a pre-recorded video distributed online and through news networks, not at a press conference where reporters would have had the chance to ask tough questions. While Muilenburg said the plane maker cared about the victims – and the company allocated

---

[63] Sheetz, M. (2019, December 20). Boeing Starliner fails key NASA mission as autonomous flight system malfunctions. *CNCB News.* https://www.cnbc.com/2019/12/20/boeings-starliner-flies-into-wrong-orbit-jeopardizing-trip-to-the-international-space-station.html

$100 million in compensation – he needed to personally show he cared, and express empathy, not just corporate platitudes.

Consider the response by Paul Hudson, President of Flyers Rights, a nonprofit group advocating for passengers:

> *"If they really wanted to fix the problem, you would think they would admit that it's their fault. You can't say, 'Oh, we own it, but we didn't do anything wrong and it's someone else's fault'"* [64].

It's little wonder that the impression spread that every statement seemed to have been filtered through the Boeing legal team rather than being led by communication professionals

There is nothing wrong with the CEO needing to understand the legal implications of what he says. That's right and proper. When you are holding well over $600 billion worth of orders for a plane which is grounded, and customers are threatening to cancel, it's very natural to be seriously worried about the legal and commercial reality[65]. After all, the troubled plane represented about one third of the company's revenue.

But Boeing is not only selling aircraft. It's selling the promise of safe travel and that needed to be a priority.

No one seriously doubts that Boeing will survive. As one of America's largest manufacturing companies, it probably fits into the category of "too big to fail." However, its recovery is likely to take

---

[64] Kitroeff, N, and Gelles, D. (2019, May 8). With 737 MAX, Boeing wants to win back trust.Many are Skeptical. *New York Times.*
https://www.nytimes.com/2019/05/08/business/boeing-737-max.html

[65] Lee, D. (2019, March 14). Ethiopian Airlines crash puts $633 billion worth of Boeing 737 MAX jet orders in jeopardy – with Asian airlines among the biggest customers. *South China Morning Post.*
https://www.scmp.com/news/hong-kong/transport/article/3001749/ethiopian-airlines-crash-puts-us633-billion-worth-boeing

a very, very long time and the world will not soon forget the biggest-ever product crisis.

Samsung Gets Hot

One obvious reason product crises gain so much attention is the megaphone effect of social media, which gives angry individuals equal voice. The other reason is that lay members of the public don't always respect the rules in a way that lawyers might imagine, which can make them very unpredictable.

Take the compelling case of the all-guns-blazing legal reaction by Samsung when a customer complained that his Galaxy S4 phone had been damaged when the charging port caught fire.

Canadian Richard Wygand (using his social media moniker *ghostlyrich*) went online saying he approached Samsung, who said they required proof of the damage. So he recorded a YouTube video showing the burned charger connector plus heat damage around the port.

The YouTube post was accompanied by the message:

> *"This video is proof the phone caught fire that Samsung was asking for. So far they have been jerking me around. Well here is a video proving my claim and a warning to Samsung S4 owners the claims are true they have been reading about"[66].*

The video quickly amassed well over 100,000 views and Samsung realized they had an emerging brand issue on their hands.

The Galaxy S4 – which reportedly sold 40 million units in its first six months – had already generated massive unwanted publicity. Just weeks earlier the South Korean manufacturer had to announce a global free battery replacement program

---

[66] Wygand, R. (2013, December 2). Samsung Galaxy s4 caught fire, proof for Samsung. *Youtube.* https://www.youtube.com/watch?v=dc4duKuPrQ0

after complaints that the original power packs were draining at an unacceptable rate and some were swelling up and distorting the casing [67.]

Given that context, the video claim of a fire risk was seemingly too much for the Samsung legal team. Their response was a letter demanding that the young Canadian take down the video before they would replace his phone under warranty. They also demanded that he agree never to divulge any settlement and to absolve Samsung of any legal liability.

The legal letter was a masterly 650-word epistle heavily larded with whereas and hereby and whatsoever. All of this, remember, for a phone worth a few hundred dollars.

It's not clear to me what reaction Samsung expected from the customer. Presumably they did not expect Wygand to make a second video in which he very publicly rejected the company's demands.

It's also not clear what, if any, of this was supported by the company's communicators responsible for the negotiations.

Far from agreeing to the proposed confidentiality clause, the Canadian read extracts from the letter on YouTube and posted the full text online[68].

The second video initially attracted more than 800,000 views and mainstream headlines such as:

---

[67] Charles, A. (2013, October 17). Samsung offers S4 owners free replacement on faulty batteries. *The Guardian*.
https://www.theguardian.com/technology/2013/oct/17/samsung-s4-faulty-battery-replacement
[68] The full text of the Samsung legal letter can be seen online at
https://pastebin.com/D3G2iKDP

"Samsung damage control backfires after Galaxy S4 fire claim." (*news.com*)[69]

"Samsung tries to smother report of Galaxy S4 fire. (*The Telegraph*)[70]

"S4 catches fire, Samsung tries to silence report." (*UPI*)[71]

Samsung changed legal tack after the second video and Wygand got a replacement phone – apparently without conditions.

There were few consequences for the young Canadian. He got his replacement phone and his classic 15 minutes of fame, perpetuated by the fact that his videos remain online, and continue to receive attention. At the time of writing, his first YouTube video had been viewed more than 1.4 million times, and the second video about the legal letter from Samsung had been viewed well over 1.5 million times.

But what were the consequences for Samsung? The immediate impact was a brief reputational crisis (a few other cases of alleged fire damage were also reported) and the potential embarrassment of a questionable legal strategy. We can perhaps guess that – as so often happens – the lawyers argued that there was "a larger principle involved."

---

[69] Michael, S. (2013, December 11). Samsung damage control backfires after Galaxy S4 fire claim. *News.com*. https://www.news.com.au/technology/gadgets/samsung-damage-control-backfires-after-galaxy-s4-fire-claim/news-story/56da1a52cf54173802c41ed44f6158a0

[70] Curtis, S. (2013, December 10). Samsung tries to smother report of Galaxy S4 fire. *The Telegraph, UK.* https://www.telegraph.co.uk/technology/samsung/10508913/Samsung-tries-to-smother-report-of-Galaxy-S4-fire.html

[71] Levy, G. (2013, December 11). S4 catches fire, Samsung tries to silence report. *UPI.* https://www.upi.com/blog/2013/12/11/S4-catches-fire-Samsung-tries-to-silence-report/5041386799076/

> "On matters of style swim with the current. On matters of principle stand like a rock."

> Thomas Jefferson

The old joke is never trust politicians, lawyers or professional communicators when they talk of "matters of principle." And the Samsung response is pretty clearly a case of focusing on the particular and losing sight of the big picture.

However, the longer-term consequence was evident just a few years later in 2017 with the company's response to the major crisis involving the Samsung Note 7 smartphone which began to overheat and explode. The issue was so serious that some airlines banned the phone being carried on board[72].

This is where you can see that Samsung learned their lesson, and it's a lesson for other companies too.

Unlike in the previous incident, Samsung rapidly initiated a global recall of over two million devices and discontinued manufacture at a cost of over $5 billion. Most importantly the company promptly held a press conference at which it took full responsibility for the crisis. It then committed to find the root cause of the issue and set up a test lab with 700 researchers, 200,000 devices and 30,000 batteries in an attempt to replicate the fires. Moreover Samsung committed to make the report public and to subject the research to third party auditors.

Setting up an investigation is sometimes just a stalling tactic. But true to their word, Samsung released the "warts and all" report – detailing flaws in battery design and manufacturing – and the company found itself praised for its handling of the crisis, in contrast to the reputation-sapping headlines from the previous incident.

---

[72] *Samsung Galaxy Note 7 banned by more airlines over fire* risk (2016, October 16). BBC World News. https://www.bbc.com/news/business-37674170

> *"From a 'cultural meme' to a comeback kid: How*
> *Samsung overcame its Galaxy note 7 fiasco.*
> *(Business Insider)[73]*

> *"Samsung explains Note 7 battery explosions, and*
> *turns crisis into opportunity." (Forbes)[74]*

Shuttering the Note 7 cost Samsung about $10 billion in direct costs and their shares on the Seoul exchange plunged by $17 billion. Yet by year's end Samsung improved from seventh to sixth place on the Interbrand Best Global Brands list for 2017, with a reported nine per cent increase in brand valuation, despite the crisis. A Reuters-Ipsos poll reported:

> *"Samsung Galaxy Note 7 exploding batteries have*
> *not damaged brand, says new poll."[75]*

Samsung's Senior VP of Marketing Communications, Pio Schunker, later revealed that the company and its agencies set up a war room in the immediate aftermath of the crisis, monitoring media reports and consumer sentiment online day in and day out to make sure everyone was on the same page. So perhaps Samsung did finally come to value public opinion and reputation over the heavy-handed legal approach.

---

[73] Dua, T. (2017, October 9). From a 'cultural meme' to a comeback kid: How Samsung overcame its Galaxy Note 7 fiasco. *Business Insider.* https://www.businessinsider.com.au/how-samsung-overcame-its-galaxy-note-7-fiasco-2017-10

[74] Lopez, M. (2017, January 22). Samsung explains Note 7 battery explosions and turns crisis into opportunity. *Forbes Magazine.* https://www.forbes.com/sites/maribellopez/2017/01/22/samsung-reveals-cause-of-note-7-issue-turns-crisis-into-opportunity/

[75] Brown, A. (2016, November 22). Samsung Galaxy Note 7 exploding batteries have not damaged brand, says new poll. *Daily Express.* https://www.express.co.uk/life-style/science-technology/734756/Samsung-Galaxy-Note-7-Explode-Battery

The real legacy of the Samsung crisis

"As the months pass in the wake of the Note 7 debacle, it will be the damage to the brand that we should be watching. Phones come and go. Profits come and go. But loss of credibility is a pain that lingers."

Fast Company. [76]

Missing the Joke

Of course, Samsung is not the only company to be embarrassed by the publication of an overzealous legal letter trying to defend a product (and doubtless won't be the last).

As its annual April Fools' Day prank in 2010, ThinkGeek, an American online retailer selling nerdy-gifts and joke products, launched "canned unicorn" as "the new white meat"[77]. However, the National Pork Board claimed ThinkGeek infringed the copyright of their slogan "the other white meat" and the Board's lawyers issued a 12-page cease-and-desist demand.

Yes, you read that right. A 12-page legal letter to defend a real product against a fictional competitor which didn't even exist.

Company owners GeekNet apologized on their website, playfully saying they had not intended to "cause a national crisis and misguide Americans regarding the difference between the pig and the unicorn."

[76] Sullivan, M. (2016, October 12). How did Samsung botch the Galaxy Note 7 crisis? It's a Failure of leadership. *Fast Company.* https://www.fastcompany.com/3064569/how-did-samsung-botch-the-galaxy-note-7-crisis-its-a-failure-of-leadership

[77] *Canned unicorn meat.* (2010). https://www.amazon.com/Think-Geek-Canned-Unicorn-Meat/dp/B004CRYE2C

As in the Samsung Galaxy S4 case, GeekNet too proceeded to publish the lengthy legal letter they had received, which led to mocking headlines across the country and what the *Washington Post* called "an internet-wide case of the giggles."

> "National Pork Board targets ThinkGeek website: Blame the unicorns." (*Washington Post*)[78]

> "Pork Board squeals over unicorn meat." (*NBC news*)[79]

> "Unicorns. They're not the other white meat." (*New York Times*)[80]

> "Pork Board threatens legal action over 'canned unicorn' parody." (*Huffington Post*)[81]

Pork Board spokeswoman Ceci Snyder explained that the board's attorneys are instructed to protect the "Other White Meat" trademark in all cases to avoid future legal challenges to the slogan. "Clearly there's some fun being had, and we can laugh, too," she said. "But in the end, they're just following the law."

It's tough to argue against following the law, but where were the Pork Board's communicators responsible for reputation, especially as the case came just a few years after the Board was berated for sending a similar cease-and-desist letter to a

---

[78] Eggen, D. (2010, June 22). National Pork Board targets ThinkGeek website: Blame the unicorns. *Washington Post*.
https://www.washingtonpost.com/wp-dyn/content/article/2010/06/22/AR2010062201657.html

[79] Skidmore, S. (2010, June 22). Pork Board squeals over unicorn meat. *NBC News*. http://www.nbcnews.com/id/37854432/ns/business-us_business/t/pork-board-squeals-over-unicorn-meat/

[80] Bilton, N. (2010, June 22). Unicorns. They're not the Other White Meat. *New York Times*.
https://bits.blogs.nytimes.com/2010/06/22/unicorns-theyre-not-the-other-white-meat/

[81] Pork Board threatens legal action over 'canned unicorn' parody. (2010, June 21). *Huffington Post*.
https://www.huffpost.com/entry/canned-unicorn-pork-board_n_619926

breastfeeding website, which sold T-shirts with the slogan: "The Other White Milk."

As *Washington Post* reporter Dan Eggen commented:

> *"If you ever wonder what kind of work the lawyers for powerful industry groups get paid good money for, consider the case of the National Pork Board versus ThinkGeek Inc."*

While we might find it easy to laugh about unicorn meat and the lawyers' self-inflicted discomfiture, there are plenty of other examples where legal advice about a genuine product problem led to genuine reputational damage.

As elsewhere, in individual examples, we can't be privy to what prior discussion took place in the executive suite or between legal and communication professionals. But we can draw conclusions based on what was said or done in public, and we can draw lessons about what might have been a more effective strategy.

One such case which seemed to have legal fingerprints all over it was in early 2019 when Mondelez recalled some batches of Chewy Chips Ahoy because of "an unexpected solidified ingredient."[82] While the imagination might run wild, the company made it clear that the problem was in fact small lumps of corn starch which didn't get properly mixed in and solidified in the baking process. But the rather ambiguous phrase "unexpected solidified ingredient" appeared in media coverage across the country and doubtless worried many anxious mothers.

Here again we don't know who thought this was a good idea, but we can guess that somewhere in the communications approval chain were lawyers who wanted to damp down the impact of any claims. In a product crisis the focus should be on

---

[82] Bever, L. (2019, April 18). Put down the Chewy Chips Ahoy — a 'solidified ingredient,' recall says, might break your sweet tooth. *Washington Post.* https://www.washingtonpost.com/food/2019/04/17/chewy-chips-ahoy-recalled-after-unexpected-solidified-ingredient-may-have-caused-gagging-dental-injuries/

clear messaging rather than an apparent effort to minimize future legal or financial risk, even when such a risk might not actually exist.

Negative Online Reviews

In another example of heavy-handed defense of brand, online retailer KlearGear sued a Utah couple for $3,500 after they posted a negative review about non-delivery of a perpetual-motion desk toy and a smiley-face keychain worth in total less than $20.

Almost four years later the retailer sued the disgruntled customers on the basis of a claimed "non-disparagement clause." The couple counter-sued for defamation and infliction of emotional distress and the company persisted in pursuing the case over three years.

In 2014 the Utah District Court eventually found in favor of the customers and awarded $306,750 against the company, plus almost $50,000 in attorney's fees and expenses[83]. Apart from the costly legal strategy – triggered by an order worth less than $20 – the case prompted California's legislature to ban non-disparagement clauses.

Lessons learned

These three cases – Samsung's exploding phone, canned unicorn meat and KlearGear's reaction to a negative online post – all illustrate the same central lesson in crisis management: namely that sometimes a heavy-handed legal approach can turn a relatively simple product-related problem into a full-blown reputational nightmare.

In my view, such cases cannot be laid solely at the feet of overzealous lawyers. It's the lawyer's proper role to set out all the possible strategies from a legal perspective – even the less desirable strategies. But it's the role of management to balance each option against the commercial and reputational risk.

---

[83] Farivar, C. (2014, 26 June). KlearGear must pay $306,750 to couple that left negative review. *Arstechnica.com*. https://arstechnica.com/tech-policy/2014/06/kleargear-must-pay-306750-to-couple-that-left-negative-review/

In none of these cases do I know who made the decision to send a threatening legal letter which had every chance of backfiring badly. Yet I do know that the reputational red flags should have been clearly recognized.

Of course, 20:20 hindsight is a wonderful thing, but:

- *After the first embarrassing video was posted, Samsung should have recognized they had a serious emerging issue and not sent the legal letter which triggered a second round of terrible publicity.*

- *The Pork Board may argue that its lawyers were "just following the law," but they needed to temper their response to "canned unicorn" with common sense, and demonstrate an ability to appreciate a joke and,*

- *When the angry KlearGear customers counter-sued, the retailer should have recognized it was probably time to settle. Looking back, which KlearGear executive could have honestly argued that a disputed $20 order was really worth over $350,000?*

But perhaps the most important lesson you can take here is that Samsung appears to have understood what went wrong and put measures in place to make sure it didn't happen again (though I would have recommended they not characterize the recall as an "exchange program" and hadn't kept referring to the decision to halt production by saying the company had "adjusted its production schedules.")

I don't know whether the Pork Board or KlearGear ever accepted that their reputational damage was largely self-inflicted. But I take heart from the fact that a corporate giant like Samsung can learn from a reputational crisis and avoid the same mistake again.

The question is whether you too can learn, and whether you would think twice before authorizing a legal letter which risks blowing up in your face.

The Pentium Chip Recall

Of all the different areas of product crises, recalls of faulty product are perhaps the richest area for conflict between legal and communication over how to minimize legal liability versus protecting brand reputation. And one of the most analyzed incidents among classic crisis management disasters is the notorious Intel Pentium chip recall.

While this much-studied case is now 25 years old, it remains very relevant because it helped set the standard for public expectation in a recall and is regarded as the first internet-generated corporate crisis. More importantly in the current context, contrary to the usual in-house secrecy, sufficient detail was eventually revealed to seemingly expose the result of cross-functional conflict and dissent within the executive suite.

In June 1994, about a year after launching the flagship Pentium processor, Intel experts discovered a flaw in the chip which would produce an occasional error in some highly complex calculations. However, after a great deal of internal discussion, the company decided not to reveal the flaw because, they argued, the fault would almost never affect most users. Indeed, their internal experts calculated that the flaw caused a rounding error in division once in every nine billion calculations and that an average user would encounter the problem only once in 27,000 years of spreadsheet use.

As a result, no-one outside Intel was notified.

Unfortunately, at around the same time, Dr Thomas Nicely, a professor of mathematics at Lynchburg College, Virginia, noticed a disparity between calculations made on different computers. After five months of exhaustive testing to eliminate possible causes he determined that the error was caused by the Pentium processor. He then contacted Intel technical support, who confirmed the error but claimed it had not been previously reported.

Lacking a satisfactory response from Intel, Dr Nicely posted his findings online, and the story rapidly spread through specialist forums and newsgroups, and inevitably out into mainstream media. Intel's response was that the problem was minor and that it was not uncommon in a new product.

It was at this point that a pivotal decision was made by Intel management which turned what could have been a standard recall into a reputational crisis.

In response to a highly critical report in the *New York Times*,[84] and a similar story syndicated to newspapers, television and radio nationwide, Intel CEO Andrew Grove assembled his management team.

It was reported that some at the conference table suggested an immediate no-questions-asked return policy. But Grove overruled objections and rejected this approach "because of the consequences."

Instead Intel announced that it would replace a Pentium chip only after the customer had contacted Intel to prove that it was used in an application in which it would cause a problem. In other words, Intel would decide whether the computer owner really needed a replacement.

---

[84] Markhoff, J. (1994, November 24). Circuit flaw causes Pentium chip to miscalculate, Intel Admits. *New York Times*.

While the angry customer response was predictable and fairly brutal, calls to the hotline soon declined and Intel convinced itself they might have weathered the storm.

Then IBM, a major Pentium purchaser as well as maker of its own competing processor, revealed that new calculations showed the average spreadsheet user might encounter an error every 24 days, not every 27,000 years as Intel predicted. IBM announced that it would immediately cease shipping computers with "Intel Inside" and offered replacements to all of its customers.

At an all-day crisis team meeting at Intel (19 December 1994) the company bowed to the inevitable and withdrew the conditional replacement policy, offering instead to provide a new processor chip to anyone who requested a replacement.

Grove told the *New York Times* the meeting was marked not by yelling or screaming but by passionate discussion, and the decision to change the policy on the Pentium replacements was adopted and rescinded several times[85]. "Finally we decided, this is the right thing to do, both morally and ethically." Which raises the obvious question, was the company conceding that previously it was *not* acting morally and ethically?

> "Finally we decided, this is the right thing to do, both morally and ethically."
>
> Andy Grove, Intel

In a media teleconference, Intel's CEO explained:

> "We got caught between our mindset, which is a fact-based, analysis-based engineer's mindset, and customers' mindset, which is not so much emotional but accustomed to making their own choice." He added: "I think the kernel of the issue we missed . . . was that we presumed to tell somebody what they should or shouldn't worry about, or should or shouldn't do." [86]

---

[85] Markhoff, J. (1994, December 21). Intel's crash-course on consumers. *New York Times*. https://www.nytimes.com/1994/12/21/business/business-technology-intel-s-crash-course-on-consumers.html

[86] Carlton, J. and Kreider, S. (1994, December 21). Humble Pie: Intel to replace its Pentium chips. *Wall Street Journal*. http://mizar.org/qed/mail-archive/volume-2/0128.html

From the same teleconference an Intel lawyer was reported as saying – somewhat unwisely – that the recall "takes care" of questions of product liability.

What we do know is that the Pentium chip debacle cost Intel a one-off charge against earnings of $475 million, though their reputation quickly recovered, and CEO Grove was named "Time Man of the Year."

Doing Business in China

Intel is certainly not the only company to impose a legalistic obstacle course in response to a product recall crisis. More than a decade later Procter and Gamble (P&G) tried the same strategy for their skincare brand SK-II... and suffered a similar hit to reputation.

The American multinational had purchased the Japan-based SK-II and launched it into China, where successful marketing made it the dominant premium brand. Like many other luxury cosmetics, SK- II was sold primarily at dedicated counters in high-end department stores across the country.

In mid-September 2008 the Chinese Government Quality Authority announced that it had detected the banned heavy metals chromium and neodymium in nine SK-II products.

P&G insisted its products were safe, and in a classic legalistic response they offered refunds, but only if the customer could show the original sales receipt, and also agreed to sign a waiver saying there was no problem with quality. Customers were told they might have to wait three weeks for the refund.

Furthermore, it was claimed that in some stores, local staff refused a refund if more than two thirds of the product had been used. Some stores were even reported demanding a certificate from the hospital saying the customer was allergic to the product.

Unsurprisingly, angry SK-II users took to social media to complain about the unfairness of the refund process, and their cause was quickly taken up by sympathetic local mainstream media. The Chinese Consumer Association (CCA) pointed out the obvious fact that "consumers are entitled by law to demand that substandard products be recalled unconditionally."[87]

CCA spokesman Wu Gaohan said companies should strictly abide by the law and set no conditions on withdrawn products. "Any new conditions that the company tries to impose are either invalid or illegal."

The emerging crisis was further inflamed by a tone-deaf P&G response (which appeared to rely on legal advice):

> *"We are not required by the law to refund customers, nor have we been notified to remove products, but we agreed to refund customers as a gesture of goodwill."[88]*

A gesture of goodwill? Really? Chinese authorities then ordered the company to stop selling the nine suspect products and added another three to the list after further contamination was detected.

A day later (22 October) P&G announced that sales of certain SK-II products would be suspended and that the deadline for seeking refunds would be 5 November.

Tempers flared and hundreds of angry customers in Shanghai stormed counters and refund centers and smashed the glass front door at the building which housed P&G's headquarters in China.

The company responded by shutting down all 97 SK-II counters across China and suspended refund operations, supposedly to protect staff. They also halted sales of all SK-II products in China "due to confusion among consumers."

All this time brand reputation was taking a battering. An internet poll taken by the popular website sina.com showed that 98.8 per cent of 150,000 respondents said they would not buy SK-II products in the future. Another sina.com survey showed

---

[87] *Substandard Japanese cosmetics asked to be recalled.* (2006, September 22). Xinhua. http://en.people.cn/200609/22/print20060922_305236.html

[88] Chow, V. (2006, September 20). SK-II products will be banned if tests find more quality problems. *South China Morning Post.* https://www.scmp.com/article/564656/sk-ii-products-will-be-banned-if-tests-find-more-quality-problems

about 90 per cent believed the banned substances in SK-II products were dangerous to human health, and a similar number believed P&G was lying.[89]

Meanwhile health authorities elsewhere in Asia tested SK-II and other luxury cosmetic brands and concluded that trace amounts of metals detected posed no health risk.

Just over one month after the crisis began, Chinese authorities gave SK-II the all-clear to resume sales... but admitted no error on their part.

> "If stakeholders *think* there is a risk or a crisis, there is one."
>
> Sherry Holladay and Tim Coombs[90]

Lessons learned

The Pentium chip and SK-II crises illustrate another crisis management lesson I have discussed before – the critical need to properly understand your stakeholders.

Intel CEO Andrew Grove admitted they got caught between the analysis-based engineer's mindset and the customers expectation that they should make their own choice. But it's also clear that they completely underestimated the likely customer response.

In fact, at one stage Grove told a reporter:

> *"What we view as an extremely minor technical problem has taken on a life of its own."[91]*

This comment was published in the wake of the critical meeting when the company decided on an unconditional replacement policy.

---

[89] Tai, S. (2008) Beauty and the Beast: The Brand Crisis of SK-II Cosmetics in China. *Asian Case Research Journal*, 12 (1), 51-71

[90] Holladay, S. J., & Coombs, T. W. (2013). Successful prevention may not be enough: A case study of how managing a threat triggers a threat. *Public Relations Review, 39*(5), 451- 458.

[91] Zitner, A. (1994, December 21). Consumers get a break on computer chip. *Boston Globe*.

I believe Intel's failure to understand the true nature of the crisis and their general inability to see it from the customer's viewpoint was most likely inexperience rather than deliberate. But you have to ask which Intel department heads spoke up at the first meeting when the CEO rejected a no-questions-asked recall? What was their reasoning? And did the communications professionals – if they were present – raise the obvious reputational risks?

Then you have to ask why it took the subsequent all-day meeting to decide to "do the right thing both morally and ethically?"

Here again we will probably never know who spoke on each side of the discussion. But the CEO admitted the replacement policy was adopted and rescinded several times, so presumably at least some participants were arguing that the company should not do the right thing. No wonder it took all day, even allowing for the time needed to agree on the legal and financial and logistical details.

As I mentioned before, the lawyer's proper role is to help in defining legal alternatives. In this case we don't know what position Intel's lawyers took, but perhaps it's a reminder that what's legal is not necessarily what's ethical or moral. You should use legal standards only to indicate what is a legal course of action, not what is a morally desirable course of action.

One thing we know from the Pentium chip case is that a full-scale crisis might have been avoided if Intel had decided on a low-key recall right at the beginning, and that the crisis was more about the company's mishandling of the situation rather than the issue itself.

There is no doubt that much of the public anger against Intel arose from their initial refusal to recognize the crisis, and the deliberately difficult process applied in the original conditional replacement program.

A similar lesson can be taken from the SK-II crisis, where a deliberately difficult product replacement process led to actual violence and long-term brand damage.

However, the key lesson here is about failure to understand stakeholders, and in the SK-II case it was about stakeholders far beyond just the angry consumers and the unfair and badly implemented refund policy. Some experts have argued that the SK-II crisis was more about politics than science, and that it was motivated by retaliation against Japanese trade policy, or by state agencies intervening to resist foreign products.[92]

That discussion is outside my scope here. Yet the case undoubtedly has important lessons for foreign companies wanting to do business in China and hoping to avoid similar crises.

First, it's unwise to say you are cooperating with local authorities then cast doubt on the validity of local testing procedures. P&G needed to understand the importance of working within local systems rather than dismissing local concerns and using "foreign" standards. Similarly, emphasizing that other countries' testing found no problems was not at all helpful.

Second, corporations must learn how to act when they are caught up in a political argument. Think no further than the crisis facing Dior in China when their brand ambassador Sharon Stone suggested the devastating Sichuan earthquake in 2008, resulting in almost 70,000 deaths, was "karma" for China's policy against her friend the Dalai Lama.[93] Dior was forced to remove all advertisement in China with Stone's image and the brand suffered badly in China for many years.

The third lesson from the SK-II example is that brand-owner P&G appeared not to recognize the difference between global and local issues and how to respond to them. For example, social media in

---

[92] Whiteman, G. and Krug, B. (2008) Beauty and the Beast: Consumer stakeholders demand action in China. *Journal of International Business Ethics* 1 (1) 36-51

[93] Olson, P. (2008, May 29). Sharon Stone's Own Bad Karma. *Forbes*. https://www.forbes.com/2008/05/29/sharon-stone-china-face-markets-cx_po_0529autofacescan01.html#39ebb9927890

China played a major role in raising the profile of the issue, but the company failed to use it establish two-way communication with their customers. At the same time what worked for P&G in their home market was not necessarily going to work elsewhere, and they seriously overestimated their influence in China.

Regardless of these specific lessons, the fact remains that P&G's legalistic mishandling of the situation and failure to respond to the local political environment severely damaged the brand.

Chalk one up for common sense

Sometimes it's not at all clear who's to blame for legal action that damages a brand, but the damage is no less real.

Inspired by the Occupy Wall Street Movement, 40-year-old Jeff Olson of San Diego scrawled anti-bank slogans in water-soluble children's chalk on the public footpath outside three local branches of Bank of America. The bank reportedly complained to local officials, who laid 13 misdemeanor charges of vandalism, which could have brought 13 years in jail and $13,000 in fines.[94]

Olson refused to have the charges reduced by agreeing to community service cleaning up the graffiti, and after a *four-day trial* a jury acquitted him. Mayor Bob Filner called it a "nonsense prosecution" and blamed the bank and an overzealous city attorney. Bank of America declined to pursue its own legal action against the lone protester, but the case generated

---

[94] *13 years in jail for a little sidewalk chalk?* (2013, July 2). *USA Today.* https://www.usatoday.com/story/news/nation/2013/07/02/san-diego-sidewalk-chalk/2482201/

months of anti-bank publicity and adverse news media and social media commentary.

Olson himself said the case had brought more attention to his views than he ever imagined possible. He concluded: "I couldn't have done better if I rented an airplane with a banner and put billboards up all over town."

A Mouthful of Mouse

While the exact role of lawyers and communicators in a crisis is often hidden behind a corporate facade, there are three notorious product cases where the heavy hand of legal advisors was unambiguously on display in the courtroom or in legal filings.

Ronald Ball of Madison County, Illinois, lodged a claim in court for $75,000 alleging he found a dead mouse in a can of the caffeinated drink Mountain Dew, produced by Pepsi. One headline writer gleefully dubbed it "A mouthful of mouse."

Contamination claims – real or fake – are one of the most common product risks faced by food and beverage companies everywhere. But it's the response in this case which raised eyebrows.

After a long period of consideration, Pepsi filed a defense citing experts who would testify that the dead mouse could not have been in the can because, they argued, Mountain Dew is so acidic it would have destroyed the tiny rodent's body and turned it into "a jelly-like substance."

Yes, the company's legal strategy was apparently to tell the world that their valued brand, intended for human consumption, can actually dissolve flesh. Not only that, but the Pepsi lawyers spelled out in gruesome detail in court documents a description of exactly how and how quickly their company's fine product would gradually destroy a mouse. [95]

---

[95] Mikkelson, D. (2014, July 22). Will Mountain Dew dissolve a mouse. *snopes.com.*
https://www.snopes.com/fact-check/mountain-ewww/

It's no secret that many soft drinks are acidic. But imagine how this strategy must have pleased the marketing department! The case became a national joke, with astonishingly unhelpful international reports such as:

"Swig of Mountain Dew Included Dead Mouse, Suit Claims." (Madison Record) [96]

"Pepsi defends lawsuit: Says Mountain Dew turns a mouse into jelly." (Digital Journal) [97]

"Apparently, Mountain Dew Can Turn A Mouse Into A 'Jelly Like' Goo." (Business Insider) [98]

"Pepsi explain why you'll never find a mouse in Mountain Dew." (Geek.com) [99]

"Drinks giant Pepsi says man who claims he found a mouse in his can of Mountain Dew must be wrong... because it would have dissolved." (Daily Mail) [100]

---

[96] Holleran, K. (2009, May 4). Swig of Mountain Dew Included Dead Mouse, Suit Claims. *The Madison-St Clair Record.* https://madisonrecord.com/stories/510566609-swig-of-mountain-dew-included-dead-mouse-suit-claims

[97] Goessl, L. (2012, January 4). Pepsi defends lawsuit: says Mountain Dew turns a mouse into jelly. *Digital Journal.* http://www.digitaljournal.com/article/317293

[98] Bhasin, K. (2012, January 5). Apparently, Mountain Dew Can Turn A Mouse Into A 'Jelly Like' Goo. *Business Insider.* https://www.businessinsider.com.au/mountain-dew-mouse-jelly-2012-1?r=US&IR=T

[99] Humphries, M. (2012, January 5). Pepsi explain why you'll never find a mouse in Mountain Dew. *Geek.com* https://www.geek.com/geek-cetera/pepsi-explain-why-youll-never-find-a-mouse-in-mountain-dew-1455209/

[100] Watson, L. (2012, January 5). Drinks giant Pepsi says man who claims he found a mouse in his can of Mountain Dew must be wrong . . . because it would have dissolved. *Daily Mail.* https://www.dailymail.co.uk/news/article-2081767/Mountain-Dew-dead-mouse-lawsuit-Ronald-Ball-wrong-dissolve.html

> *"Mountain Dew mouse case dissolves as Pepsico settles." (Beverage Daily)* [101]

While the mouse-in-the-can case was eventually settled out of court for an undisclosed sum, it raises an obvious question: where were the communication and marketing professionals when someone thought this legal defense was a good idea? Alternatively, if the reputation professionals *were* giving good advice, why was it ignored or overruled?

Chipping Away at Reputation

The second incident where the heavy hand of lawyers became evident is an example of a marathon crisis (which you will learn about in Chapter Nine) where prolonged determination to win in court can outweigh ongoing damage to reputation.

This product-related case involves Pringles Chips, coincidentally another international brand then owned by Procter and Gamble (Pringles was later sold to the Kellogg Company).

The case itself was simple enough. In Britain most foods are exempt from VAT (sales tax) but potato chips and similar are taxable. In the case of Pringles that amounted to perhaps £20 million (about US$26 million) a year. So management hit on the idea to claim that the famous chips are not potato product at all, but "savoury snacks" and therefore exempt from tax.

The VAT and Duties Tribunal disagreed, ruling that Pringles – which are marketed in the United States as potato chips – are taxable.

Not satisfied, P&G appealed the decision, arguing in court that Pringles "don't look like a chip, don't feel like a chip and don't taste like a chip." Their legal team helpfully explained that the stackable slices are only 42 per cent potato, with the remainder made up of oil, wheat starch, maltodextrin, salt, rice flour and dextrose. The lower court agreed that Pringles are made from dough and are

---

[101] Bouckley, B. (2012, August 9). Mountain Dew mouse case dissolves as Pepsico settles. *Beverage Daily.* https://www.beveragedaily.com/Article/2012/08/08/Mountain-Dew-mouse-case-dissolves-as-PepsiCo-settles

therefore more like a cake or a biscuit – which must have confused the heck out of legions of Pringles consumers – although it meant Pringles would be exempt from VAT after all.

However Her Majesty's Revenue and Customs has a duty to protect the public revenue and appealed the case to the Supreme Court of Judicature, which had little patience with what were described as "P&G's lawyerly attempts to break out of the potato chip category."

After the case had gone through three levels of the British legal system, and much argument about the "potato-ness" of the product, the three judges finally ruled that Pringles *are* legally potato chips and *are* subject to tax. With typical British understatement, Lord Justice Jacob insisted the question was "not one calling for or justifying over-elaborate, almost mind-numbing legal analysis."

He might equally have asked: who thought it was a clever idea to allow a "mind-numbing" legal strategy to potentially damage the reputation of a highly profitable brand in negative news reports published around the world?

> *"Pringles 'are not potato crisps'." (BBC)* [102]

> *"Stop everything. Are Pringles a biscuit or a crisp?" (Metro UK)* [103]

> *"Legal team says Pringles aren't potatoes. Branding Work Undone as Details of UK Tax Case Spread Across the Web." (Ad Age)* [104]

---

[102] *Pringles 'are not potato crisps.' (2008, July 4). BBC.* http://news.bbc.co.uk/2/hi/business/7490346.stm

[103] Willis, A. (2016, October 26). Stop everything. Are Pringles a biscuit or a crisp? *Metro UK.* https://metro.co.uk/2016/10/26/stop-everything-pringles-are-a-biscuit-not-a-crisp-6216352/

[104] Neff, J. (2009, May 25). Legal team says Pringles aren't potatoes. *Ad Age.* https://adage.com/article/news/p-g-legal-team-pringles-potatoes/136849

> *"The Lord Justice Hath ruled: Pringles are potato chips." (New York Times)* [105]

New owners, Kellogg's, later confirmed they had no intention of pursuing the legal argument about the status of Pringles.

Just Cruisin' Along

While the coronavirus pandemic in 2020 has focused massive amounts of negative attention on the role of cruise ships as epicenters of infection, the industry has long been the subject of news reports, prosecutions and fines for a wide range of environmental, operational and health concerns.

But there have been few cruise liner crises as nauseating and as widely reported as the so-called "poop cruise" in 2013.

The vessel *Carnival Triumph* had an engine fire which knocked out the ship's power and it drifted for four days without air conditioning and largely without lights, water, food and working toilets, before eventually being towed into Mobile, Alabama

With more than 4,000 passengers and crew aboard, raw sewage backed up into passenger areas, and plastic bags of human waste began to accumulate outside the cabins.

A random selection of headlines at the time spell out the depth of this reputational crisis.

---

[105] Cohen, A. (2009, May 31). The Lord Justice hath ruled: Pringles are potato chips. *New York Times.*
https://www.nytimes.com/2009/06/01/opinion/01mon4.html

"How Carnival went from 'Fun Ship' to 'Poop cruise'." Business Insider. [106]

"Stranded cruise ship on which 'sewage ran down the walls' and 'savages' fought over food finally docks amid jubilant scenes." The Independent. [107]

" 'Carnival Dream' becomes nightmare 'poop cruise' while stranded in the Caribbean." Raw Story. [108]

"Weary passengers head home after stinky Carnival cruise." Reuters. [109]

"The Carnival poop cruise is finally over." The Atlantic. [110]

---

[106] Austin, C. (2013, February 21). How Carnival went from "Fun ship" to "Poop Cruise." *Business Insider*. https://www.businessinsider.com.au/how-carnival-went-from-fun-ship-to-poop-cruise-2013-2?r=US&IR=T#carnival-cruise-lines-was-founded-by-ted-arison-in-1972-1

[107] Hall, J. (2013, February 15). Stranded cruise ship on which 'sewage ran down the walls' and 'savages' fought over food finally docks amid jubilant scenes. *The Independent*. https://www.independent.co.uk/news/world/americas/stranded-cruise-ship-on-which-sewage-ran-down-the-walls-and-savages-fought-over-food-finally-docks-8496330.html

[108] Ferguson, D. (2013, March 14). "Carnival Dream" becomes nightmare "poop cruise" while stranded in Caribbean. *Raw Story*. https://www.rawstory.com/2013/03/carnival-dream-becomes-nightmare-poop-cruise-while-stranded-in-caribbean/

[109] Wilkinson, K. (2013, February 15). Weary passengers head home after stinky Carnival cruise. *Reuters*. https://www.reuters.com/article/us-mexico-carnival/weary-passengers-head-home-after-stinky-carnival-cruise-idUSBRE91D0YT20130215

[110] Clarke Estes, A. (2013, February 14). The Carnival poop cruise is finally over. *The Atlantic*. https://www.theatlantic.com/national/archive/2013/02/carnival-poop-cruise-finally-over/318327/

It was inevitable that a flood of legal proceedings would follow, but it was the response by the company's lawyers which makes this case noteworthy. CNN reported that Carnival Cruise lines insisted what happened was "just an accident" and the company pointed out to passengers taking legal action that the cruise line never promised a safe trip.

CNN said the company's court filing said the ticket contract:

> *"makes absolutely no guarantee for safe passage, a seaworthy vessel, adequate and wholesome food, and sanitary and safe living conditions."[111]*

As with Mountain Dew and Pringles chips, it is hard to believe the marketing and PR people at Carnival thought this would enhance the reputation of the brand.

Lessons learned

It's not often that the legal strategy behind a product crisis becomes so fully unambiguous. But the Mountain Dew mouse, the Pringles chips not made of potato, and the cruise line not guaranteeing safety, provide three vivid examples of where the legal strategy was laid out in public, and where that strategy seemed to be driven by financial consideration at the expense of the product itself.

Allegations of "foreign bodies" in cans of soft drink – or other food for that matter – happen all the time and most often gain little public attention. That's why the Mountain Dew case is a classic which warrants in-depth review for managers today.

When I think of this incident, I can't help imagining the meeting where this debacle was born. In my mind's eye I picture the production manager saying: "We've got this claim of a dead mouse in a can. I think we should focus on showing that the canning process would make this virtually impossible."

---

[111] Griffin. D. and Bronstein, S. (2013, December 18). Carnival knew of fire danger before cruise, documents show. *CNN.* https://edition.cnn.com/2013/12/17/travel/carnival-cruise-triumph-problems/index.html

In response the lawyer says: "I've got a better idea. Let's show that the product is so acidic it would turn the mouse into jelly."

Then I imagine the marketing manager and the communications professional – if they are in the room – saying: "Are you joking?" But somehow the strategy was approved.

Of course, that exchange is just hypothetical, but something like that may well have happened because it's precisely the legal defense spelled out in the company's court documents. And not only did they say the product would dissolve a mouse, but they generously explained, step by step, exactly how the company's fine product would destroy any unfortunate rodent. With the resulting media response blindingly predictable it truly is hard to understand how the lawyers got the green light to proceed.

The case involving Pringle's chips is somewhat easier to understand because there was a potential tax bill of £20 million a year to consider. But you have to ask whether even that incentive was sufficient to warrant the high-profile brand risk – given that it relied entirely on what the Judge called "an over-elaborate, almost mind-numbing" legal strategy.

My guess is that, in reality, far fewer people noticed when P&G originally won its Pringles-is-not-a-potato-crisp argument before the lower court than the worldwide audience who read the ironic headlines when the company eventually lost their appeal.

Add to that the fact that Pringles – like Mountain Dew – is a "one-product" brand-name, albeit part of a multinational corporation, and you have a sure recipe for a brand crisis.

In the case of Carnival – whose ships operate under a variety of flags of convenience and account for about half of the world's cruise capacity – there is a long history of breakdowns at sea, onboard infections of the notorious norovirus, and fines for discharges into the environment. There is also a history of aggressive court defense, and one news report about the notorious "poop cruise" refers to

Carnival's "legendary court filing" as an example of "cruise companies' aversion to responsibility."[112]

Yet corporate brand owners like Samsung, Intel, Proctor & Gamble and Carnival have an undeniable right to defend their merchandise and brand equity. However such product crises in particular highlight how damaging and how public it can be when legal advice conflicts with the welfare of the product.

Lawyers conventionally focus on the legal niceties and winning the case. These examples suggest that approach sometimes flies in the face of broader management priorities and may damage both brand and corporate reputation.

I believe that in the end it all comes down to a simple proposition: A lawyer's role is to defend a position, while a communicator strives to improve upon or advance a position, and the executive needs to make a considered decision in the long-term interests of the brand.

---

[112] Moore, R. (2020, April 19). Is the cruise industry finally out of its depth? *The Guardian.* https://www.theguardian.com/travel/2020/apr/19/is-the-cruise-industry-finally-out-of-its-depth?CMP=Share_iOSApp_Other

Key Takeaways

- High-profile product crises are particularly vulnerable to clashes between legal and communications counsel.
- Unpredictable involvement by consumers who are personally affected may add an extra level of risk to product crises.
- An overzealous legal strategy can backfire or even turn a problem into a crisis.
- Properly understanding your stakeholders is essential to all crises, especially those involving consumer products.
- An effective crisis response strategy at home may not be successful in another country.
- Your brand value can be at risk if the legal response is not aligned to long-term reputation priorities.

Questions for Discussion

1. *Does sacking the CEO deliver any tangible benefit in responding to a major product crisis?*
2. *How has the rise of social media changed the perception of a product failure?*
3. *What made the Intel Pentium Chip crisis become such a classic of a mismanaged product recall? Does it really deserve that reputation?*
4. *Who do some high-profile products find it so hard to see the funny side of a light-hearted story about them?*
5. *Is it useful in a product crisis to say, "the customer is always right?" Or is that just a cliché?*

Chapter Four

Why Should I Apologize?

"In litigation as in life, one thing is certain: A party who feels wronged wants an apology."

Bradley M. Henry.

One of the most common areas of disagreement between lawyers and communicators is about when and how to apologize.

That probably won't surprise you. The truth is that while apologizing seems simple, it's not easy. Think about it at a personal level – how hard it is to genuinely apologize, even to your friends and loved ones. How much harder it is for corporations and CEOs having to do so on the public stage, in the glare of the news media, beset by concerns about avoiding embarrassment and protecting reputation and share value while surrounded by a phalanx of nervous lawyers and anxious communication professionals.

That prospect can generate a whole catalogue of reasons why you don't *want* to apologize. Which in turn leads to the defensive questions: "Why should I apologize at all? What's the worst that can happen?" Those issues demand both legal and communications involvement.

This chapter will help you to:

- Recognize why you *should* apologize when you've done something wrong.
- Assess the legal implications of apologizing.
- Learn from real-life examples how lack of a proper apology can trigger a crisis.
- Avoid making the crisis worse by failing to apologize.
- Know how apologizing can sometimes reduce legal liability.
- Accept why you sometimes need to apologize, even when you've done nothing wrong.
- Show how legal or political pressure can demand organizational apologies for historical issues.

What Can Go Wrong

The first and most obvious reason to apologize is that very often it's simply the right thing to do.

This seeming statement of the obvious was the conclusion of Dave Carroll in his book *United Breaks Guitars: The power of one voice in the age of social media.*[113]

Carroll is neither a lawyer nor a professional communicator. But his experience has come to be a classic example of what can go wrong when a company fails to respond. Carroll is a Canadian folksinger who was flying from Halifax to Omaha with his band Sons of Maxwell. During a stopover at O'Hare Airport, Chicago, in March 2008, United Airlines baggage handlers were seen mishandling his $3,500 Taylor acoustic guitar, which was badly damaged and cost him $1,200 in repairs. But for nine months the airline refused to apologize and brushed off his claim for compensation.

At that point Carroll could have gone to any newspaper or online platform to complain, as thousands of unhappy customers have done before and since. Instead, Carroll created a catchy song called "United Breaks Guitars" and posted it on YouTube.[114]

> *"I flew United Airlines on my way to Nebraska*
> *The plane departed, Halifax, connecting in*
> *Chicago's O'Hare.*
> *While on the ground, a passenger said from the seat*
> *behind me,*
> *"My God, they're throwing guitars out there."*

Within weeks the $150 clip had been viewed more than three million times, and millions more were exposed to criticism of the airline when Carroll appeared on TV chat shows across America. United Airlines belatedly relented and agreed to compensate Carroll, but he refused the money and the airline instead decided to

---

[113] Carroll, D. (2012). *United Breaks Guitars: The power of one voice in the age of social media.* Carlsbad, CA:., Hay House.

[114] The Dave Carroll protest song video can be seen at
http://www.youtube.com/watch?v=5YGc4zOqozo

make a $3,000 donation to the Thelonious Monk Institute of Jazz. (It was later revealed that the Institute was, at the time, chaired largely by United executives and used United Airlines exclusively for its corporate travel.)

But this modest "goodwill gesture" was dwarfed by the wider reputational and financial impact of the incident. The *Times* of London reported:

> *"Within four days of the song going online, the gathering thunderclouds of bad PR caused United Airlines' stock price to suffer a mid-flight stall, and it plunged by ten per cent, costing shareholders $180 million. Which, incidentally, would have bought Carroll more than 51,000 replacement guitars."*[115]

A respected business website commented:

> *"Can United's $180 million loss be chalked up entirely to a song on YouTube? Probably not. Did the song have a very real and very negative effect on United's brand equity? Absolutely."*[116]

When I last checked, the YouTube video had accumulated over 20 million views. And it has been reported that 150 million people overall were exposed to the negative story about the airline, largely because it chose not to apologize promptly and deal with the issue.

Carroll later wrote a book and delivered a TED talk on his experience and the power of one person on the internet. He concluded: "Sometimes saying you're sorry is not only the right thing to do, but also the least expensive."

---

[115] Ayres, C. (2009, July 22). Revenge is best served cold, on Youtube: How a broken guitar became a smash hit. *The Times*.
https://www.thetimes.co.uk/article/revenge-is-best-served-cold-on-youtube-2dhbsh6jtp5
[116] Sawhney, R. (2009, July 28). Broken guitar has United playing the blues to the tune of $180 million. *Fast Company*.
https://www.fastcompany.com/1320152/broken-guitar-has-united-playing-blues-tune-180-million

Lessons learned

Airline passengers have lost or damaged baggage every day of the week and you never hear about it. The story of Dave Carroll's damaged guitar just might have made it into the news because he was a reasonably well-known musician. And celebrity does increase newsworthiness. You may remember the incident a couple of years later when actor-director Kevin Smith was removed from a Southwest Air flight because he was "too fat to fly."[117] Smith launched a Twitter tirade and the airline promptly apologized. Most importantly, the airline had reacted quickly and, after some media attention, the story soon faded from view.

Contrast this with United's failure to promptly deal with Carroll's broken guitar. If the musician had complained to a newspaper or simply ranted online it may have generated a short-lived reputational blip. But instead, the airline's prolonged refusal to apologize, and the customer's innovative YouTube protest, turned an otherwise unremarkable incident into a genuine reputational and business crisis.

The other key lesson from the broken guitar debacle is that the issue was dealt with for some time by a low-level customer services representative (immortalized in the YouTube song as Ms. Irlweg) and was seemingly not escalated to management until far too late. I can't overstate how important it is that your employees on the ground know the rules yet have discretion to act and know when to involve more senior management. In the Kevin Smith case, while the airport staff initially implemented the airline's "customers of size" policy requiring him to purchase two seats, he was quickly and correctly rebooked on another flight the same day.

---

[117] De Nies, Y. and Yeo, S. (2010, February 15). Kevin Smith Too Fat to Fly. *ABC News*. https://abcnews.go.com/WN/kevin-smith-fat-fly/story?id=9837268

Reasons for Your Organization to Apologize

- To acknowledge that an injury or damage has occurred.
- To express responsibility and/or regret for the event.
- To limit legal or insurance liability.
- To commit to change and promise action to avoid a repeat.
- To draw a line in order to move forward.
- To avoid prolonged media attention or reduce online outrage.
- To protect reputation and share or brand value.
- To re-establish working relationships with stakeholders.
- To demonstrate executive leadership, internally and externally.
- To reduce the likelihood of unwarranted regulatory scrutiny.
- Because it's the right thing to do.

When Lack of Apology Becomes the News

United's refusal to promptly apologize and compensate Dave Carroll – which basically created a reputational crisis out of a standard damage claim – leads directly to another key reason to apologize: namely when lack of an apology in an already serious situation becomes the story rather than the incident itself.

Unfortunately, nine years later, United found itself at the center of one of the most notorious global reputational crises of recent years when lack of a proper apology was once again a feature.

Extraordinarily, the scene was again O'Hare Airport, in April 2017, where a 69-year-old passenger was physically dragged from an overbooked flight for which he held a valid ticket and was already seated.[118] Disturbing mobile phone footage of Dr. David Dao, bloodied and protesting, being dragged down the aisle by burly Chicago Aviation security officers was viewed hundreds of millions of times around the world.

---

[118] Lartey, J. (2017, April 11). United Airlines passenger violently dragged from seat on an overbooked flight. *The Guardian*. https://www.theguardian.com/us-news/2017/apr/10/united-airlines-video-passenger-removed-overbooked-flight

It was unquestionably time for a prompt and profound apology, but United CEO Oscar Munoz instead praised his employees for "following established procedures" and blamed the passenger, who he described as "disruptive and belligerent."

In a letter to employees he said: "There are lessons we can learn from this experience."[119] Yet nowhere did he appear to concede the airline had done anything wrong. This from the man who just one month earlier had been declared PR Week's "Communicator of The Year."

Contrast United's support for employees supposedly following procedure with the Chicago Department of Aviation, which said the incident was "not in accordance with our standard operating procedures." They immediately suspended the three officers involved pending a review and one was later discharged for excessive use of force.

I would agree with PR writer and blogger Ed Zitron who told CNN News that United's response was "a classic case of a company too afraid to make a categorical statement of compassion for fear of a lawsuit."[120]

With the share value of United Airlines tumbling more than $1 billion in a single day,[121] Mr. Munoz issued a poorly executed statement in which he appeared to place the interests of the airline first:

---

[119] Horton, H. (2017, April 11). United Airlines CEO sends letter praising staff after doctor was forcibly removed from an overbooked plane. *Telegraph UK.* https://www.telegraph.co.uk/news/2017/04/11/read-united-ceos-painfully-tone-deaf-letter-employees-man-forcibly/

[120] Griffiths, J, and Wang, S. (2017, April 11). Man filmed being dragged off United flight causes outrage in China. *CNN.* https://edition.cnn.com/2017/04/11/asia/united-passenger-dragged-off-china-reaction/index.html

[121] United Airlines loses $1.3 billion in market value after passenger is dragged off plane (2017, April 13). *News.com.au.* https://www.news.com.au/travel/travel-updates/united-airlines-loses-13-billion-in-market-value-after-passenger-is-dragged-off-plane/news-story/ae121d39a770b85cfcb70eea3a9c5b8b

> *"This is an unsettling event to all of us here at United. I apologize for having to reaccommodate these passengers."[122]*

This tone-deaf response, which failed to apologize to the passenger himself, provoked further outcry, and the unfortunate euphemism "reaccommodate" was widely mocked across social media.

The so-called "involuntary denied boarding process" occurred on a Sunday, and only the following Tuesday, after several attempts, did the CEO issue what could be regarded as an adequate apology.

> *"The truly horrific event that occurred on this flight has elicited many responses from all of us: outrage, anger, disappointment. I share all of those sentiments, and one above all: my deepest apologies for what happened. Like you, I continue to be disturbed by what happened on this flight and I deeply apologize to the customer forcibly removed and to all the customers aboard. No one should ever be mistreated this way."[123]*

His statement went on to say: "It's never too late to do the right thing." However, it surely was too late to apologize.

Never forget though that "doing the right thing" can be very costly. When Hollywood actor Kevin Spacey was accused of predatory sexual behavior, Netflix dumped him from their highly acclaimed series *House of Cards*, and scrapped a biopic about Gore Vidal which was already in post-production. Netflix later

---

[122] Sakzewski, E. (2017, April 13). United Airlines: What we can learn from the company's 'breathtakingly bad' crisis management. *ABC News, Australia.* https://www.abc.net.au/news/2017-04-13/united-airlines-what-went-so-wrong-pr/8441796

[123] Winchel, B. 2017, April 12). Learning from United's vow to 'do better' *Ragan's PR Daily.* https://www.prdaily.com/learning-from-uniteds-vow-to-do-better/

announced that the decision to sever all ties with their former star cost them $39 million.[124]

Lessons learned

There is a maxim much loved by motivational speakers: You only get one chance to make a good first impression.

In the same way, you only get one chance to apologize promptly and properly. Huffington Post's headline on the case said it all:

> *"United Airlines Boss FINALLY makes proper apology to passenger pulled screaming from plane."[125]*

On the same theme I really liked the post by Chicago-based PR commentator Marylou McNally: "You don't swing and miss at your first apology and think you can hit a home run later."[126]

The victim's lawyer Thomas Demetrio, later said:

> *"United has taken full responsibility for what happened, without attempting to blame others. For this acceptance of corporate accountability, United is to be applauded."*

---

[124] Menta, A. (2018, January 23). Netflix lost $39 million from firing Kevin Spacey. *Newsweek.* https://www.newsweek.com/kevin-spacey-netflix-lost-money-788690

[125] Sommers, J. (2017, April 12). United Airlines Boss FINALLY makes proper apology to passenger pulled screaming from plane. *Huffington Post.* https://www.huffingtonpost.co.uk/entry/united-airlines-oscar-munoz-apology_uk_58ed3274e4b0c89f91224bcc

[126] McNally, l. (2017, April 12). Let's stop the non-apology apology: The do's and don'ts of 'I'm Sorry.' Blog *Original Content Matters.* https://ocmsite.wordpress.com/2017/04/12/lets-stop-the-non-apology-apology-the-dos-and-donts-of-im-sorry/

But it is only fair to point out that was after his client had received an undisclosed "amicable settlement," rumored to be over $100 million.

Most importantly, I have to emphasize that you should not take any of this to suggest that the United Airlines de-planing debacle was simply a communication or legal problem. The disturbing mobile phone images meant it was always going to be a major reputational crisis dominating the headlines, regardless of what the CEO said and regardless of the compensation paid. However, I believe that a prompt and proper apology would have reduced the impact.

Sometimes it's Just too Late

A BBC headline a few years ago claimed "It's never too late to apologize." [127] But I would argue that sometimes an apology is so late as to have little value.

While Mr. Munoz of United was just a few days too late, some apologies have been so far overdue that they lost any significant meaning, such as when the German drug-maker Gruenenthal waited more than 50 years to apologize for the morning sickness pill Thalidomide which had caused devastating deformities to over 10,000 babies born in the 1950s before it was withdrawn in 1961.

In 2012, CEO Harald Stock offered a cautious apology, which showed every sign of having been carefully crafted by lawyers concerned more with legal liability than compassion.

> *"We ask for forgiveness that for nearly 50 years we didn't find a way of reaching out to you from human being to human being. We ask that you regard our long silence as a sign of the shock that your fate caused in us." [128]*

---

[127] It's never too late to apologise (2009, February 9). *BBC News.* http://news.bbc.co.uk/2/hi/uk_news/magazine/7875005.stm

[128] German thalidomide maker Gruenenthal issues apology (2012, September 1). *BBC.* https://www.bbc.com/news/health-19443910

Victims groups said the apology was welcome yet was of little value if the company wouldn't open discussions on financial compensation. In addition the statement appears remarkably insensitive and more about the company than the victims.

For years the drug maker consistently defended itself by arguing that the potential impact of Thalidomide could not have been detected by tests before it was marketed. But four years after this apology an official report, produced by the University of Muenster for the German state of North-Rhine Westphalia, confirmed the long-held suspicion that Grunenthal had early knowledge about possible side effects and gave out intentionally false information and hushed up its knowledge.[129]

Similarly, the New York Police Department waited five decades to formally apologize for the notorious raid on a gay Greenwich Village nightclub – the Stonewall Inn – which triggered a serious riot in 1969. Demonstrators were protesting not only against heavy-handed police tactics, but also against being arrested for simply patronizing a gay establishment or for being "out" in public. With the 50th anniversary of the raid approaching, in June 2019, Police Commissioner James O'Neill declared:

> *"The actions taken by the NYPD were wrong, plain*
> *and simple. And for that I apologize."*[130]

The raid wasn't the first time that LGBT people had demonstrated or clashed with police, but it proved a turning point that spurred a wave of activism.

A more blatant example of the lack of an apology becoming the story involved controversial Australian radio host Alan Jones who used every legal means at his

[129] Martin, M. (2016, May 14). Thalidomide maker hushed up drug's side effects, German report says. *Reuters*. https://www.reuters.com/article/us-germany-thalidomide/thalidomide-maker-hushed-up-drugs-side-effects-german-report-says-idUSKCN0Y4281

[130] Brockwell, G. (2019, June 6). 'Wrong, plain and simple': 50 years after the Stonewall raid, New York City's police commissioner apologizes. *Washington Post*. https://www.washingtonpost.com/history/2019/06/06/wrong-plain-simple-years-after-stonewall-raid-new-york-citys-police-commissioner-apologizes/

disposal to delay an apology for nearly eight years. In on-air comment in April 2005 Jones called Lebanese men "vermin and mongrels" who "simply rape, pillage and plunder a nation that's taken them in."[131] His incendiary views are widely believed to have contributed to a race riot at Cronulla, in Sydney, a few months later.

After prolonged legal wrangling and appeals, in 2009 the New South Wales Administrative Decisions Tribunal found that these remarks incited hatred and contempt of Lebanese Muslims and ordered Jones to apologize within eight weeks.

The broadcaster then launched more than two years of further legal proceedings in an attempt to overturn the decision. Only when his legal options ran out in December 2012 did the broadcaster finally state publicly that his comments were unlawful and that he apologized for making them (using a script directed by the Tribunal after they deemed an earlier apology was "an inadequate statement of wrongdoing.")[132] But this was almost eight years after the original offense and, remarkably, the amended apology was broadcast via a prerecorded message when the man himself was on leave.

It's not often that an individual or organization will go to such exhaustive legal lengths to evade having to make an apology. By then of course the apology had little or no value, which we can only guess is what he intended

It's important to remember that the cost of failing to apologize and failing to be apologetic doesn't just apply to business corporations. The international aid charity Oxfam enjoyed a stellar reputation until revelations in early 2018 that some staff had sexually exploited female disaster victims in the wake of the devastating Haiti earthquake in 2011, and that Oxfam covered up the scandal for years.

---

[131] Nguyen, K. (2007, April 11). Jones 'incited' Cronulla violence on air. *The Age*. https://www.theage.com.au/national/jones-incited-cronulla-violence-on-air-20070411-ge4mti.html

[132] Wells, J. (2012, December 14). Jones forced to apologize over racist comments. *ABC News*, Australia. https://www.abc.net.au/news/2012-12-13/jones-to-apologise-after-calling-lebanese-muslims-vermin/4426692

In the face of falling donations and severely damaged reputation, CEO Mark Goldring gave an extraordinarily ill-judged interview in which he accused critics of "gunning" for the charity and that the response was "out of proportion:"

> *"The intensity and the ferocity of the attack makes you wonder, what did we do? We murdered babies in their cots? Certainly, the scale and the intensity of the attacks feels out of proportion to the level of culpability. I struggle to understand it. You think: 'My God, there's something going on there'."*[133]

Lessons learned

The main lesson in each of these cases comes not from the fact that the apology was delayed, but from why. While the reasons were very different in each instance, the cases tell you a lot about the balance between legal and communication objectives and also a lot about the difference between focusing on yourself or on those affected by your actions.

The occasion for the apology by Grunenthal was unveiling a bronze statue of a child born without limbs because of thalidomide, though the words used were very clearly more about the company than the victims, of whom 5,000-6,000 still survive. While CEO Stock said he was sorry his company had remained silent for so long, they never admitted liability.

As usual, the behind-the-scene reasoning before his apology is not publicly known, but this appears to be a case where legal considerations prevailed. In fact the official report released four years after the CEO's statement said the firm had used delaying tactics and legal threats of potential claims against the state to keep the drug on the market as long as possible. There are some cases where legal advice should rightly take precedence over reputation,

---

[133] Aitkenhead, D. (2018, February 17). Oxfam boss Mark Goldring: 'Anything we say is being manipulated. We've been savaged.' *The Guardian.* https://www.theguardian.com/world/2018/feb/16/oxfam-boss-mark-goldring-anything-we-say-is-being-manipulated-weve-been-savaged

and it could be argued that – from the company's perspective – Grunenthal's medico-legal strategy may have been their best option.

By contrast the New York Police Department apology for the Stonewall nightclub raid was almost entirely about the victims rather than the organization. Commissioner James O'Neill declared that the raid was a clear example of discrimination which was no longer acceptable in society. The apology may have been five decades in coming, but from a communication perspective you would have to agree that the eventual timing was perfect. Commissioner O'Neill spoke in June 2019, just days before the 50th anniversary of the riot, which was marked by WorldPride Weekend in New York City, claimed to be the largest LGBTQ event in history with five million attending in Manhattan alone.

Sadly, the same focus on victims was glaringly absent from the strategy of radio host Alan Jones, whose hard-fought and very public resistance to apologizing seems to have been to protect himself rather than defending any significant legal principle. He appeared to have little or no regard for the ethnic group he had denigrated and apologized reluctantly and only after intense legal pressure.

However, Jones has a long history of outspoken and sometimes offensive commentary and was evidently playing to his massive and generally conservative radio audience. He probably did little to harm his reputation among that audience and in fact his reputation may even have been enhanced by his steadfast defence of his opinions. Despite a record defamation payout for other on-air comments; threats of advertising boycotts; and management warnings to tone down his controversial style; Jones continued as one of the highest paid and most popular radio hosts in Australia (he retired in June 2020).[134] I suspect he would argue that he knew

---

[134] Carmody, B. (2009, May 28). Alan Jones signs on for another two years at 2GB. *Sydney Morning Herald*. https://www.smh.com.au/entertainment/tv-and-radio/alan-jones-signs-on-for-another-two-years-at-2gb-20190429-p51i6o.html

his audience better than anyone, and that pursuit of reputation trumps legal caution.

In the other case of a long-delayed apology, Oxfam CEO Mark Goldring mirrored Alan Jones' example and made it about himself rather than the victims, but the outcome for him was very different. When the aid charity was accused of covering up a staff scandal from some years earlier, Goldring failed disastrously in an attempt to portray the organization and himself as victims of disproportionate criticism. It was reported at the time that the CEO gave the interview "unchaperoned by press officers" and it is hard to imagine that, with proper legal and communication advice, any responsible executive would have made such unguarded and provocative remarks. His comment that he "struggled to understand" the situation was probably his most accurate statement. Goldring later excused himself by saying "I do apologize. I was under stress."[135] But unlike in the case of Alan Jones, the charity's reputation and finances had suffered severe damage and the CEO was soon forced to resign.

Each of these cases offers you some very different perspectives on the legal and communication elements of apologizing for events long passed. But all four examples highlight one of the most important lessons about making an apology – It's not about you. It's about the people affected.

[135] Rawlinson, K. (2018, May 17). Oxfam chief steps down after charity's sexual abuse scandal. *The Guardian.*
https://www.theguardian.com/world/2018/may/16/oxfam-head-mark-goldring-steps-down-sexual-abuse-scandal

Crisis is an equal opportunity risk

The distressing experience of the charity Oxfam is a salutary reminder that crisis is an equal-opportunity risk that doesn't discriminate among organizations. In a workshop I was running, two attendees from a high-profile children's organization told me: "We are a charity, so we don't have issues that might turn into crises."

When I suggested a couple of fairly basic potential crisis scenarios which might affect them – the accountant absconding with donated funds, or the CEO arrested for having child-porn on his computer – they seemed genuinely offended at the idea that their long-serving colleagues might behave in such a way.

A few months later the organization was on the front page of all the local newspapers because they had knowingly allowed street kids to take drugs on their premises. Not-for-profits are especially vulnerable to reputational damage and the predictable outcry put future donations and grants at risk. Never forget, no one is immune from crisis, no matter how pure their intentions.

Apologizing to Reduce Liability

While delaying or declining to apologize can seriously damage reputations, a timely and appropriate apology can serve to reduce legal liability.

I discuss the broader question of liability versus responsibility in crisis in Chapter Eight and how it can impact your success in responding to a crisis. For the moment I want to focus on the strategic use of an apology to reduce legal exposure in civil proceedings.

Make no mistake, this is a contentious area of management where the decision is most often led by the lawyers rather than communicators. Yet it's typically a legal decision with very definite reputational as well as legal consequences.

You would probably expect this is a topic more often found in legal journals than in a book like this. In fact, there is a massive library of legal articles about this subject. To take just one example, a leading academic review of the power of apology cites over 120 mainly legal sources and unhelpfully concludes – after 50 pages of analysis – that it is *still* unclear how apologies function in relation to civil liability and how the relationship between the law and apologies works.[136] If legal experts find it difficult, what hope for everyone else?

Richard Ingrams, co-founder of the frequently-sued British satirical magazine *Private Eye*, was hardly joking when he famously said: "When lawyers talk about the law, normal human beings begin to think about something else."

However, my purpose here is not to attempt to analyze the law, but to focus on circumstances which show you when executives have accepted the principle that an apology may yield a positive legal outcome.

Although you may not be involved in the provision of health services, you can learn a lot about the effect of apologies from the extensively studied area of medical malpractice. For instance, an American study of factors which prompted families to file medical malpractice claims following perinatal injuries found that 24 per cent filed suit when they realized that physicians had failed to be completely honest with them about what happened, allowed them to believe things that were not true, or intentionally misled them.[137] The study concluded that such filings may have been prevented by an apology.

Similarly, a study of British patients and families suing doctors found that 37 percent might not have brought malpractice suits had there been a full explanation

---

[136] Vines, P. (2007). The power of apology: Mercy, forgiveness or corrective justice in the civil liability arena? *The Journal of Law and social justice* Vol 1, 1-51.
[137] Hickson, G.B., Clayton, E.W., Githens, P. B. & Sloan, F.A. (1992). Factors that prompted families to file medical malpractice claims following perinatal injuries. *JAMA* 267, 1359-1361.

and apology, factors which to them were more significant than monetary compensation.[138]

And, more specifically, when the University of Illinois Medical Center introduced a new program of patient disclosure, apology and compensation, the number of malpractice suits halved in two years and in the 37 cases where the hospital acknowledged a preventable error and apologized, only one patient filed suit.[139]

As crisis expert James Lukaszewski has boldly written with no room for ambiguity:

> *"An apology may be the trigger to settlement. Failure to apologize is always a trigger for litigation."*[140]

Would an apology satisfy you?

Think about it from a personal perspective. If you or one of your loved ones was adversely affected by a preventable medical mishap, how much would an explanation and apology influence your decision whether to lodge a lawsuit for malpractice against the doctor or the hospital? Would you really be satisfied or simply less inclined to sue?

It is important to recognize that reputation is valuable not only as a business asset but is also valuable as a legal asset in the event of litigation. There is good evidence that when lawsuits do proceed, both judges and juries tend to appreciate apologies and look upon them favorably in terms of modifying penalties.[141] This

---

[138] Vincent, C., Yong, M. & Phillips, A. (1994). Why people sue doctors: A study of patients and families taking legal action. *Lancet*, 343, 1609-1612.

[139] Sack, K. (2008, May 18). Doctors start to say 'I'm sorry' before 'See you in court'. *New York Times*. https://www.nytimes.com/2008/05/18/us/18apology.html

[140] Lukaszewski, J. E. (2019). The Perfect Apology: the atomic energy of empathy. From *PR News Tipsheet*. https://www.e911.com/the-perfect-apology/

[141] Cohen, J. R. (1999). Advising clients to apologize. *Southern California Law Review*, 72, 1009-1069.

has been shown not only in cases of medical malpractice but also in other types of civil suits, including allegations of libel or defamation.

However, there is an important caveat. While I have said that in some cases the offer and acceptance of an apology can help an organization to pre-empt accusations and negative publicity, diffuse public anger and even help avoid a lawsuit entirely, you should *never* expect an apology to allow your organization off the hook for what has happened.

But I've Done Nothing Wrong!

In contrast to trying to reduce or avoid punishment for wrongdoing, another – more controversial – reason to apologize is when you *need* to, even though you believe you have nothing to apologize for.

This is not just about denial or refusal to accept responsibility. It's about when you genuinely believe you've done nothing wrong and *still* need to apologize.

You'd be right to think this situation causes conflict between lawyers and communicators. And it also causes disagreement between crisis management experts themselves.

The contrarian New York crisis consultant and writer Eric Dezenhall has championed this approach and even coined a label for it. Dezenhall calls it the "marital apology" which, he says, arises in cases fraught with so much tension that there is no chance of a resolution until that tension is released.

> *"Long-married people know this phenomenon well. Even though it's not in the sanctioned marital relations handbook, there are times that you apologize even when you're not sure what you did wrong. Or even if you're convinced you were actually right in the first place."*[142]

Dezenhall argues that the same principle can apply to corporations, and he cites the case of Toyota following multiple reports of alleged uncontrolled sudden

---

[142] Dezenhall, E. (2014). *Glass Jaw: A manifesto for defending fragile reputations in the Age of Instant Scandal*. Chapter Eight, The Three Apologies. (pp 133-142). New York: Twelve.

acceleration. That crisis led Toyota to recall millions of cars at a cost of billions of dollars, and the company paid nearly $50 million in fines and saw a massive fall in its share price.

Motor vehicle recalls are common and the Toyota case in particular has been widely reported. But what makes the Toyota recall different – and why it's relevant to you in this context – is that the Japanese carmaker was convinced there was no manufacturing fault.

However, the company faced a firestorm of allegations and devastating news media coverage, especially in the United States, and CEO Akio Toyoda – for legal and reputation reasons – eventually had little choice but to issue an apology.

How To Apologize When You Believe You've Done Nothing Wrong

Speaking to a press conference in Japan, the Toyota CEO Akio Toyoda said he "deeply regretted" the concern the acceleration faults had caused to customers and said it was his "personal responsibility" to fix the problem.

"The recalls are affecting several models in several regions and have caused anxiety among customers who are wondering if their cars are OK. For that we are very sorry."

"I believe we will soon win back the trust of Toyota owners. Believe me, Toyota cars are safe. We always put the customer first."

A subsequent investigation by the National Highway Traffic Safety Administration (NHTSA) cleared Toyota by announcing that the company's electronic throttle system was not to blame for reported episodes of runaway acceleration.[143] This supported the company's belief that there was not a fundamental manufacturing fault and helps explain why the CEO's apology

---

[143] For more detail on how Toyota cars were tested see Chapter Nine on Marathon cases.

carefully avoided admitting having caused the problem. Yet at the same time Toyota also avoided blaming its customers.[144]

Contrast this with the response by Audi to a similar "sudden acceleration" crisis in the 1980s which devastated the company's sales and caused long-term damage to reputation.[145] Here too human error was found to be the main cause, and many years later the woman whose story triggered the Audi allegations admitted she had pressed the accelerator instead of the brake. Although Audi was eventually vindicated, many crisis experts at the time faulted Audi for blaming drivers and consequently suffering added damage.

Lessons learned

Despite these dissimilar outcomes, the question of whether to apologize when you believe you have done nothing wrong remains a contentious one for both lawyers and communicators.

John Doorley, a recognized expert on reputation, disagrees with Dezenhall's concept of the "marital apology:"

> *"Apologizing, even when the individual or organization did nothing wrong – despite what some crisis communicators advise – may stop the bleeding, but is untruthful and bad behavior. It will, therefore, harm reputation over the long term."[146]*

---

[144] McCurry, J. (2010, February 6). Toyota president Akio Toyoda 'very sorry' for safety recalls. *The Guardian.* https://www.theguardian.com/business/2010/feb/05/toyota-president-very-sorry-recalls

[145] Risen, J. (1989, September 14). Audi Sales Still Weak, Despite Federal Report That Car Is Safe. *Los Angeles Times.* https://www.latimes.com/archives/la-xpm-1989-09-14-fi-357-story.html

[146] Doorley, J. (2019). To manage reputation is to treat it as an asset: Not to do so is to make it a liability. In T. Langham (Ed.), *Reputation Management: The future of corporate communications and public relations* (pp 71-76). Bingley, UK: Emerald Publishing.

So, was Toyota right to apologize even though their vehicles were not at fault? The bottom line is that Toyota regained its position as top global carmaker within 12 months.

I don't think there is a "right answer" to this question, although the Toyota example is very instructive. Consider the unusual circumstances of the case. On one hand Toyota was able to call on an enormous reserve of goodwill (which many companies do not enjoy) while on the other hand the alleged faults arose in the context of reported faults across a number of different brands of motor vehicles, and amidst greatly heightened media interest in vehicle safety.

Moreover, it seems clear that if Toyota had not apologized, the media story would have become the company's "hostility to consumer safety." In other words, the real impact is sometimes not what the apology does but what the lack of an apology may do.

I think the case also highlights another important consideration, namely the difference between apologizing when you know you have done nothing wrong as opposed to apologizing when you don't yet know whether in fact you have done something wrong.

On balance perhaps Dezenhall and Doorley are both correct. That conclusion may not be helpful, but this issue could truly be one of those times when each case must be considered on its individual circumstances.

The Political Apology

My final reason for apologizing is also legally controversial and has the added challenge that it is often deeply entangled in politics: when you are pressed to apologize for the actions of someone else, or on behalf of someone else, for historical misdeeds.

It's most often seen in the area of national politics, but can also apply to businesses, NGOs and other organizations.

While such apologies may be regarded as largely symbolic, they nevertheless attract widespread publicity and sometimes generate passionate debate. Similarly, *failure* to apologize for historical events can also generate passionate current debate – witness the long-standing refusal by the Government of Turkey to acknowledge or apologize for the so-called Armenian Genocide at the time of the First World War.

The political sensitivity of this issue, even 100 years later, was reinforced in late 2019 when the US Senate voted to recognize the Genocide and Turkey immediately threatened retaliation.[147]

However, to apologize for a wrongdoing decades or even centuries ago has, or is often intended to have, a positive impact on reputation and reconciliation.

Let me list just a small sample:

Governments

- US Senate apologized (2009) for slavery, though added a disclaimer that the resolution couldn't be used as a rationale for reparations.[148]

- Australia's Parliament issued a "National apology" (2008) for the "stolen generation" – thousands of mainly mixed-race aborigine and Torres Strait Island children forcibly removed from their families between 1910 and 1970 as part of an assimilation policy and placed in state institutions or fostered to non-indigenous families.[149]

---

[147] Ortega, R. (2019, December 16). Turkey threatens to close air base that hosts US nuclear warheads in response to proposed sanctions and genocide declaration over mass killings of Armenians. *Daily Mail* https://www.dailymail.co.uk/news/article-7795427/Turkey-threatens-close-air-base-hosts-nuclear-warheads-response-proposed-sanctions.html

[148] Becker, B. (2009, June 18). Senate Approves Slavery Apology, With Reparations Disclaimer. *New York Times*. https://thecaucus.blogs.nytimes.com/2009/06/18/senate-approves-slavery-apology-with-reparations-disclaimer/

[149] Welch, D. (2008, February 14). Kevin Rudd says sorry. *Sydney Morning Herald*. https://www.smh.com.au/national/kevin-rudd-says-sorry-20080214-gds0vu.html

- Norway's government apologized (2018) to Norwegian women targeted for reprisals by the authorities for having relationships with members of the German occupying forces during World War II. [150]

- US President Reagan apologized (1988) to over 100,000 Japanese-American citizens and residents removed to remote internment camps during World War II as a "security risk."[151]

- British Prime Minister **Gordon Brown** apologized (2010) for the UK's role in sending an estimated 150,000 underprivileged children aged between three and 14 to countries such as Canada and Australia from the 1920s to the 1960s, where many ended up being abused in foster homes, state-run orphanages and religious institutions. [152]

- The West African Country of Benin apologized (2000) for its role in selling fellow Africans to the American slave trade. [153]

- South Korean police finally apologize (2019) for massacres during a communist uprising on Jeju island in 1948. The Prime Minister had apologized in 2003. [154]

---

[150] Norway apologizes to women punished for relationships with German soldiers (2018, October 18). *The Guardian.* https://www.theguardian.com/world/2018/oct/17/norwegian-women-get-apology-for-reprisals-over-wwii-friendships

[151] Bishop, K. (1988, August 11). Day of apology and 'sigh of relief" (1988, August 11). *New York Times.* https://www.nytimes.com/1988/08/11/us/day-of-apology-and-sigh-of-relief.html

[152] Gordon Brown to apologize for UK's role in child migrant scandal (2010, February 24). *The Guardian.* https://www.theguardian.com/politics/2010/feb/24/gordon-brown-apology-child-migrants

[153] Benin apologizes for role in slavery (2000, May 1). *Globe and Mail.* https://www.theglobeandmail.com/news/world/benin-apologizes-for-role-in-slavery/article22402977/

[154] South Korean Police apologize for Jeju Island massacre (2019, April 13). *Channelnewsasia.* https://www.channelnewsasia.com/news/asia/south-korean-police-apologise-jeju-incident-massacre-11408500

- On the 80th anniversary of the Nazi invasion of Poland, German President Frank-Walter Steinmeier apologized (2019) and begged for forgiveness.[155]

Organizations

- The Church of England General Synod voted unanimously (2006) to apologize to descendants of slaves for its role in benefiting from slave labor in the Caribbean in the 18th century.[156]

- Pope John Paul II apologized (2004) on behalf of the Catholic Church for the sack of Constantinople by Christian Crusaders in April 1204.[157]

- Boy Scouts of America apologized (2019) to more than 12,000 victims of sexual abuse from 1944 through 2016 for harm during their time in scouting.[158]

---

[155] Waterfield, B. (2019, September 1). President apologizes to Poland for Nazi invasion. *The Times.* https://www.thetimes.co.uk/article/president-apologises-to-poland-for-nazi-invasion-0g857s0t0

[156] Church of England apologizes for having been at the heart of slavery (2006, February 10). *Sydney Morning Herald.* https://www.smh.com.au/world/church-of-england-apologises-for-having-been-at-the-heart-of-slavery-20060210-gdmxvu.html

[157] Connolly, K. (2004, June 30). Pope says sorry for crusaders' rampage in 1204. *Telegraph, UK.* https://www.telegraph.co.uk/news/worldnews/europe/italy/1465857/Pope-says-sorry-for-crusaders-rampage-in-1204.html

[158] Hanna, J., Joseph, E.& Squeglia, K. (2019, April 25). The list of Boy Scouts leaders accused of sexual abuse has nearly 3,000 more names than previously known. *CNN.* https://edition.cnn.com/2019/04/24/us/boy-scouts-sexual-abuse-allegations/index.html

Companies

- Georg Krayer, President of the Swiss Bankers Association, apologized (1999) on behalf of Swiss banks which were said to have hoarded millions of dollars deposited by Jews who later perished in the Holocaust[159]

- To mark the 70th anniversary of the end of World War II, Mitsubishi, one of the largest companies in Japan, apologized (2015) for mistreatment of prisoners of war. [160]

- France's state railway SNCF apologized and paid compensation (2010) for its role in transporting innocent victims to the Nazi death camps. The Dutch national railway NS did the same in 2019.[161]

Lessons learned

When you look at these examples you might think corporations and other organizations are not likely to find themselves in such a high-profile "political" situation.

It's a comforting thought, but such exposure is not as uncommon as you might imagine.

Over recent years hundreds of Japanese and German companies, and some major British and American multi-nationals, have been forced to confront their role during World War II.

---

[159] Drozdiak, W. (1999, December 7). Panel finds 54,000 accounts of Nazi victims. *Washington Post.* https://www.washingtonpost.com/wp-srv/WPcap/1999-12/07/070r-120799-idx.html

[160] Ripley, W. (2015, July 20). Mitsubishi apologizes to WWII Japanese prisoners of war. *CNN.* https://edition.cnn.com/2015/07/19/asia/mitsubishi-japan-pow-apology/index.html

[161] Cuskey, P. (2019, June 28). Dutch railway operator to pay compensation for role in Holocaust. *Irish Times.* https://www.irishtimes.com/news/world/europe/dutch-railway-operator-to-pay-compensation-for-role-in-holocaust-1.3939610

For example, IBM has had to address persistent claims that the company knowingly supplied the punch card tabulating technology which helped Nazi Germany implement their Final Solution.[162]

The reality is that such companies, and many others, find themselves facing a variety of different reasons why they need to apologize.

To summarize, I'd like to give the last word to my friend Peter Sandman, one of the world's leading authorities on risk and risk communication, who created the famous formula "Risk = Hazard + Outrage."

"Clients often claim the barrier to apologizing is legal. They say they're afraid that greedy 'victims' will take advantage of an apology to sue for damages... In fact, an apology can actually improve a defendant's legal position, by reducing the impulse of prospective plaintiffs to sue and by reducing the impulse of jurors to impose punitive damages. Both of these effects result from the powerful effect of apologies on outrage. It's hard to stay angry at people who say they're sorry – which makes apologizing one of the best and certainly one of the cheapest outrage reducers around."[163]

I couldn't have said it better myself.

---

[162] Jackson, B. (2011, June 20). IBM's darkest chapter: Controversy over Second World War. *ITBusiness, Canada.* https://www.itbusiness.ca/news/ibms-darkest-chapter-controversy-over-second-world-war/16394

[163] Sandman, P.M. (2001, May 4). Saying you're sorry. *Peter Sandman Blog* http://www.psandman.com/col/sorry.htm

Key Takeaways

- Apologizing is often the right thing to do and may be the least expensive.
- Failing to apologize can make a reputational crisis even worse.
- A delayed apology risks losing all meaningful purpose.
- Apologizing can reduce legal liability, especially in civil suits.
- The "marital apology" is when you need to apologize, even when you've done nothing wrong.
- Sometimes you have to apologize for historical wrongdoing committed by other people.

Questions for Discussion

1. *Would United Airlines' notorious "deplaning" reputational crisis at Chicago Airport have ever mattered if it wasn't captured on mobile phones?*
2. *Is it ethical to issue a so-called "marital apology" when you know you've done nothing wrong just to avoid further controversy or liability?*
3. *Does a political apology delivered after 50 or 100 or even 600 years serve any useful purpose beyond making the apologizer feel better?*
4. *As a member of the jury, would it make any difference to your opinion if the organization on trial had issued an apology? Or had refused to apologize?*
5. *Is a delayed apology worse than no apology at all? How long would be perceived as "delayed"?*

Chapter Five

How to Apologize

"People will forgive a screw up, but they will never forgive a cover up."

Steve Hayworth, CNN.

If you want to be a good violinist, you will probably study the technique of the leading musicians. If you aspire to be a good painter, you will most likely analyze the style and brushstrokes of the masters. If you want to be a good lawyer, you'd study the cases of the great litigators. And so on for most pursuits.

Yet for communications practitioners, the learning process is often focused on studying what was done badly rather than what was done well. And understanding how to apologize is a prime example of this paradox. There are certainly far more articles, blogs, and presentations on how *not* to apologize than on how to do it effectively. That's not surprising. It's much more interesting for you to read about other people's failures, and much more satisfying to smugly conclude: "We're too smart to have made *that* mistake."

This chapter will help you to:

- Focus on how to apologize rather than how not to.
- Design well-planned and well-executed apologies to help protect your reputation.
- Implement practical guidelines to prepare and deliver an effective apology.
- Evaluate the key risks and apply lessons from occasions where apologies were issued against explicit legal advice,
- Recognize and avoid a list of the words and phrases which undermine the authenticity and credibility of an apology.
- Learn from a classic case of a bad apology in a high-risk legal context just how quickly it can all go wrong.

Despite the importance of effective apologies, it's the bad apologies and non-apologies which make the headlines and tend to dominate discussion.

There are even long-running blogs and online video resources devoted solely to examining apologies and highlighting what are called "PR disasters." For example, Sorrywatch.com, run by American writers Susan McCarthy and Marjorie Ingall, is a treasure trove of advice and examples about how not to apologize, as well as occasionally how to do it properly. Similarly, publicapologycentral.com, managed by Utah academic Kevin Stein, provides a rich catalogue of apologies, many illustrated by video or movie clips.

There is, alas, no shortage of terrible apologies (and a few good ones too) for such sites to analyze.

As Marjorie Ingall of SorryWatch has concluded:

> *"Apologizing well is hard because pride and shame get in our way. Even when we want to apologize beautifully and generously, our wee brains hate acknowledging the fact that we screwed up. So, we find ways to convey (implicitly or explicitly, consciously or unconsciously) that the other person is actually at fault."*[164]

Blaming the other person is just one of the many ways *not* to apologize, and most practitioners and experts agree that a bad apology may be worse than no apology at all. In other words, if you don't *feel apologetic*, you might as well not even try to apologize. Remember, you not only have to *be* sincere, but you also have to be *perceived to be* sincere by the other party.

And not just the other party. Executive credibility is in fact under challenge even within top management. A major study of C-suite executives (excluding the CEO)

---

[164] Ingall, M. (2014, August 17). How *Not* to Apologize. *Real Simple*. https://www.realsimple.com/work-life/life-strategies/marjorie-ingall-apologies

found 74 per cent reported that CEO apologies in general are genuine.[165] Think about that. It leaves a worrying 26 per cent who thought that CEOs in general are "rarely or almost never" genuine in their apologies.

That's worth repeating. Even one in four senior executives don't believe CEO apologies. Is it any wonder that the public and the stakeholders directly involved have their doubts?

Moreover, it goes without saying that to apologize well you need to listen to the advice of the lawyers and communications professionals. But in the end, most apologies are seen as personal statements from the person who needs to apologize and who typically has the capacity to make things right.

Unfortunately, poor advice can lead to a frightening assortment of bad apologies and non-apologies. And it certainly isn't always the cliché of bad legal advice. But it's all too easy to identify and analyze terrible apologies.

Take for example cybercrime or data security, which is one of the very worrying reputational and organizational crisis risks today. It happens so often you'd think organizations would know how to apologize well. Sadly it isn't so.

Consider the explanation by the Australian political consultants Hawker Britton after they inadvertently exposed the private email addresses of about a thousand clients and associates:

> *"We obviously apologize if anyone is in the slightest*
> *way upset. It's a human error. We don't want them*
> *to occur, but sometimes they do."* [166]

How would you have felt about that "apology" if your private information had been exposed? It certainly didn't seem to convey any spirit of sympathy or

---

[165] WeberShandwick (2015). *The CEO reputation premium: Gaining advantage in the engagement era.* https://www.webershandwick.com/news/the-ceo-reputation-premium-a-new-era-of-engagement/ The study surveyed 1700 executives in companies of $500 million or more revenue, across 19 countries.
[166] Dumas, D. (2015, July 24). Labor lobbyist Hawker Britton makes embarrassing email error. *Sydney Morning Herald.* https://www.smh.com.au/politics/federal/labor-lobbyist-hawker-britton-makes-embarrassing-email-error-20150724-gijzmp.html

contrition or genuine regret. In fact it was a pretty poor effort by a company of professional communicators.

Some other recent data breaches have been on a very different scale.

When Reddit revealed a major data breach in August 2018, they described in detail actions being taken to protect users in the future, but as one commentator wrote: "Noticeably missing from the announcement was any kind of apology."[167]

Also in August 2018 it was reported that Comcast Xfinity inadvertently exposed the partial home addresses and Social Security numbers of more than 26.5 million customers.[168] Again, technical explanation but no apology.

A few months earlier hackers accessed five million credit card accounts at Sax Fifth Avenue and the company said: "We deeply regret any inconvenience or concern this may cause." [169] Shortly afterwards Marriott revealed a hacker attack on a database containing information for up to 500 million hotel customers, and followed the same approach, saying: "Marriott deeply regrets this incident happened." [170]

Expressing regrets may feel "safe," but it hardly counts as a meaningful apology to the customers affected, and I will come shortly to some of the other words and phrases to avoid.

Frankly, crafting a half-decent apology isn't so difficult.

---

[167] Kitterman, T. (2018, August 3). Reddit reveals major data breach, promises security fix. *PR Daily*. https://www.prdaily.com/Main/Articles/24823.aspx

[168] Nguyen, N. (2018, August 3). A Comcast security flaw exposed millions of customers' personal information. *Buzzfeed*. https://www.buzzfeednews.com/article/nicolenguyen/a-comcast-security-flaw-exposed-millions-of-customers?utm_

[169] Kitterman, T. (2018 April 3), Saks, Lord & Taylor tackles data breach with FAQ, reassurances. *PR Daily*. https://www.prdaily.com/saks-lord-taylor-tackles-data-breach-with-faq-reassurances/

[170] Winchel, B. (2018, November 30). Marriott reveals data breach for up to 500 million guests. *PR Daily*. https://www.prdaily.com/Main/Articles/25395.aspx

Around the same time in 2018 as the previous on-line security failures, British Airways had a data breach which compromised payment and personal information for about 500,000 customers. The company statement said:

> *"We're deeply sorry, but you may have been affected... Please accept our deepest apologies for the worry and inconvenience that this criminal activity has caused."[171]*

I think you'd agreed that's a considerable improvement on other cases. (A year later, in July 2019, the Information Commissioner's Office proposed a £183 million (US$230 million) fine because of the airlines "poor security arrangements" in protecting data [172]).

More recently another airline, the British budget operator EasyJet, was also caught up in a data breach, with hackers accessing 9 million customer files, including just over 2,000 with full credit card details. The CEO issued an adequate apology, but the breach reportedly began in January 2020 and the apology and official public notification was not until May.[173] The company said it had taken time to identify which credit card information had been accessed, but the case is a clear reminder that an apology must not only be genuine, but must also be timely.

A good example of a remarkably prompt apology was after American audio system maker Sonos announced in January 2020 that older models of their high-end equipment would be cut off from future software updates.

---

[171] Winchel, B. (2018, September 7). British Airways apologizes as data breach hits 380,000+ customers. *PR Daily*. https://www.prdaily.com/Main/Articles/24995.aspx

[172] Sweney, M. (2019, July 8). BA faces £183m fine over passenger data breach. *The Guardian*. https://www.theguardian.com/business/2019/jul/08/ba-fine-customer-data-breach-british-airways

[173] Schwartz, M. J. (2020, May 19). EasyJet Data Breach Exposes 9 Million Customers' Details. *Bank Info Security*. https://www.bankinfosecurity.com/easyjet-data-breach-exposes-9-million-customers-details-a-14300

The predictable result was customer outrage.[174] In the face of some very obvious brand and legal risks, CEO Patrick Spence quickly issued a blog post and customer email which said, in part:

> *"We heard you. We did not get this right from the start. My apologies for that and I wanted to personally assure you of the path forward.*
>
> *First, rest assured that come May, when we end new software updates for our legacy products, they will continue to work just as they do today...Whilst legacy Sonos products won't get new software features, we pledge to keep them updated with bug fixes and security patches for as long as possible.*
>
> *Thank you for being a Sonos customer. Thank you for taking the time to give us your feedback. I hope that you'll forgive our misstep and let us earn back your trust. Without you, Sonos wouldn't exist and we'll work harder than ever to earn your loyalty every single day."[175]*

His policy reversal and apology were remarkable for a number of reasons.

- It was issued just two days after the original announcement.
- It showed empathy – "We hear you."
- It showed honest contrition – "We did not get this right from the start... Forgive our misstep."
- It contained a clear and personal apology from the CEO, not on behalf of "the company."

---

[174] Hern, A. (2020, January 24). Sonos to deny software updates to owners of older equipment. *The Guardian*. https://www.theguardian.com/technology/2020/jan/23/sonos-to-deny-software-updates-to-owners-of-older-equipment

[175] Spence, P. (2020, January 23) A letter from our CEO: All Sonos products will continue to work past May. *Sonos Blog*. https://blog.sonos.com/en-gb/a-letter-from-our-ceo/

- It explained how Sonos planned to act to resolve the problem.

… simple, forthright and not sounding like a corporate statement polished to within an inch of its life by cautious lawyers.

A Job Well Done

Just as failure to apologize, or apologizing badly, can become the story, so too apologizing well can actually generate positive media.

I have never favored the notion that within every crisis is an opportunity. And no sensible manager would welcome a crisis as a chance to shine. But some apologies after a crisis have proved not only to deflect or reduce criticism but to actually garner genuine praise.

> "The gentle language of genuine empathy, delivered in the right tone at the right time, is a powerful human response which can fundamentally alter the perception of how the company is dealing with the crisis."
>
> Sydney communication expert Craig Badings.[176]

While bad apologies are not hard to recognize, it is also not that hard to recognize and appreciate an apology well executed.

So in this chapter I'd prefer my focus to be on showing you further examples of apologies done well, especially where there were clear legal consequences or potential legal risk.

For a great example of an apology by the CEO personally – and returning to the theme of cyber security – I invite you to consider what happened when hackers

---

[176] Spencer-Smith. T. (2019). Why good crisis control relies on the language of empathy. *Exclaim, 46.* http://www.icontact-archive.com/archive?c=796724&f=4026&s=4257&m=449121&t=83b983455212693ea215dd91e9bd23404af73666021ed7c8a0350afae10d86ec

attacked Anthem Blue Cross, America's second largest health insurer, in 2015, potentially exposing personal details of up to 80 million customers.[177]

Their tactical response was textbook. Anthem provided assurance that there was no evidence credit card or medical details had been accessed; they hired a global cybersecurity firm to check systems and offered two years of free credit monitoring; and they set up a dedicated website and a new toll-free number to provide information and answer questions.

That response was very much in line with what has come to represent technical best practice. But it was the written apology by CEO Joseph Swedish which attracted special attention. His public letter included the following statements:

> *"Anthem's own associates' personal information – including my own – was accessed during this security breach. We join you in your concern and frustration and I assure you we are working around the clock to do everything we can to further secure your data."*

> *"I want to personally apologize to each of you for what has happened, as I know you expect us to protect your information. We will continue to do everything in our power to make our systems more secure and I hope that we can earn back your trust and confidence in Anthem."*[178]

You couldn't deny it was a masterly blend of personal empathy and corporate assurance, and it was widely applauded. Crisis expert Jonathan Bernstein, for

---

[177] Mathews, A. and Yadron, D. (2015, February 4). Health insurer Anthem hit by hackers. *Wall Street Journal*. https://www.wsj.com/articles/health-insurer-anthem-hit-by-hackers-1423103720

[178] Terhune C. (2015, February 5). Anthem hack exposes data on 80 million; experts warn of identity theft. *Los Angeles Times*. https://www.latimes.com/business/la-fi-anthem-hacked-20150204-story.html

example, called it "A rare corporate apology done right" and said it hit all Three Cs of an effective response – Credibility, Confidence and Compassion.[179]

Another CEO who won widespread praise a few years earlier for a heartfelt personal apology was Domino's boss Patrick Doyle after two employees at a pizza outlet in North Carolina in 2009 filmed themselves doing disgusting things to food then posted it on YouTube, viewed over a million times in a few days.

Doyle filmed his own YouTube response.

> *"We sincerely apologize for this incident. Although the individuals in question claim it's a hoax, we are taking this incredibly seriously. The store has been shut down and sanitized from top to bottom.*
>
> *"There is nothing more important or sacred to us than our customers' trust. It sickens me that the actions of two individuals could impact our great system. We want to thank you for hanging in there with us as we work to regain your trust."[180]*

I suggest you read those words again, because they are so unlike typical corporate language. And it wasn't a slick business video. The CEO was filmed inside a Domino's store, wearing a logo branded shirt, speaking directly to camera. You might think that saying he was "sickened" by what had happened, and referring to a "sacred trust," might be a little overblown when talking about selling fast food. But there is no doubting the CEO's honesty and commitment, and it was reported that the script was entirely his own work.

The media had little doubt about the impact. One TV food news channel carried the headline; "Domino's pizza and its brilliant apology" and the case has been

---

[179] Bernstein, J. and Bernstein, E. (2015, February 25). Anthem's apology hits all three C's of credibility. *Bernstein crisis blog.* https://managementhelp.org/blogs/crisis-management/2015/02/24/anthems-apology-hits-all-three-cs-of-credibility/?utm_

[180] Domino's Pizza Patrick Doyle apologizes for employees' Youtube prank. (2009, April 15). *Youtube.* https://www.youtube.com/watch?v=xvg4-E2C8UE

extensively analyzed as a classic example of how to do it, which remains very relevant today.[181]

More recently, another CEO earned praise for doing and saying the right things. When two African American men were arrested in April 2018 for trespassing at a Philadelphia Starbucks while waiting for a friend, CEO Kevin Johnson travelled to Philadelphia to meet the arrested men as well as the city's Mayor and Police Commissioner. But he also announced they would close all 8,000 US stores for half a day for about 175,000 employees to attend racial bias education to address implicit bias and prevent discrimination.

While Mr. Johnson's decision to close every store generated predictable controversy, his words were a model of an effective apology.

> *"I want to offer a personal apology to the two men who were arrested in our store. What happened in the way that incident escalated, and the outcome, was nothing but reprehensible, and I am sorry. We are going to learn from this and we will be better for it. These two men did not deserve what happened and we are accountable. I am accountable.*
>
> *"Now there's been some calls for us to take action on the store manager. I believe that blame is misplaced. In fact, I think the focus of fixing this: I own it. This is a management issue, and I am accountable to ensure we address the policy and the practice and the training that led to this outcome."* [182]

---

[181] Flandez, R. (2009, April 20). Domino's response offers lessons in crisis management. *Wall Street Journal.* https://blogs.wsj.com/independentstreet/2009/04/20/dominos-response-offers-lessons-in-crisis-management/

[182] Schwantes, M. (2018, April 17). Starbucks' CEO showed a classy example of what a great leader does when managing a crisis. *INC.* https://www.inc.com/marcel-schwantes/starbuckss-ceo-showed-a-classy-example-of-what-a-great-leader-does-when-managing-a-crisis.html

As INC magazine added, the CEO took three textbook steps: (1) He genuinely apologized as his first course of action (2) He admitted fault and took ownership of the problem, and (3) He pledged to take action and fix the problem at all cost. Their headline said it all

> *"Starbucks CEO showed classy example of what a great leader does when managing a crisis." (INC)*

Others followed suit:

> *"The CEO of Starbucks just passed his biggest leadership test yet." (Bloomberg)*[183]

> *"Zuckerberg should look to Starbucks CEO Kevin Johnson on how to handle a crisis." (CNBC)*[184]

The Great Chicken Disaster

Another recent apology which gained widespread praise was not by an individual but was an advertisement on behalf of a corporation.

One of the first things a young communicator learns is never to mess with the corporate logo. During many years working for a major global corporation, I knew from personal experience that the corporate design manual was sacrosanct, and that the company lawyers would crash down upon my head if I made play with the logo, even in the face of the most serious crisis.

Yet that is exactly what happened with one of the cheekiest and most memorable corporate apologies of the last decade.

---

[183] Halzack, S. (2018, April 18). The CEO of Starbucks just passed his biggest leadership test yet. *Bloomberg.*
https://www.bloomberg.com/opinion/articles/2018-04-18/starbucks-ceo-kevin-johnson-aces-this-leadership-test
[184] Zhao, H. (2018, April 18). Zuckerberg should look to Starbucks' CEO Kevin Johnson on how to handle a crisis. *CNBC.com*
https://www.cnbc.com/2018/04/18/zuckerberg-should-look-to-starbucks-ceo-on-how-to-handle-a-crisis.html

In early 2018, KFC in Britain ran out of chickens as a result of a major logistical failure and had to temporarily close down more than 750 branches across the country.[185] It was an organizational crisis which received huge publicity and generated what you could only call hysteria. There were calls for government intervention and the police even had to issue a statement asking people not to report it as an emergency.

Near the end of the nine-day crisis KFC published a full-page newspaper apology advertisement which featured an empty chicken bucket with the KFC logo rearranged to spell FCK. The advertising text began:

> *"We're sorry. A chicken restaurant without any chicken. It's not ideal. Huge apologies to our customers, especially those who travelled out of their way to find we were closed."[186]*

But it was the image – with its almost spelling of a very different word – that was reproduced around the world and gave rise to hundreds of approving reports and online memes.

For example, one British commentary site carried the headline:

> *"The KFC apology ad is so good it's almost worth running out of chicken for."(The Poke)[187]*

[185] Ma, A. (2018, February 20). 750 KFCs in Britain closed down because they ran out of chicken. *Business Insider*. https://www.businessinsider.com.au/kfc-shuts-750-uk-stores-in-chicken-logistics-crisis-2018-2?r=US&IR=T

[186] Oster, E, (2018, February 23). KFC Responds to UK chicken shortage scandal with a timely "FCK, we'sorry". *Adweek*. https://www.adweek.com/creativity/kfc-responds-to-u-k-chicken-shortage-scandal-with-a-timely-fck-were-sorry/

[187] The KFC apology ad is so good it's almost worth running out of chicken for. (2018, February 23). *The Poke*. https://www.thepoke.co.uk/2018/02/23/kfc-apology-ad-good-almost-worth-running-chicken/

While the cheeky "brand transformation" was seen by millions of people who were not in Britain, were not affected by the crisis, and may never have been KFC customers, what's really interesting from my perspective is the reasoning and strategy behind the decision. To fully appreciate the apology campaign, it's worth taking a moment to hear from the person involved with this rule-challenging decision, Jenny Packwood, Head of Brand Engagement.

> *"There were certain principles established pretty quickly: we stuck to our brand voice, and we tackled the issue head on. We didn't try to shift blame or responsibility elsewhere, and put our hands up and said it was a massive cockup. We had a huge amount of goodwill from the media because we weren't hiding.*

> *"The ad enabled us to say sorry with a big platform, in a way that felt human and bold. It didn't stop the crisis, but it totally shifted the media focus onto our response and handling, rather than the crisis itself."* [188]

No mention, you will note, of what the KFC corporate lawyers might have thought, although Ms Packwood went on to say that when you're under pressure the easiest thing is to default to a corporate statement that comes from lawyers and sounds insincere. But if people don't buy it, she said, it does more harm than good.

> *"It wouldn't be appropriate to use our light-hearted, irreverent tone if someone has got hurt. But you have to find a way to be true to your brand and find a balance, treading that fine line between being credible and sincere, and corporate and formal."*

---

[188] Sims, M. P. (2018, December 3). Crisis Lessons From KFC: "Ultimately We Needed To Be Brave". *The Holmes Report.*
https://www.holmesreport.com/latest/article/crisis-lessons-from-kfc-ultimately-we-needed-to-be-brave?utm

My guess is you can be sure the KFC apology and its cheeky image will continue to feature in lectures on marketing and crisis management in years to come as an example of how you can turn a reputational crisis into a sort of triumph.

Needless to say, there are other examples of a truly effective corporate apology. And some are very evidently the result of an open and constructive relation between communicators and lawyers.

Doing it right.

Have you read or heard examples of a truly effective organizational apology?

What made it good?

Why was it memorable?

Did it appear to reflect legal or communicator input?

What can you learn from it?

Have you or your organization had to issue a public apology?

How good was it?

While good apologies might indeed be rare – as Jonathan Bernstein said regarding the Anthem case – the mechanics of good apologies are not difficult to understand. Fundamentally good apologies are about stepping up, while bad apologies typically avoid taking full responsibility.

Eight basic steps towards an effective apology	
1	Say what you are apologizing for, what you did wrong. Not vague phrases like "I'm sorry for what happened."
2	Make it clear who you are apologizing to. Be specific. Name names of people or groups if necessary. Not just "anyone who was offended."

Eight basic steps towards an effective apology	
3	Express remorse and demonstrate some humility.
4	Empathize with the feelings of whoever you are apologizing to.
5	Hold yourself accountable for what went wrong. An apology is best from the leader rather than a lawyer or spokesperson.
6	Do it quickly and voluntarily, not only after damaging media attention or under legal duress.
7	Give a genuine assurance it won't happen again.
8	Describe what you will do to rectify the wrongdoing... and carry through on that promise.

So, if the basics are not difficult to understand, why do we so often see terrible apologies, or non-apologies masquerading as the real thing?

There are two important preconditions. The first is that you need to *be* sorry, not just *say* you're sorry. The second is that your apology must be *seen to be* genuine in the eyes of the offended party or parties. Which means, to be effective it must be focused on the other person's needs and feelings, not your own

There is no doubt that some poor apologies are the result of bad legal or communications advice. But it's simplistic and misguided to lay all the blame on advisors. Executives and politicians can't legitimately avoid responsibility for what they write and say.

Take the notorious case of American Senator Bob Packwood who famously responded to accusations of sexual harassment by saying:

"I'm apologizing for the conduct that it was alleged that I did, and I say I am sorry." [189]

Packwood refused to say what he was apologizing for, and this embarrassingly vague response was the first step in a long decline which led to his eventual resignation in the face of certain expulsion from the Senate.[190]

It is hard to imagine any lawyer or public relations advisor – even in the 1990s – suggesting this was a smart choice of words.

Indeed, it's rare for legal and communications advice about apologizing to become public. And it's even more uncommon for an executive to publicly repudiate such advice.

One such case involved the British travel company Thomas Cook when two children, aged six and seven years, died of carbon monoxide poisoning at a holiday cottage on Corfu. The gas leaked from a faulty boiler which had not been correctly repaired.

For nine long years the company argued that, while the holiday was booked through Thomas Cook, the fault lay with the Corfu hotel and the travel company "had nothing to apologize for." This was the line continued by the company's newly appointed CEO Peter Fankhauser at the inquest into the deaths, in 2015, which found that Thomas Cook had breached its duty of care.

However, soon after the inquest, Fankhauser met with the children's parents and offered a sincere and heartfelt apology. He later admitted he should have done so the moment he walked in as chief executive.

---

[189] Battistella, E. (2014, May 7). The art of the political apology: From Bill to Monica and everyone in between - a guide to saying sorry. *Politico.* https://www.politico.com/magazine/story/2014/05/the-art-of-the-political-apology-106458

[190] Keith, T. (2017, November 27). When Bob Packwood was nearly expelled from the Senate for sexual misconduct. *National Public Radio.* https://www.npr.org/2017/11/27/566096392/when-bob-packwood-was-nearly-expelled-from-the-senate-for-sexual-misconduct

"I was confronted with a situation that had gone on for nine years and was dragging and dragging. Even though I was new to the job, I somehow got stuck in this legacy. I got caught in this corporate behavior. I listened too much to lawyers."[191]

It was a startling about-face for Britain's second-largest travel operator. "I listened too much to lawyers." In that simple phrase the Swiss-born CEO expressed the essence of this chapter: Yes, listen to legal and communications advice, but in the end it is an executive decision which needs to be made in the best interests of the organization as a whole, preferably made promptly, without delay.

Referring to his initial decision to maintain the nine-year refusal to apologize, Fankhauser later said it was the biggest mistake in his 27 years in the travel industry. (The company eventually collapsed in 2019 in the face of an unrelated financial crisis.)

For another of those rare cases where an organization explicitly stated in public that it was going against legal advice, I need to take you back to 2011 to consider a Presbyterian church in Vienna, Virginia, where a Youth Ministries Director was convicted in court after inappropriate relationships with female students.

Following a long period of soul-searching, the church concluded that they had not adequately cared for the young victims of abuse and decided to admit to these lapses and to apologize. A lawyer for the church's insurance company warned against making any such statements, but they proceeded anyway. A spokesman for the church elders said:

---

[191] Arlidge, J. (2010, May 15). I learnt a lesson from our crisis: don't listen to lawyers. *Sunday Times*. https://www.thetimes.co.uk/article/i-learnt-a-lesson-from-our-crisis-dont-listen-to-lawyers-995sz0l67

"The direction from the insurance company and its lawyer were clear and possibly correct from a legal perspective. They did their job, but as elders we had to do ours. We still have lots of work cleaning up the mess created (by the youth leader) but not following their legal advice was a good start."[192]

The church Pastor went even further and told his congregation; "We won't hide behind lawyers... Jesus said the truth will set us free."

"The truth will set us free" might not be a popular sentiment in the average corporate boardroom, or in their legal department, but the case is another worthy reminder that in the end it's organizational leaders who need to assess the communications and legal advice and make the decisions.

Lessons learned

Although the common tendency is to focus on crisis apologies gone wrong, there are valuable lessons to be taken from good apologies, especially about balancing advice in the face of potential legal risk.

Joseph Swedish at Anthem, Patrick Doyle at Domino's and Kevin Johnson at Starbucks all set the tone from the top by positioning themselves personally and speaking directly to the people affected

In addition, Swedish emphasized his own direct involvement in the crisis, explaining that the hackers had not only threatened the data of millions of customers but also the personal data of himself and his management group.

It followed the example set by Queen Elizabeth, The Queen Mother, when Buckingham Palace in London was hit by German bombs during World War II. In one of her best-known statements she said: "I am glad we have been bombed. Now we can look the East End in the eye." As the Anthem CEO showed, when making an apology in

---

[192] Eisler, P. (2011, October 5). Church abuse cases and lawyers an uneasy mix. *USA Today.* https://usatoday30.usatoday.com/news/religion/2011-05-09-vienna-virginia-church-abuse-case-lawyers-insurers_n.htm

a crisis there can be no better way you can convey genuine empathy than by saying "Yes, and it happened to me too."

I believe an important lesson from the Domino's case was that the company took the threat seriously, despite the fact that the individuals concerned said it was a hoax and despite the fact that none of the food adulterated on video was served to the public. This was a crisis driven by customer perception where the CEO left no room at all for any doubt.

Similarly, the Starbucks example also concerned a very high-profile consumer brand where perception was essential. The CEO launched what I would call a "full court press" response, integrating both effective words and a plan of focused action in which he was personally involved.

It is also particularly notable that Johnson at Starbucks acknowledged and addressed the online clamor for action against the manager of the store where the incident happened. Very often in a crisis, managers are tempted to point the finger at some individual way down the organization hierarchy, and I have given you examples elsewhere in this book. But in this case the CEO not only took personal responsibility, but he went out of his way to explicitly state why the store manager should be not be punished.

The KFC chicken crisis too posed a major threat to a global consumer brand, but in that case it was a corporate rather than an individual apology. The objective was to maintain reputation and goodwill, which was brilliantly delivered. As Ms. Packwood explained, they couldn't stop the crisis, but they did manage to shift the media attention away from what had gone wrong. And they carefully resisted the temptation to lay all the blame on their new distribution contractor.

There is an important subsidiary lesson from the KFC case and that relates to the concept of the "full page apology." This is a tactic which has also been recently used by, among others, Facebook CEO Mark Zuckerberg to promise consumers he would "do better for you" in a full-page letter published in newspapers across the world following the Cambridge Analytica scandal,[193] and by media mogul Rupert Murdoch to declare he was sorry for the News of the World phone-hacking scandal.[194] In neither case was the apology regarded as particularly genuine.

Such full-page apology advertisements seem to be unimaginative and formulaic, and hint at a "tick the box" response. While they may attract momentary media attention, there is very little evidence that they actually change opinion in any meaningful way. And they can easily divert resources and distract from the main game.

Yet it is notable that, despite the digital revolution, when it comes to a large-scale corporate apology, big companies continue to turn to traditional newspapers as the preferred medium. Whatever you might think about the true effectiveness of a "full page apology," it seems clear that a large format print advertisement in a newspaper is still regarded as credible and trustworthy, and offers a permanent record which can cut through the online clutter. As my friend Gerry McCusker, a recognized authority in crisis management, said: "It's better than doing nothing, but not by a massive amount."[195]

In the case of Thomas Cook in Britain and the Church in Virginia, both apologies came in direct public contradiction of legal advice. I am not for a moment suggesting you should carelessly ignore what the lawyers have to say. But sometimes it can be the right thing to do.

---

[193] McKenzie, S. (2018, March 25). Facebook's Mark Zuckerberg says sorry in full-page newspaper ads. *CNN News.* https://edition.cnn.com/2018/03/25/europe/facebook-zuckerberg-cambridge-analytica-sorry-ads-newspapers-intl/index.html

[194] Plunkett, J. (2011, July 16). Rupert Murdoch says 'sorry' in ad campaign. *The Guardian.* https://www.theguardian.com/media/2011/jul/15/rupert-murdoch-sorry-ad-campaign

[195] Landis-Hanley, J. (2019, December 16). Westpac's grovelling apology letter the latest in a long line of full-page mea culpas. *Crikey.* https://www.crikey.com.au/2019/12/16/westpac-newspapers-apology/

Similarly both apologies came a good time after the event – in the case of Thomas Cook so long after that it was easy to say, "too little too late."

In fact, you might question whether I am correct to classify the Thomas Cook example as an apology well done. But I think it does fit into that category. Yes, the company spent years refusing to apologize, but the new CEO made the decision to put that right. I believe in this instance it truly was a case of "better late than never."

Setting aside for a moment the detail of specific cases, lawyers have some legitimate reasons to argue against an apology. Most importantly, they may argue that an apology will seemingly concede liability or jeopardize defense in subsequent legal proceedings.

From the point of view of a senior executive making a decision about an apology, it is essential you remember that this is precisely the lawyer's job. Their professional role is to protect your organization from needless liability and to defend you in court if necessary. So lawyers are by nature conservative and are prone to err on the side of caution.

It is no cliché that communicators inherently tend to see the need to communicate while lawyers tend to favor the organization saying as little as possible.

In fact, there is a cynical old legal maxim that every word used to persuade the public is a word which the other side can use to persuade the judge and jury.

At the same time, good lawyers understand that organizational crises are about a lot more than just the law and in Chapter Eight you will learn in more detail about the broader issue of liability versus responsibility.

However, the present focus is on how to apologize and how to balance legal and communications considerations.

How Not to Do It

I said earlier I wanted to focus here on examples of good apologies. But my judgement is you can't fully appreciate how to do that, and how to do that well, without giving thought to bad apologies and some of the pitfalls to avoid.

I'd like to spend just a little time on a classic case which relates to an old crisis but will give you insight today into what can go wrong, especially in the face of heavy legal consequences.

An example of how this misalignment can occur was shown in one of the most intensively studied and analyzed environmental disasters in recent decades, namely the 1989 *Exxon Valdez* oil spill crisis along the coast of Alaska.

The public and the media at the time consistently accused Exxon of not taking responsibility for the spill, and this belief has lived on in countless case studies and textbooks.

However, the fact is that the Exxon officer on the scene, the Chairman and the President all repeatedly apologized, and an apology advertisement in the name of the Chairman appeared in about 100 major magazines and newspapers (although critics complained that the advertisement kept referring to the disaster as an accident).

The frustration of Chairman Lawrence Rawl was evident in an interview with *Time* magazine:

> *"I went on TV and said I was sorry. I said a dozen times that we're going to clean up. But people keep saying that I don't commit. I don't know what the hell that means. Do you hang yourself or hold a gun to your head and say I'm gonna squeeze it five times, and if there's not a bullet in there I'll be all right?"*[196]

In the same ill-advised interview he made the extraordinarily tone-deaf statement that the thing that bothered him most about the disaster was the embarrassment: "I hate to be embarrassed, and I am."

Really? The thing that bothered him most about a major environmental disaster was that he was embarrassed?

---

[196] Behar, R. (1990, March 26). Exxon strikes back. *Time*. http://content.time.com/time/magazine/article/0,9171,969673,00.html

Here again, as in my previous reference to Senator Packwood, it's hard to imagine any lawyer or communications advisor suggesting that this was an appropriate response.

It certainly didn't help that the Exxon Chairman was apparently isolated and failed to understand what the public was thinking. He was also well known to be very suspicious of reporters. At a press conference soon after the disaster, the hapless Mr. Rawl confessed to an anguished frustration about public reaction.

> *"I'm angry myself. Now you get up in the morning*
> *and you think about Valdez; it colours your thinking*
> *till you go to bed at night. But it was an accident. It's*
> *not clear to me why people are so angry at us."[197]*

It might not have been clear to the Chairman why people were so angry with the company, but their opinion certainly had an impact. Before the spill Exxon held sixth place on Fortune's list of most admired companies. One year later it had fallen to 110th place.

Lessons Learned

The Exxon Valdez crisis may have been three decades ago, but it remains an extraordinarily valuable example for managers today.

The first obvious lesson is that Rawl clearly needed some media training. As I have said elsewhere, while crisis management is a lot more than a media management, failing to manage the media well can be a fatal flaw. Media training is like trying to get fit. You don't go to the gym just once and think that's enough to get the job done. The same applies to media training. It has to be done well and done frequently.

> "Media training is like trying to get fit. You don't go to the gym just once and think that's enough to get the job done."

---

[197] Spill damages oil company's credibility (1989, May 1). *South Florida Sun-Sentinel.* https://www.sun-sentinel.com/news/fl-xpm-1989-05-01-8901220570-story.html

The second lesson from this important case is that you can see Exxon didn't seem to understand the difference between making an apology and being apologetic. This distinction was once captured in an unrelated headline which appeared in the New York Times: "Too busy apologizing to be sorry."[198]

In my view it wasn't that Rawl and his company didn't apologize, but that society and the offended parties were reluctant to accept it as a genuine sign of contrition. And, anyway, there are perhaps some offences so egregious that no apology will ever suffice. One study of the case carried a headline which seems to me to capture the whole problem in just a few words: "Exxon Valdez: How to spend billions and still get a black eye."[199]

Finally, calling the spill an accident looks like an attempt to make it appear as some sort of unavoidable Act of God rather than a preventable result of human error (as the courts later found). In addition, I think this attitude might make executives less likely to work to prevent such events in the future. Obviously, corporate executives who insist that the disaster would not have occurred if Exxon rules had been followed are less likely to examine those rules, and more likely to perceive themselves as victims.

William K. Reilly, then head of the US Environmental Protection Agency, said later that Rawl "provided a casebook example of how not to communicate to the public when your company messes up."[200]

---

[198] Sontag, D. (1997, June 29). Too busy apologising to be sorry. *New York Times.* https://www.nytimes.com/1997/06/29/weekinreview/too-busy-apologizing-to-be-sorry.html

[199] Small, W. J. (1991). Exxon Valdez: How to spend billions and still get a black eye. *Public Relations Review 17(1), 9-25*

[200] Reilly, W. K. (1999, 24 March). The lessons we've learned in years since Exxon Valdez. *San Francisco Chronicle.* https://www.sfgate.com/opinion/openforum/article/The-Lessons-We-ve-Learned-In-Years-Since-Exxon-2940524.php

A casebook example, certainly, but so many executives still seem not to have learned the lessons.

Beyond setting the right tone and properly reading the situation, there is the question of choosing the right words to apologize, and that has its own challenges. You need to choose words which genuinely communicate your sincerity, and the sincerity of your organization, and at the same time don't needlessly create legal risk.

As I said at the start of this chapter, communication practitioners often focus on studying what was done badly rather than what was done well and my catalogue of sorry words and phrases to avoid in an apology is sure to be all too familiar.

Words and phrases to avoid in an effective apology	
It is regrettable or **I am regretful**	This approach is about you, not the offended party.
Mistakes were made	Denial of personal responsibility. Instead say: I made mistakes.
This is not who we are	More denial. Instead say: This is not who we want to be. Or: This is not who we would like to be.
But . . .	I am sorry, BUT I was upset/drunk/angry/stressed at the time. This is an excuse, not an apology.
If...	I am sorry IF you were offended. Instead say: I am sorry that I offended you.

Words and phrases to avoid in an effective apology	
It was not our intent to...	Denial of the outcome.
People close to me know that...	Blaming the offended party.
Let's move forward / Let's start a new chapter	Hopeful optimism. Instead say: Let's make sure we don't miss the important lesson here.
That was a different time	Possibly true, but no excuse.
My heart goes out to...	A platitude to avoid meaningful action.
It distresses me that...	This is about you, not the offended party.
I am paying the price...	More about you, not the offended party.
My Black / Jewish / Muslim / Gay / Christian / ethnic friends were not offended.	Perhaps, but someone or some group was offended.
My humor is edgy	Instead say: It was a very poor attempt at humor. I should have known better and I am extremely sorry.
The real party at fault here is...	It is never helpful to blame someone else... even when it truly is not your fault.

Words and phrases to avoid in an effective apology	
I was reacting to...	An excuse, not apology.
I'm sorry you feel that way	Blaming the offended party.
If only our critics...	A genuine apology is not an opportunity to lash out at your critics . . . even when they deserve it
This hasn't had as big an impact as most people think	Never minimize what you are apologizing about.
It was just a PR stunt. Our agency came up with the idea	It's your organization and you are responsible
I didn't think that people would take offense at my behaviour...	Making it worse by exposing your original poor judgement.
My words were taken out of context	Almost never true. A cliched attempt to reposition ill-advised words.
I misremembered/mis-spoke	An excuse, not an apology. Instead say I made a mistake.
This apology does not authorize nor support any settlement claims against...	Oh No! Lawyers in full control.

You can easily understand why these approaches seem attractive, especially to communicators and nervous lawyers who are reluctant to take responsibility in a crisis.

Within this shameful catalogue there are two terms in particular which are favored by risk-averse executives and their advisors.

The first of these is "It's regrettable," as opposed to "I am really sorry." The term "It's regrettable" may put your lawyers at ease in the belief that it means you aren't admitting guilt, and it may make you feel less at risk.

However, it's not an apology. Your upset customers or stakeholders won't see it as one, and it won't help you regain control of the crisis. Moreover, it truly *is* regrettable since the longer it takes you to acknowledge and admit your responsibility the more negative consequences you will suffer because of the crisis.

The other dire non-apology – which has been around for longer but still retains its popularity – is "Mistakes were made." Social commentator Mark Memmot once called it the "king of non-apologies"[201] and it has famously been used by (among others):

- President Richard Nixon to justify the Watergate scandal.
- British Prime Minister David Cameron commenting on UK Middle East policy.
- American General David Richards trying to explain how an air strike killed 70 Afghan civilians.
- Henry Kissinger responding to claims that his role in US foreign policy amounted to war crimes.
- New Jersey Governor Chris Christie describing the George Washington Bridge scandal in his State of the State address.

---

[201] Memmot, M. (2013, May 14). It's true: 'Mistakes were made' is the king of non-apologies. *National Public Radio*. https://www.npr.org/sections/thetwo-way/2013/05/14/183924858/its-true-mistakes-were-made-is-the-king-of-non-apologies

- Jamie Dimon, CEO of JPMorgan Chase, explaining huge bonuses paid to executives after a government bail-out saved the company from bankruptcy.

Indeed, it's so popular that social psychologists Carol Tavris and Elliot Aronson devoted an entire book to the subject called *Mistakes Were Made (but Not by Me): Why we justify foolish beliefs, bad decisions and hurtful acts.*[202] The title itself neatly sums up why this is such a trendy but sorry excuse for an apology.

Apart from the fact that it tries to evade or divert personal responsibility, it conveys no compassion; doesn't indicate any commitment not to make the same mistakes again; and it's a statement of the blindingly obvious. Of course mistakes were made. That's why you're in the spotlight.

So next time you hear an organization or individual in trouble trying to avoid a genuine apology by saying "Mistakes were made," your best response should be, "Yes, and you just made another one!"

---

[202] Tavris, C. and Aronson, E. (2015). *Mistakes Were Made (but Not by Me): Why we justify foolish beliefs, bad decisions and hurtful acts.* New York: Houghton Mifflin Harcourt.

Key Takeaways

- Authentic leaders have shown that apologizing well can generate positive media.
- The mechanics of good apologies are not difficult to understand.
- When apologizing, you need to *be* sorry, not just *say* you are sorry.
- Your apology should focus on the other person's needs and feelings, not your own.
- Sometimes it's the right thing to publicly ignore legal advice.
- The decision to apologize and how to do it is truly a senior executive responsibility.

Questions for Discussion

1. *Is using evasive non-apology words more likely to reflect legitimate legal concerns or simply unwillingness to accept responsibility?*
2. *How can you bridge the perception gap between making an apology and being genuinely apologetic?*
3. *Why do executives fall into the trap of making the apology about themselves?*
4. *Is there any benefit in publicly stating that you are ignoring legal advice? Why say it?*
5. *Did Kevin Johnson of Starbucks go too far by closing all 8,000 US stores for racial bias education or not far enough? Was it just a "publicity stunt"?*

Chapter Six

Case Studies:

Patently Obvious Risk

"What do lawyers learn in law school? They learn to win. What we've got to start thinking about is how do we solve problems."

Ben Carson

In November 2019 billionaire American rapper Jay-Z launched legal action against an Australian mother over her self-published book designed to help young children learn to read.[203]

---

[203] Kwai, I. (2019, November 28). "99 Problems but My ABCs Ain't One": Jay-Z Sues Over Children's Book. *New York Times.* https://www.nytimes.com/2019/11/28/world/australia/jay-z-children-book-copyright.html

Jessica Chiha's hip-hop picture book was titled *AB to Jay-Z* and refers to well-known rappers to help teach the alphabet. It includes the line "ZZ is for Jay-Z and he has 99 problems, but his ABCs ain't one" – an allusion to one of his best-known songs.

Documents filed by Australian lawyers for the uber-wealthy musician and father of three claimed they had twice asked the author to stop selling the book on-line, and that their client "has suffered, and will continue to suffer, loss and damage."

The rapper's legal action made headlines around the world, not only regarding alleged copyright infringement but also provoking angry online discussion about claimed cultural appropriation. The case was quietly settled in April 2020 after court-ordered mediation, with no terms of agreement disclosed.

While we don't know the detailed outcome in this case, I guess you will have your own opinion about a celebrity using litigation to protect their personal brand, which is not uncommon these days. The Jay-Z example certainly highlights the perceived importance of intangible assets and the increasing involvement of lawyers to protect individuals as well as companies.

This is the second of three chapters devoted to in-depth review of situations where lawyers and communicators often come into conflict, in this case legal action to protect patents and trademarks.

This chapter will help you to:

- Learn from some high-profile cases where lawyers pursued brand and trademark rights at the risk of reputational damage.
- Balance your intellectual property rights against the cost of bad publicity.
- Appreciate the impact of the dramatic rise in financial value of intangible assets.
- Assess the role of communications advice in an area which seems to be home turf for lawyers.
- Avoid trademark and brand disputes which can escalate into reputational crises if not correctly managed.

While over-reach by celebrities keeps lawyers and social media happily occupied, the impact of trademark overreach by corporations and other organizations is much more likely to result in a serious and persistent reputational crisis.

To fully appreciate the scope of this risk I need to take just a few paragraphs of basic revision to remind you of the importance of intangible assets in general and in terms of reputation.

Accounting 101 teaches us that the classic intangible assets include reputation, goodwill, contracts and permits, as well as intellectual property assets such as patents, trademarks, copyrights, software, data, research and trade secrets (such as secret formulas and recipes).

It's pretty well known that the whole range of intangible assets is enormously valuable to any enterprise. Experts around the world calculate that reputation alone typically makes up 40-60 per cent of an organization's market value, and even more in some businesses.

Less well understood is how dramatically the relative scale of intangible assets, including reputation, has shifted over the last 40 years.

The intellectual property specialists Ocean Tomo monitor the intangible asset value of the S&P 500 and found that in 1975 the cumulative value of all those companies showed 17 per cent of market value comprised intangible assets while 83 per cent was made up of tangible assets.[204]

Just four decades later their ten-yearly review showed that ratio had completely reversed. The components of S&P 500 market value in 2015 showed a remarkable 84 per cent intangible assets and just 16 per cent tangible.

Over that time there were some very obvious changes in the nature and structure of modern business which help to explain this reversal, such as the rise of tech companies and growing reliance on online business. More importantly, those changes also explain why management of your intangible assets has become critical across all executive functions.

---

[204] Strathis, K. L. (2015). Ocean Tomo Releases 2015 Annual Study of Intangible Asset Market Value. https://www.oceantomo.com/insights/ocean-tomo-releases-2015-annual-study-of-intangible-asset-market-value/

One of my favorite statements about the value of reputation comes from the General Motors Corporate Crisis Communication Manual written back in 1991:

> *"There are few assets on GM's balance sheet worth more than its reputation. A damaged reputation that is left untended can lead to a loss of organizational self-esteem and erosion of long-standing external relationships."*[205]

What was true for a corporate giant 30 years ago is equally true today for organizations of all sizes. In fact the rise of social media has made reputation even more important and even more vulnerable. Reputation comprises a significant proportion of intangible value and how to protect it is a common area of controversy between lawyers and communications professionals.

The focus of this chapter is patents and trademarks, which is one area of intangible assets which would seem to be legitimate home turf for lawyers. Indeed, some companies employ armies of lawyers to vigorously defend their patents and copyrights around the world.

You will know, for instance, that Coca-Cola is one of the world's most valuable and recognized brands. But their enviable status follows decades of tireless legal action to defend the lettering of their name (the company calls it their "dynamic ribbon device"); to protect the unique shape of their classic bottle; and to defeat wannabee rivals such as Kandy-Kola, Coke-Ola, Kola-Coca, Gay-Ola, Caro-Cola and even Klu-Ko Kola.[206]

From its earliest days, when the brand was still being established, Coca-Cola was a formidable legal opponent. More recently Apple has been recognized as another company with an international reputation for its relentless pursuit of legal options to defend the company's brand, seemingly intended to strike fear into the hearts of would-be infringers at home and abroad.

---

[205] Cited in Law, J. W. (1998). *Conflict Resolution: The relationship between Air Force public affairs and legal functions.* Thesis, University of Florida.
[206] Petty, R. D. (2012). Coca-Cola brand protection before World War II – it's the real thing. *Journal of Historical Research in Marketing 4(2)*, 224-244

Similarly, it was reported in late 2019 that the celebrity Kardashian/Jenner extended family have filed more than 700 trademark applications to protect their brand, their names and their children's names.[207]

What's In a Name?

Young socialite and fashion billionaire Kylie Jenner (or her lawyers) decided it would be a great idea to copyright the name Kylie. Unfortunately, she had failed to allow for another Kylie, namely Australian-British pop princess Kylie Minogue, a "one name" star who has sold more than 70 million records world-wide, and won a Grammy Award almost before Jenner was old enough to go to school. The teenage entrepreneur also hadn't allowed for the intransigence of the US Patent Office. After a slew of legal proceedings and unhelpful publicity, the case was settled in 2017 in Minogue's favor.[208]

What do you think we can learn from this example?

While individuals and companies large and small have the right to legally defend their intangible assets, there is a sorry library of cases where such action has

---

[207] Voytko, L. (2019. July 5). Kardashian Clan's 716 Trademarks: How Kim, Kanye, Kylie, And Kendall Protect Their Brands. *Forbes*. https://www.forbes.com/sites/lisettevoytko/2019/07/05/kardashian-clans-716-trademarks-how-kim-kanye-kylie-and-kendall-protect-their-brands/#1f7685254e67

[208] Knox, P. (2017, February 7). Kylie Minogue wins legal battle with Kylie Jenner over name trademark. *The Sun*. https://www.news.com.au/finance/business/kylie-minogue-wins-legal-battle-with-kylie-jenner-over-name-trademark/news-story/a2586769344bf8ec3ca479514b33edef

backfired badly, resulting in costly loss of reputation – when what may have seemed like a valid legal strategy led to communications calamity and even crises.

Some have been full-scale legal endeavors which did serious reputational damage. For example, in early 2019 when PepsiCo sought legal damages from Indian subsistence farmers in Gujarat who they claimed were growing a registered type of potato used in Lay's chips. In the face of adverse publicity, activist pressure and a threatened boycott, PepsiCo eventually dropped the lawsuit.[209]

Backcountry Claims a Natural Word

The first of my in-depth reviews of legal advice in cases about trademarks features the Utah-based online outdoor gear seller Backcountry.com.

In what one report called "a cautionary tale of overzealous trademark protection"[210] the company launched legal action against dozens of small brands for alleged trademark infringement of the word "backcountry."

The story gained traction when an investigative report in the *Colorado Sun* exposed the flurry of lawsuits after the company deployed IPLA, a large intellectual property firm based in California. The headline on the story posed the question: "Is it bullying or just business?"[211]

The October 2019 newspaper report said Backcountry eBikes and Backcountry Denim had already been forced to changed their names, and it identified the ongoing legal threat to Michigan entrepreneur David Ollila over a short ski

---

[209] Pepsi withdraws lawsuit against Indian farmers over potato used in Lay's chips (2019, May 3). *CNN.* https://edition.cnn.com/2019/05/02/business/pepsico-india-withdraws-farmer-lawsuit/index.html

[210] Gilman, A. (2019, December 12). Legal has its role, but PR must have a decision-making voice. Here's why. *Ragan's Daily Headlines.* https://www.ragan.com/legal-has-its-role-but-pr-must-have-a-decision-making-voice-heres-why/?utm

[211] Blevins, J. (2009, October 31). Backcountry.com sues anyone who uses its namesake. Is it bullying or just business? *Colorado Sun.* https://coloradosun.com/2019/10/31/backcountry-com-sues-anyone-who-uses-its-namesake-is-it-bullying-or-just-business/

designed for climbing snowy hills which he called the Marquette Backcountry Ski.

Several news outlets picked up the original story and the reaction online was rapid and comprehensive. Anger against Backcountry.com erupted on Twitter, Instagram and Reddit, and a Facebook boycott group[212] soon had more than 20,000 members.

It was also reported that dozens of people messaged and phoned in protests to Backcountry.com's sales channels, and sales staff said they had been instructed not to comment on the situation.

In addition, activists created an online legal defense fund to support Marquette in fighting the lawsuit,[213] where Backcountry.com's lawyers claimed three times the ski company's profits since it launched in 2010, plus legal fees and unspecified punitive damages.

Within days, in the face of consumer outcry, the company ran up the white flag. Founder and CEO Jonathan Nielsen dropped lawsuits including the Marquette case, fired his law firm, and issued a public apology which said in part:

> *"We have heard your feedback and concerns, and understand we fumbled in how we pursued trademark claims recently. We made a mistake.*
>
> *"In an attempt to protect the brand we have been building for nearly 25 years, we took certain actions that we now recognize were not consistent with our values, and we truly apologize.*
>
> *"Backcountry has never been interested in owning the word "backcountry" or completely preventing anyone else from using it. But we clearly misjudged*

---

[212] https://www.facebook.com/groups/boycottbackcountry/
[213] https://www.documentcloud.org/documents/6541317-Backcountry-Lawsuit.html

the impact of our actions. We intend to learn from this and become a better company."[214]

In a less formal statement to *Outside*, Nielsen outlined the steps the company would take to repair the brand's relationship with the outdoor community.

> *"We messed this up and we are sorry for that. The important thing for us to do is to show some action. We want that action to focus on community. We want to learn from what we did and learn what we can do better going forward."*

> *"I recognize that we need to do more, but the most important thing right now is to address this breach of trust and do it in a way that brings people together and coalesces community. This is not our last step."*[215]

Lessons learned

From my perspective the most important lesson from the Backcountry.com case is that the CEO not only made a mistake, admitted it, and issued a seemingly genuine apology, but that he undertook to take corrective action and spelled out what he planned to do.

He also took personal responsibility for the crisis. While he dismissed his legal advisors – and made it clear why – he recognized that this was not the time for finger-pointing. "IPLA was working on our behalf," he said, "and we take full responsibility for their actions."[216]

---

[214] A letter to our community. (2019, November 6). *Backcountry.com.*
https://www.backcountry.com/sc/a-letter-to-our-community

[215] Reimers, F. (2019, November 11). Backcountry Is Making Amends After Angering Consumers. Outside.
https://www.outsideonline.com/2405311/backcountry-com-lawsuits-amends

[216] Reimers ibid

As usual I am not privy to what legal advice was given in this crisis, but you can assume the lawyers likely recommended the proceedings which were launched.

Similarly, we will never know whether communicators were consulted before the company embarked on their legal strategy, nor whether the obvious reputation risk of such a strategy was even considered.

One thing we do know is that it was a mistake not to keep the online sales agents in the loop, and to let them say so to the public.

In all the scores of crisis simulations I have facilitated, one of the common mistakes is failing to keep receptionists, sales staff and other public-facing people fully informed. It is a cliché that they are the public face of your organization, but in the heat of a crisis – where the focus is on high-level strategic decision-making – it's too easy to overlook them. Indeed, all your employees can play a role as "ambassadors" in a crisis and it's a serious oversight to leave them out of the communication plan.

Another important lesson from the Backcountry.com example is about the power of social media in helping small companies resist trademark litigation from corporate giants. One thing for certain is that you could never say "all publicity is good publicity" when it comes to online shopping, with competitors just a click away.

This case was a clear example where the social media community stood together, holding a brand to a proper standard, and demanding they act with integrity.

That was also a lesson learned by Monster Cables of Brisbane, California, which has a reputation for aggressive legal action against anyone using the word Monster. [217] *They hold more than 70*

---

[217] Evangelista, B. (2004, November 8). Monster fiercely protects its name. Cable products company sues those who use M-word. *San Francisco Chronicle*. https://www.sfgate.com/bayarea/article/Monster-fiercely-protects-its-name-Cable-2675907.php

trademarks on the word and their catalogue of lawsuits includes suing Disney over the movie "Monsters Inc" and Discovery Channel over the television program "Monster Garage."

But they eventually came unstuck in the face of social media after taking legal action against Christina and Patrick Vitagliano, founders of the Monster Mini Golf franchises, based on monster-themed mini-putting courses.[218]

After two years of legal disputation and failed mediation with the company, the Rhode Island couple launched an internet-based guerrilla campaign to generate public support, blogging non-stop and selling symbolic "slices of justice" on eBay to help fund their defense.

The result was a decisive victory. Monster Cable CEO Noel Lee admitted the company had received at least 200 angry consumer complaints, and eventually agreed to drop the lawsuit. He also agreed to pay the Vitagliano's up to $200,000 in legal expenses... but there is no public record of any apology.

The final lesson from these two cases relates to choosing a brand name which is a natural word, such as backcountry or monster. It's true, of course, that Apple and Visa are among the world's biggest brands, but their challenges in tradename protection reinforce the legal and reputational risk of making this choice.

---

[218] Stecklow, S. (2009, April 4). The scariest monster of all sues for trademark infringement. *Wall Street Journal.* https://www.wsj.com/articles/SB123869022704882969

How the "Head Monster" explained

In the aftermath of controversy about aggressive legal action to support his trademark, Noel Lee, CEO of Monster Cable, agreed to a very sympathetic TV interview in Fox Business.[219]

"People don't really understand how you protect the brand. So we've had to balance what we do with trademark protection with what the public think we should do. We can't protect to the extent that we used to protect."

Do you think it was an effective explanation?

What else could he have said?

Should he maybe have not said anything at all?

Fast Food Fiascos

Fast food companies frequently feature in this book regarding legal versus communication counsel, and it probably won't surprise you to learn that protection of their high-profile brands has led to some extraordinary legal proceedings.

Consider the Tan Hill Inn in the Yorkshire Dales, whose only claim to fame was that it is the highest pub in Britain, at 1,732 feet above sea level. Back in 2007 landlady Tracy Daly received a legal letter from KFC demanding she stop using the slogan "Family Feast" to promote the traditional Christmas dinner she serves on just one day a year. She told the media:

> *"It beggars belief. I am dumbfounded. They are a multi-million-pound international organization and I am a little lady up a mountain."*

---

[219] Interview with Noel Lee (2009, April 27). *Fox Business News.* https://www.youtube.com/watch?v=D3BwIyt1dnU

And she pointed out the blindingly obvious fact that her family feast of Christmas turkey with all the trimmings could hardly be confused with KFC's deep-fried chicken with chips and a sugary soft drink.

Only days after confirming the legal proceedings, KFC advised no further action would be taken. Attempting to play down the media chorus of terrible publicity, the company's spokesperson declared:

> *"KFC has to protect its trademarks against those who seek to trade off its brand... It's an unusual situation that has been blown out of proportion."*[220]

As landlady Daly concluded: "Common sense has prevailed." Which might be more than could be said for that other fast-food giant McDonald's, which spent eight years in their pursuit of a small curried chicken restaurant on the outskirts of Kuala Lumpur, Malaysia.

Although terms such as McMansion and McJob have entered into common use, and there is a British TV series called McMafia, McDonald's legal department is generally unrelenting in its defense of the "Mc" prefix. Over the years their claim to "Mc" has been tested in various courts, with mixed success, for example winning against Quality Inn who wanted to open a chain of economy hotels under the name McSleep, but losing against Chinese takeaway outlets in London called McChina Wok Away.

However, one of their most humiliating trademark defeats was against the Kuala Lumpur restaurant called McCurry. Owners A.M.S.P. Suppiah and his wife Kanageswary argued that the "Mc" in their name stands for Malaysian Chicken and pointed out that their logo was not the Golden Arches but a chicken giving the thumbs-up. McDonald's lawyers were unconvinced and began what became a legal marathon and a reputation nightmare.

In 2001 McDonald's sued the restaurant, claiming that use of the "Mc" prefix infringed its copyright. After lengthy delays the Malaysian High Court ruled in favour of McDonald's, but the restaurant appealed and in early 2009 the Appeal

---

[220] KFC backs down in legal challenge against country pub (2007, May 10). *Daily Mail*. https://www.dailymail.co.uk/news/article-453871/KFC-backs-legal-challenge-country-pub.html

Court overturned the verdict, ruling that McDonald's could not claim an exclusive right to the prefix in the country.

Ever hopeful, McDonald's took the matter to the Federal Court, the highest court in Malaysia, which dismissed the McDonald's appeal and ordered them to pay Mr. and Mrs. Suppiah 10,000 ringgit (a little over US$2,000). The court also refused McDonald's application to appeal the precedent-setting decision.

The case received extensive publicity around the world, much of it focused on the David versus Goliath victory for the plucky little restaurant.

> *"McCurry beats McDonald's in Malaysian lawsuit." (Reuters)*[221]

> *"McCurry, the restaurant that defied the Big Mac wins eight-year battle." (Daily Mail)*[222]

The damage to McDonald's reputation was exemplified by a scathing report in the *Guardian*, which referred to the company's "stupidity and corporate hubris." Reporter Tim Hayward wrote:

> *"It's no surprise to see a multinational 'protecting' their brand in this way and the tactics of stalling and attrition are pretty much what you'd expect from an organization of that size attempting to defend a case of such obvious daftness. How can anyone claim ownership over a Gaelic ancestral prefix, millennia old?*

> *"McDonald's, of course, do have one point in their favor. If they let operations like Mr. Suppiah's proliferate with no quality control, there would be a*

---

[221] McCurry beats McDonald's in Malaysian lawsuit. (2009, April 29). *Reuters.* https://www.reuters.com/article/us-malaysia-courts-mcdonalds/mccurry-beats-mcdonalds-in-malaysia-lawsuit-idUSTRE53S34O20090429

[222] McCurry, the restaurant that defied Big Mac wins eight-year battle (2009, September 9). *Daily Mail.* https://www.dailymail.co.uk/news/article-1211873/McDonalds-vs-McCurry-Fast-food-giant-loses-year-trademark-battle-local-Malaysian-restaurant.html

danger that the 'Mc' suffix would become associated in people's heads with poor quality fast food, made with dreadful ingredients and served by underpaid drones. And we can't have that, can we?"[223]

Ouch! Legal defeat is one thing, but such sarcasm in a globally circulating newspaper is quite another.

In the wake of this humiliating loss, McDonald's spokesman Liam Jeory evidently concluded enough damage had been done. "We respect the finding of the court and beyond that we have no further comment."[224] Apparently nothing to say about the wisdom of the action or its implications for future defenses of that contentious little prefix.

Remembering Goliath

Everyone remembers that David fought Goliath, though hardly anyone remembers what they were fighting about. But just about everyone knows that David won and that Goliath was the villain of the piece.

You should bear that reputation risk in mind if your organization is likely to be seen as the Goliath setting the lawyers onto a smaller opponent.

Being the giant doesn't necessarily make you wrong, but can you think of a strategy which

---

[223] Hayward, T. (2009, September 8). McDonald's loses McCurry legal battle. *The Guardian.*
https://www.theguardian.com/lifeandstyle/wordofmouth/2009/sep/08/mcdonalds-mcurry-court-case-legal

[224] Ahmed, S. (2009, September 8). McCurry wins battle against McDonald's. *CNN.*
https://edition.cnn.com/2009/WORLD/asiapcf/09/08/mcdonalds.mccurry.legal.malaysia/index.html

Lessons learned

KFC were right when they said the "family feast" case had been "blown out of proportion." But they were wrong to imply that this was somehow the fault of irresponsible news media. They were also right when they said that the company had to protect its trademarks against "those who seek to trade off its brand." However, there was no evidence that the landlady in the north of England was even thinking of KFC when she advertised her Christmas Dinner special. As she said: "It beggars belief."

*So there was always an obvious risk the case would be "blown out of proportion," but that would have been good advice from the Communications Department to the Legal Department **before** they sent the threatening letter which triggered the whole story.*

The case involving the Malaysian curry restaurant seems to have a little more merit in that McDonald's has a long history of acting to protect the "Mc" prefix. It may even be that the owner and his wife had chosen their name deliberately to somehow associate with the hamburger giant.

So far so good. At that point it might have been little more than a short-lived news item like the case of the Christmas Family Feast. However, McDonald's dogged pursuit of the case through the courts, in the face of terrible publicity which spread far beyond Malaysia, appears to have been where legal advice and communications advice were likely in conflict.

I can easily understand the legitimate desire of McDonald's to protect their brand, but that has to be balanced against the reputational damage of an eight-year legal fight.

McDonald's is of course no stranger to marathon lawsuits, and you will read in Chapter Nine about their role in the infamous McLibel case which became the longest trial ever in English courts and has been consistently described as the "Biggest Corporate PR Disaster in History." That reputation-sapping fiasco was heard well before the McCurry case but appeared not to have diminished McDonald's willingness to engage in risky, high-profile legal proceedings.

Taking it Up to the Big Boys

What the *Guardian* called "corporate hubris" in my Malaysian example has often been at the heart of cases where companies make assumptions about themselves which differ substantially from general perception, and lead to adverse public attention and media coverage.

Take the time when Walmart decided to claim legal rights to the yellow Smiley Face. The big-box retailer had been using the Smiley since the early 1990s on staff uniforms and on signage to publicize special prices. And they certainly weren't alone, as the iconic image had been used worldwide since the 1970s. Several people claim to have first developed the design (including the fictional Forrest Gump in the 1994 movie of the same name). But it was former French journalist Franklin Loufrani, who began to systematically merchandise the Smiley and trademarked the symbol in about 100 countries through his London company SmileyWorld Ltd.

However, when he applied to control the famous yellow face in the United States the Patent Office told him he couldn't, ruling that it was a "widely used decorative symbol." So he lodged a request to trademark the word Smiley, and Walmart lodged a counter claim, triggering a protracted legal dispute.

Not surprisingly the case produced unhelpful headlines such as:

> *"Walmart seeks smiley face rights." (BBC)* [225]

> *"Walmart not joking with smiley face lawsuit." (Los Angeles Times)*[226]

---

[225] Walmart seeks smiley face rights (2006, 8 May). *BBC.* http://news.bbc.co.uk/2/hi/business/4984138.stm

[226] Goldman, A. (2008, May 14). Walmart not joking with smiley faced lawsuit. *Chicago Tribune.* https://www.chicagotribune.com/news/ct-xpm-2006-05-14-0605140121-story.html

It would be reasonable to feel some sympathy for Walmart because, as they told the *Los Angeles Times*, they had not moved to register the trademark until Mr. Loufrani threatened to so do.

But as the case dragged on – with the potential for reputational damage blindingly obvious – Walmart lawyers decided to open a second front in the battle for the Smiley face.

Charles Smith of Conyers, Georgia, a persistent critic of Walmart's business methods, created a line of merchandise featuring the terms WAL and OCAUST, separated by a star, placed above a Nazi-style eagle, holding in its talons a smiley face similar to Walmart's beloved symbol.

Walmart was understandably annoyed and, despite the Loufrani case remaining before the courts, made the fateful decision to sue Smith on the grounds of infringement of its trademark right, unfair competition and trademark dilution.

Unfazed, the creative Mr. Smith then proceeded to launch a new series of merchandise under the name Wal-Qaeda to protest what he perceived as an attack on his free speech.

After lengthy legal argument by Walmart, the Federal District Court ruled that Smith's designs were parodies and refused to allow the matter to proceed to a jury. "No fair-minded jury," the judge concluded, "could find that a reasonable consumer is likely to be confused by the two challenged marks."[227]

Lessons learned

The Smiley case was an embarrassing defeat which led to needless negative media coverage for Walmart, and at the same time drew welcome attention to Mr. Smith's little company and its products, which might otherwise have never been heard of beyond his limited online customer base.

---

[227] Reed Smith (2008, May 5). Walmart loses trademark battle against parodies. *Lexology.com.* https://www.lexology.com/library/detail.aspx?g=77638e21-32d4-4d4f-83f5-32d10b880991

I believe it started as a legitimate response to an external legal challenge, but then seemed to go off-track with a fresh initiative which brought needless ridicule and reputational damage.

It was then presented by Walmart's critics as a victory for free speech and a demonstration that even a corporate giant is subject to parody.

That could be a matter of opinion, but I agree with the Public Citizen attorney who argued the case when he said the verdict sent a clear message to big corporations who would try to use their deep pockets to intimidate and silence their critics.

Whatever your view of Walmart, a key lesson here is that the public love an underdog and resent what they perceive as corporate bullying.

While the two outcomes may or may not be related, two years later, in 2011, Walmart and Mr. Loufrani's SmileyWorld company reached a confidential agreement to bring that case to an end. In 2016 Walmart brought back the smiley face after a decade-long hiatus.

Who Thought This Was a Good Idea?

Cases involving patents and trademarks don't need to be prolonged, or necessarily even make it to court, to produce reputational damage where legal opinion appears to have over-ruled prudent communications counsel.

One short-lived case of apparent legal over-reach took place in the aftermath of the 2011 raid by US Special Forces who killed al Qaeda leader Osama bin Laden in Pakistan. The Navy's most elite hunter-killer team is officially called the United States Naval Special Warfare Development Group, or DevGru, but is widely known by the much more marketable name SEAL Team 6.

Sure enough, two days after the world learned of the raid, the Walt Disney Company applied to the US Patent and Trademark Office seeking exclusive right to use the name on its merchandise.[228]

It must be assumed that the Disney communications people knew the move would be – at the very least – controversial. But perhaps even they underestimated the likely extent of the public outrage.

Disney said the application was mainly because they were considering a TV show about the elite squad. But their legal people had ensured the application would also cover a generously comprehensive assortment of products including "gymnastic and sporting articles (except clothing); hand-held units for playing electronic games... Christmas stockings; Christmas tree ornaments and decorations; snow globes."

Late night comics and other critics ridiculed Disney for trying to profit from the death of the al Qaeda leader, and for what they regarded as crass commercialism. Snow globes? Really?

In a segment on *The Daily Show,* cutely called "Well, that was fast", host Jon Stewart said:

> *"Putting a trademark on SEAL Team 6 is like copyrighting 'The guys who stormed the beach at Normandy'. It belongs to all of us."* [229]

Meantime the Navy lodged applications for the phrases "SEAL team" and "Navy SEALS" – though not for "SEAL Team 6."[230]

---

[228] Disney trademarks 'Seal Team 6' for toys, games, movies, snow globes and Christmas stockings TWO days after daring Bin Laden mission. (2011, May 16). *Daily Mail.* https://www.dailymail.co.uk/news/article-1387208/Osama-Bin-Laden-dead-Disney-trademarks-US-Navy-Seal-Team-6-toys-movies.html

[229] Choi, C. (2011, May 26). Mickey's Retreat: Disney withdraws 'SEAL Team Six' bid. *Time.* http://newsfeed.time.com/2011/05/26/mickey%E2%80%99s-retreat-disney-withdraws-seal-team-six-patent-application/

[230] Carbone, N. (2011, May 24). Claiming What's Theirs: Navy Files Trademarks for 'SEAL TEAM' and 'NAVY SEALS'. *Time.*

Within a month, in the face of continuing criticism and negative news stories, someone in Disney's management made the decision to give up the legal strategy, leaving the communications people to try to spin the company's embarrassment.

> *"Out of deference to the navy's application for these trademarks, we have withdrawn ours."* [231]

Unfortunately, the reputation pain persisted as headline writers made merry with the situation.

> *"Walt Disney surrenders to Navy's SEAL Team 6."* *(Wall Street Journal)* [232]

> *"Mickey's Retreat: Disney withdraws 'SEAL Team Six' bid." (Time)* [233]

> *"Navy Defeats Disney in Copyright Flap." (CBS News)* [234]

Six years later, Disney JV A&E Studios did in fact launch a TV series which they called "Six," said to be "inspired by the real-life missions of Navy SEAL Team Six." It was cancelled after two seasons, partly because of competition by the comparable CBS series "SEAL Team."

---

http://newsfeed.time.com/2011/05/24/claiming-whats-theirs-navy-files-trademarks-for-seal-team/

[231] Smith, E, and Barnes, J. E. (2011, May 26). Walt Disney surrenders to Navy's SEAL Team 6. *Wall Street Journal.* https://www.wsj.com/articles/SB10001424052702304066504576345752703592770

[232] Smith and Barnes ibid.

[233] Choi op cit.

[234] Von Hoffman, C. (2011, May 26). Navy Defeats Disney in Copyright Flap. *CBS News.* https://www.cbsnews.com/news/navy-defeats-disney-in-copyright-flap-other-regulators-could-learn-something/

The new Battle of Bull Run

When the Walt Disney Company announced plans to build a high-profile historical theme park close to a bloody Civil War battlefield west of Washington DC in the 1990s they thought the issues would be mainly bureaucratic matters such as air and water quality, noise, traffic and property values. They emphasized that the project would generate 12,000 new jobs and $1.86 billion of tax revenues.

However, the company had focused on courting local political and business bosses about the project and ignored many influential community opinion leaders who decided the real issue was "desecration of American history." When angry public and military historians created a reputational crisis, the company claimed to be surprised and the plan was eventually dropped.[235]

The Value of a Sense of Humor

It's sometimes said that the best antidote for corporate hubris is a good dose of ridicule, and that's exactly what happened when the iconic London store Harrods of Kensington decided to flex its legal muscles against a small family business on the other side of the world.

Henry Harrod was the long-time owner of Harrods Family Restaurant in the New Zealand provincial city of Palmerston North. To his surprise he received a cease and desist letter from lawyers for the London store, then owned by Egyptian business magnate Mohamed Fayed, a man who was no stranger to using publicity to his own advantage.

---

[235] Wiebner, M. (1995). The Battle of Bull Run: How insurgent grassroots lobbying defeated Disney's proposed Virginia Theme Park. *Campaigns and Elections,* 16 (1), 44–48.

But the tables were quickly turned in a totally unexpected way. A cunning plot was being hatched 200 miles to the north in the tiny dairy town of Otorohanga, which prides itself on representing "the true Kiwi spirit."

With support from the District Council, and after weeks of planning, the town – normally best-known as the gateway to the famous Waitomo Caves – temporarily renamed itself Harrodsville, and 72 of the 74 local business adopted new signage. Suddenly, there was Harrods bakery, and Harrods dry cleaner, and Harrods fish and chip shop, and Harrods bank and even the Harrodsville post office and town hall. And the local Chinese outlet briefly became Harrods Flying Horse Takeaways.

The unique demonstration of support for Henry Harrod in Palmerston North became a media sensation, and newspapers around the world – especially the merciless British tabloids – made fun of the colorful businessman. He eventually gave up and ordered his lawyers to back off.

Lessons learned

The Disney attempt to cash in on the assassination of a terrorist group leader should have been a predictable reputation risk. Asserting that their claim was withdrawn "in deference to the navy" gives every appearance of attempting to cloak a dubious legal decision with an illusion of patriotism.

The reality is that Disney pursued a marketing strategy with little apparent appreciation of its reputational consequences. Naturally we have no inside information about what communications advice they may have received, but it's not the first time Disney misread public perception about a military-related issue. Their failed Civil War theme park proposal in Virginia was another example.

In both cases Disney failed to properly understand the viewpoint of the people affected. In the language of issue and crisis management it's called stakeholder analysis. Without it mistakes will continue to be made and legal and communicator advice will continue to be out of balance. And as the failed theme-park proposal showed, a purely top-down approach just doesn't work these days.

The case of the small New Zealand town getting together to ridicule a famous London department store is just as easy to understand – even allowing for the notoriously quirky kiwi sense of humor.

It may not have been a reputational crisis, but it was certainly a major embarrassment – even for the publicity-hungry Mohamed Fayed – and a lesson about the potential reputational damage from indiscriminate use of the legal option at the cost of broader common sense.

Here again the company underestimated the "other side" and failed to understand them. Properly knowing your stakeholders is central to effective crisis prevention and that means seeing them not just through a legal or a communication lens but taking the time to consult and truly see the issue from their perspective.

Perhaps Harrods could have represented this as a good-humored "tribute" rather than a challenge. Compare their heavy-handed legal response with what happened when Colorado father Sterling Backus and his son decided to use 3D-printed parts to create their own replica Lamborghini Aventador. Obviously, the Italian supercar maker is opposed to anyone counterfeiting their luxury vehicles and could have called in the lawyers.

Instead they visited the family at Christmas 2019, loaned Backus a real $460,000 Aventador to drive for two weeks, and told him the company wanted to shoot a holiday commercial with his family.[236] That's how to turn a potential trademark problem into a communications triumph.

[236] Kim, A. (2019, December 28). A family making a 3D-printed Lamborghini replica is surprised with the real thing when the carmaker heard about the project. *CNN.* https://edition.cnn.com/2019/12/27/us/lamborghini-3d-trnd/index.html?iid=ob_lockedrail_topeditorial

Taking on a Charity Icon

Not every trademark case is so easily disposed of or is without at least some merit on both sides.

But it would be a mistake to end this chapter on trademark debacles without including perhaps the grand-daddy of them all – when lawyers for one of the words biggest healthcare companies decided to challenge the trademark of the largest and best known charity on the globe.

While the case was finally resolved in 2008 it vividly highlights the conflict between legal advice and reputation consequences, and it's worth exploring in depth because it's a case in which expert critics were divided over that central question: what's legally right and what's the right decision?

I have deliberately included quite a few different voices here to underscore the divergence and (in some cases) the intensity of views on this important case.

The background takes you all the way back to the end of the nineteenth century, when health consumer products Johnson and Johnson (J&J) started using the red cross as a trademark in 1887 – six years after the creation of the American Red Cross (ARC) but before it obtained its congressional charter in 1900.

The company reached agreement with ARC in 1895 which acknowledged J&J's exclusive right to the trademark for chemical, surgical and pharmaceutical goods, but allowed ARC to use it for their humanitarian work and on commercial goods such as first aid kits.

The problem began in 2004 when ARC began licensing third parties to make Red Cross-branded products, some of which J&J argued competed with theirs and were a breach of their trademark and the 100-year-old agreement.

To put the dispute into context for you, ARC had made about $10 million dollars from these products compared with J&J's global revenue at that time of over $53 billion. J&J was very aware that the public might see this simply as a multinational giant bullying a much-loved and respected charitable organization. But the company's judgement was that it was an important issue of trademark protection and, when negotiations broke down, the decision was made to proceed to litigation.

J&J's communication strategy (as evidenced by what followed) was to lay out the facts; to reach out to potential allies; to emphasize that it had taken legal action only reluctantly as a last resort; and to state that it had donated $5 million to ARC over the previous three years.

However, the response was predictable. The day after the case against American Red Cross was lodged in the Federal Court in Manhattan (9 August 2007) ARC President Mark Everson responded:

> *"For a multibillion-dollar drug company to claim that the Red Cross violated a criminal statute... simply so that J&J can make more money, is obscene."*[237]

Yet at the same time, many of the mainstream media remained neutral-to-positive and reflected an understanding of the company's dilemma.

New York Magazine, for example, even called Red Cross "healthy do-gooders."

> *"When we first came across this news in the Times, we immediately nominated it for our Chutzpa of the Year award: Johnson & Johnson has filed a federal lawsuit seeking to wrest the red-cross logo from the American Red Cross... As we read on, however, we found ourselves involuntarily siding with the health-product giant over the disaster-relief non-profit... And that the two had peacefully co-existed... under a deal that allowed the non-profit use of the logo so long as they not step on each other's toes. This meant that the health org wouldn't go into retail (and that*

---

[237] Johnson and Johnson sues American Red Cross (2009, August 9). *Sydney Morning Herald.* https://www.smh.com.au/business/johnson-and-johnson-sues-american-red-cross-20070809-gdqtia.html

*the conglomerate wouldn't go solving health crises,
we suppose)."[238]*

There was a similar reaction from Steve Woodruff in the *Impactiviti* blog;

> *"Of course, it appears, on the surface,
> like unconscionable bullying. But I actually
> sympathize with J&J's business stance here. I'm no
> trademark lawyer, but it appears to me that the Red
> Cross folks took a couple of steps down a slippery
> slope, and the J&J people recognize that once this
> mark starts getting used commercially, there will be
> no end of violations."[239]*

Some were even critical of the ARC position. The influential blogger Seth Godin argued that Red Cross was wrong to go up against "a good corporate citizen, a significant donor to the Red Cross and the original and rightful owner of the trademark."

> *"I'm not asserting that J&J is legally or morally
> right, nor do I have expertise or knowledge in the
> history of the issue or the role of the International
> Red Cross. My point is this: The mission of the Red
> Cross in the US isn't advanced by this fight.
> Thumbing a nose at a long-time supporter and
> contributor doesn't help them. Having a lawsuit
> doesn't help them. Distracting senior management
> from the urgent issues at hand is silly. It tarnishes the
> group in the eyes of other corporate supporters,*

---

[238] The fight for the Red Cross: In which we ended up siding with the multinational conglomerate over the healthy do-gooders. (2007, August 9). *New York Magazine.*
http://nymag.com/intelligencer/2007/08/the_fight_for_the_red_cross_in.html
[239] Woodruff, S. (2007, August 9). How to get entangled in a no-win situation: H&J sues the Red Cross" *Imperactiviti.wordpress.com*
https://impactiviti.wordpress.com/2007/08/09/jj-red-cross/

> *because companies don't like to do business (or charity) with groups that are intransigent."[240]*

The company spokesperson reinforced the official line:

> *"What we're talking about here is their deviation from a longstanding partnership and collaboration around the use of this trademark and their push to commercialize this trademark in the for-profit arena. We deeply regret that it has become necessary to file this complaint. The company has the highest regard for the American Red Cross and its mission."[241]*

And the company's in-house blogger Ray Jordan provided an optimistic assessment in their staff webpage:

> *"We felt most every journalist we engaged with (including bloggers) gave a fair hearing to both sides of this matter."[242]*

But many in the media did not hold back in their criticism of the legal action. *Adweek* made its view clear in the headline: "How could the public not side with Red Cross."

> *"Memo to Johnson & Johnson: Suing the American Red Cross over the use of the small red-cross symbol might not be the best way to build your brand and curry favour with the public... Here's the thing: The Red Cross, for the most part, is about providing aid and comfort in times of disaster. J&J makes some useful products, but I don't recall any members of its board of directors offering assistance outside my*

---

[240] Godin, S. (2007, August 9). What to do when you're wrong. *Seth Godin Blog.* https://seths.blog/2007/08/what-to-do-when-2/

[241] Saul, S. (2007, August 9). Johnson and Johnson sues Red Cross over symbol. *New York Times.* https://www.nytimes.com/2007/08/09/business/09cross.html

[242] Jordan, R. (2007,August 9). You're doing what? Johnson and Johnson corporate blog *JNJ BTW.* https://www.jnj.com/our-company/youre-doing-what

*apartment building after a fire. Guess who was there.
Hint: They wore red crosses.* "[243]

Some specialist writers in the Pharma blogosphere were similarly unsympathetic. Ed Silverman at *Pharmalot* said this could not be a good public relations move:

> *"J&J, like any company, is entitled to defend its property, including trademarks. But in an environment where big drugmakers are regularly criticized for putting profits over patients, does it make sense to run to court and take on an institution that, for many Americans, is seen as an angel who appears in time of need?"* [244]

And Peter Rost at *NRx* was even more blunt:

> *"So seriously folks: Is this about the most foolish PR move by any drug company this year? Or is it the worst move in a decade?"* [245]

> **"Is this about the most foolish PR move by any drug company this year? Or is it the worst move in a decade?"**

Mike Masnick at *Techdirt.com* was particularly concerned of that the lawsuit wanted ARC licensed products destroyed and sought punitive damages.

> *"That's going well beyond the 'we're forced to protect the trademark under the law' claim. It just*

[243] Griner, D. (2007, August 9). How could the public not side with Red Cross. *AdWeek.*
https://www.adweek.com/creativity/how-could-public-not-side-red-cross-17014/
[244] Silverman, E. (2007, August 9). J&J sues Red Cross over its symbol. *Pharmalot.* Cited John Mack, Blogger Brouhaha over the cross. *Pharmablogosphere.*
http://pharmablogosphere.blogspot.com/2007/08/blogger-brouhaha-over-cross.html
[245] Rost, P. (2007, August 9). Red Cross sued over its . . .red cross. *NRx.* Cited Silverman, ibid

> *makes them look like a bunch of bullies who would kick babies if it would make them money. While J&J was clearly concerned about the value of its trademark, it's not clear if they realized the value of good PR.*[246]

A few weeks later J&J filed an amended complaint, withdrawing the demand that ARC surrender the products; hand over the sale proceeds (with interest); and pay J&J punitive damages and all their legal costs related to the case.

However, I think you will agree that the reputational damage was clearly already done.

Three months later the judge issued an interim ruling which rejected the ARC motion to dismiss, and also threw out one of J&J's eight claims, namely the contention that ARC had promised not to engage in certain commercial activity.

Predictably, both sides claimed victory. Red Cross said the judge had dismissed "a very significant part" of the case and called on J&J to end the proceedings. For its part, the company declared themselves pleased with the judge's decision which, they said "allows the case to move forward as planned."[247]

After another eight months of legal argument the judge finally threw out virtually all of J&J's case, except for the company's contention that ARC had purposefully interfered with their business relationship with two health care supply companies. At the same time he dismissed the ARC counterclaim that J&J itself had engaged in trademark violations.

Lawyers might have argued that it was a mixed result, but the news media headline writers had little doubt.

---

[246] Masnick, M. (2007, August 9). Trademark law gone mad: J&J sues American Red Cross over use of red cross. *Techdirt.com.* https://www.techdirt.com/articles/20070809/095011.shtml

[247] Court throws out a J&J claim in Red Cross suit. (2007, November 7). *Reuters.* https://www.reuters.com/article/americanredcross-lawsuit/update-2-court-throws-out-a-jj-claim-in-red-cross-suit-idUSN0641147420071106

> *"American Red Cross defeats Johnson & Johnson in trademark spat." (Wall Street Journal)*[248]

> *"J&J's Red Cross suit sent (mostly) packing." (CBS News) "*[249]

> *"Most of Johnson and Johnson lawsuit against Red Cross dismissed." (New York Sun)*[250]

The two parties soon agreed to resolve the matter and set aside any remaining issues.

It was left to J&J CEO, William Weldon to put the best possible face on the outcome:

> *"Johnson & Johnson brought the lawsuit very reluctantly only to protect what we believed were important trademark issues."*

> *"The decision of the court has brought clarity to those issues, including its ruling that Johnson & Johnson has properly used its valued Red Cross trademark over the years, and we have no desire to continue our dispute through trial and appeal."*[251]

---

[248] Slater, D. (2007, May 16). American Red Cross defeats Johnson and Johnson in trademark spat. *Wall Street Journal.* https://blogs.wsj.com/law/2008/05/16/american-red-cross-defeats-johnson-johnson-in-trademark-spat/

[249] Hamilton, D. (2008, May 19). J&J's Red Cross suit sent (mostly) packing. *CBS News.* https://www.cbsnews.com/news/jjs-red-cross-suit-sent-mostly-packing/

[250] Caruso, D. B. (2008, 16 May). Most of Johnson & Johnson lawsuit against Red Cross dismissed. *New York Sun.* https://www.nysun.com/new-york/most-of-johnson-johnson-lawsuit-against-red-cross/76511/

[251] Berkrot, B. (2008, June18). J&J, American Red Cross settle emblem dispute. *Reuters.* https://www.reuters.com/article/us-johnsonandjohnson-redcross/jj-american-red-cross-settle-emblem-dispute-idUSN1737719320080617

Lessons learned

Unlike the other examples in this chapter – where the case may have originated in dubious judgement or where enthusiasm momentarily outweighed common sense – the Johnson and Johnson/American Red Cross case is one where the lessons learned are much harder to identify.

And unlike some of the other occasions – where massive corporations brought legal pressure to bear on small businesses – this is a case where both sides were able to mobilize teams of lawyers armed with volumes of black letter law and legal precedents.

I am not qualified to comment on the legal merits of either side, but it was obviously a case where both parties deeply believed in their position and where the media were divided. Furthermore, it was also a case where both parties had so much to lose and where the risk of reputational damage was so obvious.

You could easily argue that – despite the failure of early negotiations – it was a case where legal and communications advisors on both sides needed to swallow their pride and help reach an agreement (which they ultimately managed to do).

The simple truth is that this case unambiguously demonstrated that the court is sometimes no place to resolve a trademark dispute and at the same time protect reputation.

Key Takeaways

- The court of public opinion often trumps a win in court, especially with high-profile consumer brands.
- The public don't like a "corporate bully" – even if the facts are on your side.
- Your trademarks and brand value may be your greatest assets and cannot be treated solely as legal responsibilities.
- A cheeky response to a trademark challenge is sometimes more effective than calling in the lawyers.
- Social media has dramatically changed the role of consumers and other external stakeholders in brand perception.
- In some cases, the court is simply no place to resolve your trademark dispute and still hope to protect your reputation.

Questions for Discussion

1. *What makes some companies with a beloved brand so apparently blind to legal risks?*
2. *Is it ever right for a big brand to exert maximum legal pressure on what will likely be publicly seen as a trivial trademark breach?*
3. *Is it good or bad for reputation when a company becomes known as an aggressive litigator in defense of its brand?*
4. *Does anyone really believe companies which blame a public trade-mark controversy on their lawyers being "over-enthusiastic" in protecting the brand? What would be a better response?*
5. *Can a company pursue brand protection with high-profile litigation and still retain consumer sympathy?*

Chapter Seven

Dealing With the Media

Untidy truth is better than smooth lies that unravel in the end anyway.

Colin Powell

Dealing with the media in a crisis is not just about what to say to reporters and who should say it.

It's also about a range of other executive questions you will need to address such as, should the CEO go to the scene; how you can have multiple spokespersons and maintain "one voice"; what social media platforms are important; should you respond to every critic; how to sustain consistent messaging across different stakeholders; and how do you keep the rest of the business operating while the crisis plays out. And – over-riding all of these issues – how to protect reputation while at the same time complying with the law and avoiding needless legal liability.

This chapter is not a general manual for how to speak to the media. My focus here is specifically on how you deal with the media in the event of a crisis and, in particular, how to protect your reputation and your legal position.

This chapter will help you to:

- Respond effectively to the media in a crisis while protecting your legal position.
- Make no comment where appropriate without actually saying "no comment."
- Establish who should be the spokesperson in a crisis.
- Execute the tricky task of telling the CEO they may not be the best choice to talk to the media.
- Implement basic reputational and legal rules for your crisis media communication.
- Identify when the lawyer could be the proper spokesperson.

The first key area here is about leadership in dealing with the media, while other chapters focus on apologizing; on liability versus responsibility; and on how your words and actions can set the tone for an entire organization's response – for better or worse.

For the present it is critical to remember that a crisis is the ultimate test of executive leadership. Crises are, by definition, highly fluid and stressful situations which can place executive management under enormous pressure. How you respond to that pressure is crucial.

It's no secret that the *perception* of an organization during a crisis often has a far greater impact on reputation and recovery than the crisis itself. And sometimes the CEO gets the balance just right.

In 2014 Mary Barra, the newly appointed CEO of GM, found herself facing a massive reputational and financial crisis after the company admitted they had waited 11 years before starting to recall millions of cars with an ignition key fault linked to 124 deaths and hundreds of injuries.

She could have followed what *Fortune* called "the company template for handling these situations – minimize their importance, fight them, drag them out, settle grudgingly."

Instead she said the opposite: "I never want to put this behind us. I want to put this painful experience permanently in our collective memories."[252] Little wonder *Fortune* dubbed her "Crisis Manager of the Year."

She later said the ignition switch crisis taught her that the best leaders are transparent with their employees and clear about their expectations. "We have 200,000 employees at General Motors – they want to do the right thing," she said. "Just make sure they know *you* want them to do the right thing."[253]

---

[252] Colvin, G. (2015, September 18). How CEO Mary Barra is using the ignition-switch scandal to change GM's culture. *Fortune*. https://fortune.com/2015/09/18/mary-barra-gm-culture/

[253] Feloni, R. (2018, November 15). GM CEO Mary Barra said the recall crisis of 2014 forever changed her leadership style. *Business Insider*. https://www.businessinsider.com.au/gm-mary-barra-recall-crisis-leadership-style-2018-11?r=US&IR=T

Lessons learned

Mary Barra had just arrived in the CEO's chair but was a GM lifer and she understood that this was a critical learning moment for the organization. While the recall cost GM a $900 million fine to settle criminal charges for wire fraud and withholding information from regulators, she recognized that this was not primarily about the law but about culture. She had to dismantle a decades-old culture that resulted in employees not voicing concerns and committees dismissing concerns when they did arise. In the process she sacked 15 senior managers or executives for misconduct or incompetence.[254]

She also made it very clear that it was about the company and not about her. Contrast her statement with the response of Volkswagen CEO Martin Winterkorn to the emission cheating scandal which emerged the following year. Winterkorn said: "I am stunned that misconduct on such a scale was possible in the Volkswagen group." Under immense pressure he resigned, but claimed he knew nothing about the scandal and added: "I am not aware of any wrongdoing on my part."[255]

Barra's leadership changed internal and external perceptions of GM. In her first year on the job, the company broke sales records despite the recall scandal.

---

[254] GM Fires Executives Linked to Faulty Ignition Switches (2014, June 5). *NBC News.* https://www.nbcnews.com/storyline/gm-recall/gm-sacks-15-workers-fallout-over-faulty-ignition-switches-n123331

[255] Tovey, A. (2105, September 23), VW boss Martin Winterkorn quits, and says: 'I did nothing wrong'. *Telegraph, UK.* https://www.telegraph.co.uk/finance/newsbysector/industry/11886523/VW-boss-Martin-Winterkorn-quits-and-says-I-did-nothing-wrong.html

When it All Goes Wrong

Sadly, any perception of failed crisis communication at the top in response to a crisis can have a devastating and prolonged effect.

Look no further than the long-lasting damage to reputation caused by the famously misjudged statements from BP CEO Tony Hayward after the notorious oil spill in the Gulf of Mexico. It will probably be a generation before people forget his infamous plea that he would like to "get his life back." The *New York Times* called it the "sound-bite from hell."[256]

Or consider when faulty "see-through" yoga pants sold by the American sports apparel company Lululemon caused a major hit to reputation and share price. A product recall was successfully implemented, but six months later chairman Chip Wilson chose to give an interview in which he tried to "explain" the excessively sheer pants problem by saying: "Quite frankly, some women's bodies actually just don't work for them." Facing a predictable backlash, he issued a much-criticized mea culpa, which ABC News suggested might be "the worst apology ever."[257] The result was a genuine reputational crisis and he soon resigned from the company he had founded.

And how about Malcolm Walker, CEO of Iceland, a British supermarket caught up in the infamous horse meat scandal in 2013. After blaming local authorities for "driving down food quality" through low-cost catering contracts to supply schools, hospitals and prisons, he told the BBC in an angry interview the company did not routinely test the genus of its meat.

---

[256] Reed, S. (2012, September 1). Tony Hayward gets his life back. *New York Times.* https://www.nytimes.com/2012/09/02/business/tony-hayward-former-bp-chief-returns-to-oil.html?

[257] Lustrin, M. & Janis, L. (2013, November 14). Is Lululemon chairman's apology the worst ever? *ABC News.* https://abcnews.go.com/blogs/lifestyle/2013/11/is-lululemon-chairmans-apology-the-worst-ever

"Did we test for horse? No, but we haven't tested for dog or cat either. I mean, there might be dog or cat. You can't test for everything."[258]

> "Speak when you are angry – and you will make the best speech you'll ever regret."
>
> Laurence J. Peter

Then there was Edward Burkhardt, Chairman of the Montreal, Maine & Atlantic Railway who faced a crisis when one of his company's trains, loaded with petrol, ran out of control downhill and virtually destroyed the small Canadian town of Lac-Mégantic through a deadly fireball which killed 47 people. After waiting four days before going to the scene, Burkhardt failed to show sincere sympathy and empathy for the victims and their families and friends; tried to blame fire fighters and a company employee before the cause of the disaster had been investigated; and tried to present himself as a victim because of his personal financial loss through the company's plunging share value.

Little wonder that *Forbes* called him "clueless as well as careless, not to mention disrespectful in handling a crisis of this magnitude"[259] and *Bloomberg* described him as "Canada's public enemy No 1."[260] Contrary to Burkhardt's assertions, the official inquiry subsequently concluded that "no one individual or single factor" caused the derailment and that the railway had a weak safety culture and no

---

[258] Horsemeat scandal: Retailers to give regular food test updates (2013, 18 February). *BBC.* https://www.bbc.com/news/uk-21495300

[259] Baldoni, J. (2013, July 15). How Edward Burkhardt is making the Lac-Megantic accident even worse. *Forbes.* https://www.forbes.com/sites/johnbaldoni/2013/07/15/how-edward-burkhardt-is-making-the-lac-megantic-accident-even-worse/#5a1683ff35c4

[260] Catts, T. (2013, July 13). Quebec train crash taints railroad CEO's legend status. *Bloomberg.* https://www.bloomberg.com/news/articles/2013-07-12/quebec-train-crash-taints-railroad-ceo-s-legend-status

functioning safety system to manage risks.[261] Facing massive losses, lawsuits and a huge clean-up bill, the company later sued for bankruptcy and was sold.

Lessons learned

In all four cases a serious crisis was made worse by ill-judged comments from the CEO. As Mary Barra at GM showed, it's not about you, but about the company, the people affected by what has gone wrong and how you plan to put it right.

Tony Hayward appealing to get his life back and Edward Burkhardt bemoaning his loss of share value were remarkably tone-deaf examples of the CEO putting themselves first.

While Lululemon's Chip Wilson had a long history of inappropriate remarks to the media, the key learning in his case was that he had no apparent reason to give the television interview at all. The faulty product recall had been adequately handled and the reputational risk had been addressed six months earlier. He had no strategic or tactical reason to appear on TV.

Iceland CEO Malcolm Walker's ill-advised response to suggestions of horsemeat in his company's hamburger patties – in not one, but two television interviews – was a powerful reminder not to speak in anger and not to ignore the feelings of your customers.

Hayward, Walker and Burkhardt made damaging statements in the heat of a major crisis, which just might be understandable. By contrast Wilson appeared in a television interview months after the crisis was over and was very obviously unprepared for what must have been the most obvious questions.

It may be ego and it may be hubris which leads people to imagine they can "control" a media interview, and the results can be devastating. Just ask Britain's Prince Andrew, who thought he could

---

[261] Lac-Megantic oil train disaster inquiry finds string of safety failings (2014, August 20). *The Guardian.*
https://www.theguardian.com/world/2014/aug/20/lac-megantic-oil-train-disaster-inquiry-finds-string-of-safety-failings

use a television interview to "draw a line" under the scandal surrounding his involvement with convicted sex offender Jeffrey Epstein.

I have had to deal with some executives who were determined to talk to the media, even when they didn't need to, and it was difficult to dissuade them. In some cases they thought they didn't require preparation or rehearsal. I find that one useful tool of persuasion is to use "horror stories" about just how wrong it can go. Sometimes – but not always – that can cool their enthusiasm to see themselves on television.

Try Humor

Then of course there are the CEOs who think dealing with the media is an opportunity to try for humor.

Take the case of Tesla CEO Elon Musk who chose April First 2018 as the opportunity for a seasonal prank tweet.

> *Palo Alto, California, April 1, 2018 – Despite intense efforts to raise money, including a last-ditch mass sale of Easter Eggs, we are sad to report that Tesla has gone completely and totally bankrupt. So bankrupt, you can't believe.*

Coming on top of weeks of negative news about the company, investors were not amused and the share price fell seven per cent.[262]

Musk then posted another tweet:

---

[262] Higgins, T. (2018, April 2). Tesla shares sink as Musk jokes about bankruptcy. *Wall Street Journal.*
https://www.wsj.com/articles/tesla-shares-sink-as-musk-jokes-about-bankruptcy-1522682691

Palo Alto, California, April 3, 2018 –Seriously!
Obviously, I'm not going to do an April Fool's joke
about going bankrupt if I thought there was any
chance it would actually happen (sigh).[263]

People who are expert in such things say the essence of comedy is timing. The controversial Tesla CEO's timing could hardly have been worse. What would you have thought if you were a Tesla shareholder?

Another CEO who thought a light-hearted approach might be appropriate was Stephen Duckett, CEO of Canada's Alberta Health Services. With the organization facing serious financial issues and a reputational crisis, Dr Duckett came out of a meeting and found himself followed by reporters down a flight of stairs and out into the snowy street.

In a video which rapidly went viral, he brushed off shouted questions by repeatedly saying he was more interested in eating a cookie. At one point he waved the cookie in a reporter's face.

"We have issued a media advisory that says the
media is available to talk in about 30 minutes. Isn't
it ridiculous that the media are not prepared to go to
the media scrum? And I'm eating my cookie."[264]

The following day he was sacked, though the Board said the infamous "cookie interview" was only one contributing factor.

[263] McGregor, J. (2018, April 3). Elon Musk's April Fools' tweets were 'not a joking matter,' experts say. *Washington Post.* https://www.washingtonpost.com/news/on-leadership/wp/2018/04/03/elon-musks-april-fools-tweets-were-not-a-joking-matter-experts-say/?utm_term=.d38c46ffbd8b

[264] Alden, W. (2010, November 23). Stephen Duckett, Alberta Health Chief, Too Busy Eating Cookie To Address Health Care Issues. *The Huffington Post.* https://www.huffingtonpost.com.au/2010/11/22/stephen-duckett-cookie-video_n_787058.html?ri18n=true

Lessons learned

Elon Musk is famous for jokes and pranks, and some of his tweets have become notorious. But joking in public about bankruptcy after what one analyst called the company's "worst month on the stock market for seven years" was a step too far. Enough said.

In the case of Dr Duckett, his attempt at humor was extraordinarily unwise and created headlines around the world which would never have happened had he simply declined to speak to reporters. All he needed to say was: "This is a very serious topic and I don't think it is appropriate to be discussing it standing out here in the snow. I have a press conference scheduled in 30 minutes where I will be happy to answer all your questions." Instead his cookie antics led to a viral video and an incident which is memorialized forever in his Wikipedia biography.

Dr Duckett apologized the next day:

> *"Most regrettably, I did not convey what I deeply feel, which is the greatest respect for the difficult challenges our health care providers face every day, and their innumerable achievements, and what those challenges and achievements mean for our patients and their families. We are all striving to do our best, but I know I got it wrong this time."[265]*

Unfortunately, his well-crafted words were never going to make up for a failed attempt at humor.

Dwight Eisenhower once commented: "A sense of humor is part of the art of leadership." My answer to the former President would be: "Yes, but not during a crisis and not when it risks creating a crisis."

---

[265] Aussie 'Cookie Monster' Dr Stephen Duckett gets the sack from Alberta Health Services (2010, November 25). *Courier Mail.* https://www.couriermail.com.au/news/queensland/aussie-cookie-monster-dr-stephen-duckett-gets-the-sack-from-alberta-health-services/news-story/2fc35eaf81f1048e94719fe004a4fd9a

The Role of Spokesperson

I am not suggesting for a moment that you would demonstrate such a worrying capacity to do the wrong thing. But it's a regrettable fact that spokespersons are much more likely to make the headlines by awful decisions which undo good crisis response work or make a crisis worse. The previous examples, and a sorry catalogue of other high-profile communication failures, prompt the core question, what are the desired qualities for the spokesperson in the event of a crisis?

One of the challenges I sometimes encounter is when the individual who is a good spokesperson in normal times may not be the right person in a crisis. After all, a crisis is, by definition, a high-stress, high-risk situation which is most definitely not business as usual. The executive who is professional and respected when announcing business results or a new corporate takeover to an audience of shareholders and financial analysts, or appearing as a witness in court, may appear awkward or even uncaring when speaking to the families of people killed in a terrible accident; or when talking to angry community leaders about a chemical leak which has poisoned the local town water supply; or meeting distraught mothers frantic about a faulty product which they believe has endangered their children.

The other challenge is the CEO or senior executive who imagines themself as a great communicator though may in fact be plain terrible when facing the media. The old saying is that there is no deception like self-deception, and executives who reach high positions sometimes have limited self-awareness. Moreover some think they can "wing it" or they are "too busy" to rehearse.

Such over-confident senior executives sometimes actively discourage candid feedback and that's a problem not just for them but for your whole organization. This is a role for legal and communications advisors: to politely but firmly explain that maybe someone else might be the best choice as spokesperson – even if this requires a few white lies and some subtle flattery.

If that doesn't work, there are some steps you can take to shield a less-than-effective executive communicator who insists on speaking on a crisis. In these circumstances, fronting up to a full-scale and potentially damaging media conference is not the only option. You might be able to arrange a one-on-one interview with a known friendly reporter, though that has some obvious risks of backfiring: the reporter is never truly your friend. He or she has to satisfy their editor, not you. Another possibility is to release a short video, where the script and image can be better controlled, filmed in a workplace environment where the CEO feels most comfortable. You could develop a personalized message as an email to employees which can then be released to the media.

Testing self belief against reality

Business continuity expert Philip Jan Rothstein, FBCI, says CEOs can have huge egos and excessive confidence in their ability to perform better than anyone else in crisis situations. He says where that confidence isn't matched by reality, a harsh intervention may be necessary.

"I was charged with training the crisis response team for a multinational Fortune 50 enterprise. The CEO was competent and professional but came across as overconfident to the point of awkwardness, particularly when it came to operational aspects of the crisis scenario.

"We simulated a one-on-one television interview with a real news anchor from a local station who was prepared by the exercise planning team for just this moment. On cue from the exercise leader, the interviewer leaned in close to the CEO, while the huge studio camera rolled in uncomfortably close, and in a soft voice asked the CEO, "*What about the dead babies?*"

"The question, of course, had no relevance to the exercise scenario, nor to any situation the CEO could ever imagine. For perhaps thirty seconds, he gulped, breathed heavily, started and abandoned sentences, and finally asked the interviewer, "uhhh... could you repeat the question?"

"A different person was later designated to serve as the primary crisis communicator."

Such strategies are important because *what* the spokesperson says, *how* it is said, and *where* it is said are all critical elements of helping to determine the public perception of how well – or how badly – your organization is responding to a crisis.

To help make this decision you need to think about what qualities make a good spokesperson. Some can be taught – and that's where regular media training is essential. But some qualities are more about character and personality.

Desired Qualities of a Crisis Spokesperson

- Capacity to communicate empathy as well as authority,
- A good understanding of the crisis and organizational response.
- Enough technical knowledge to avoid embarrassing mistakes.
- Authority to make commitments on behalf of your organization.
- Ability to stay calm under pressure.
- Previous experience with news media and other stakeholders.
- Capacity to operate in a highly fluid and unstructured situation.
- Ability to avoid jargon and corporate speak.
- Willingness to listen as well as talk.

Who Should be the Crisis Spokesperson?

So, who should take on the responsibilities of crisis spokesperson? There are not many options. The CEO? Another senior executive? The lawyer? The communications manager? I have found that when a crisis strikes there is almost never a queue of volunteers lining up to take on this often-thankless task.

One option is to have the lawyer speak on behalf of the organization. This has some merit, especially when the issue is strictly a legal one. Most lawyers are trained to speak in public; they usually have a good understanding of the precise meaning of words; they tend to be good on their feet; and are generally less prone to verbal gaffes. They are also less prone to say something which could compromise liability or confidentiality. At the same time, they are also more likely to be rather conservative and adhere to the maxim that the less you say the better, or that you can't get into trouble for what you don't say.

A much-cited quip from the famous American trial lawyer Edward Bennett Williams sums up this view of lawyers:

> *"Nothing is always a good thing to do, and almost always a brilliant thing to say."*

In this respect a survey of senior corporate lawyers in the United States found that more than half said their litigation communications were overly conservative, and nearly 80 per cent named fear of negative media coverage as a factor preventing them communicating more aggressively.[266]

Finally, of course, lawyers also have the inherent hurdle of the nature of their profession. As a non-lawyer, it might be more tactful if I let an American attorney describe this challenge when selecting a corporate spokesperson:

> *"It's generally best if this person is not a lawyer. Like it or not, many Americans think that lawyers are paid to hide the truth. When seeing a lawyer speaking for a corporate client many think 'Here comes the mouthpiece'."[267]*

Needless to say, the exact same hurdle applies to another option for the spokesperson, namely the organization's communicator. Indeed, the hurdle they face may be even less manageable because, while the lawyer has an acknowledged expertise in matters of the law, some people think the communications professional is a non-expert merely trying to sell a story.

Indeed, one early survey of 1,000 American adults by Porter Novelli found that only 46 percent said company spokespersons were very or somewhat believable

---

[266] Litigation Communications survey report (2016). *Green Target*. https://greentarget.com/wp-content/uploads/2016/02/LitigationCommunicationsSurveyReport.pdf

[267] Metrick, A. (1994). Crisis Management in the public eye. *The Practical Litigator* 5(6) 13-18.

in a crisis – the least believable sources.[268] Worryingly, 57 per cent believed that in times of crisis, companies lie or withhold damaging information.

> "It is always a risk to speak to the press: they are likely to report what you say."
>
> US Vice President Hubert H. Humphrey

Over time it has become less and less common for a person officially designated as, for example, Public Relations Director or Corporate Affairs Manager, to take a personal role in speaking for the organization. How often do you see such a title under the "talking head" on television? However, there are some high-profile exceptions – look no further than the White House Press Room where a clearly described communications professional speaks on behalf of the President.

But in the corporate world that is less frequently seen these days, especially in the context of a crisis. The reasons are fairly self-evident, and not just the inherent suspicion of a "paid mouthpiece." There has been a clear evolution in both public and media expectation – hastened by social media – that the CEO *should* necessarily speak for the organization. In fact some sections of the public believe they have a *right* to accurate information and should be able to access the highest possible authorities. For example, in a recent survey of UK and US consumers, 59 per cent said they wanted the response in a brand crisis to come from the CEO.[269]

Yet in a major organizational crisis the information available is often confusing or incomplete and the highest executives may have critical and urgent duties such as saving lives or protecting the environment rather than talking to reporters.

Despite this reality, journalists in particular have become increasingly reluctant to accept communicators as quotable sources. They understand (and hopefully respect) the role of the communications professional in activities such as providing background, facilitating interviews, developing statements and speeches, liaising with management and even being an "off the record source."

---

[268] Corporate US lacks credibility. (1993, August 14). *Calgary Herald.* https://www.newspapers.com/newspage/485013178/
[269] How consumers react to a brand crisis (2019). *Crisp Thinking*, UK. https://s3.amazonaws.com/media.mediapost.com/uploads/2019CrispCrisisImpact Study.pdf

But when it comes to providing public comment on an important issue, those same journalists want and expect to be able to quote someone with a clear executive position.

Regardless of how important it is to say the right things – especially in a crisis – the challenges presented by using the lawyer or the communicator often lead organizations to revert to the default position that "our CEO is our only spokesperson."

It may just be a case of yielding to conventional wisdom, sometimes encouraged by a CEO with a strongly developed view of their own importance. It's fitting that the CEO feels a need to show leadership in a crisis, to be seen to be taking responsibility for the response strategy. And it's quite natural to believe that when the stakes are so high, the buck stops at the top. However, that's not the same as being the spokesperson or, more accurately, not the same as being the primary or only spokesperson.

So, all other things being equal, should your CEO be the crisis spokesperson? The problem here is that the question itself is easily misunderstood. Certainly the CEO should be visible and speak when there is a crisis, especially to address issues of policy and to show the organization cares.

That does not mean the CEO should be the *only* spokesperson; nor does it mean they should speak on each and every aspect of the crisis on a 24/7 basis. The CEO should speak to demonstrate compassion and underline commitment to fixing the problem. Yet it is entirely appropriate – and often desirable – to have different spokespersons to talk about technical or operational details, or to provide routine media updates. Or a different person to address internal, as opposed to external, audiences.

Speaking With One Voice

Using multiple spokespersons can appear to challenge another aspect of conventional wisdom, namely the idea that, in the event of a crisis, the organization must "speak with one voice."

This broad statement is true, but here's the crucial distinction: speaking with one voice does not mean having only one spokesperson. That's a common misunderstanding. Speaking with one voice actually means consistency of message. It means that while new facts may emerge about the crisis, your overall message doesn't keep changing from hour to hour. And it means that your message remains unchanged across all the designated spokespersons – a calm, consistent and qualified voice. The end result is your organization having what I call a cohesive voice.

Speaking with one voice does not mean having only one spokesperson.

One of the advantages of having qualified and well-trained alternative executives speaking on specific matters, or to specific audiences, is that it's an effective way to help reduce the risk of over-exposing your CEO, and also allows the CEO to focus on providing leadership to manage the crisis. Furthermore, it allows the CEO to be held in reserve to step in if things start to go wrong, or a dispute arises. In other words, don't use your CEO as a last resort if in fact it's not the last resort.

There is another challenge when you are facing a crisis, and that's the credibility gap. Many CEOs and other senior executives cling to a firm belief that what they say is heard and believed. Unfortunately, the evidence suggests this is a case of woefully misplaced confidence.

Repeated research in many countries into public perception of the ethics and honesty of professions places business executives well down the list, alongside journalists, politicians, telemarketers and used-car salespeople. The respected Edelman Trust Barometer in 2019, for example, showed that only 47 per cent of the public surveyed around the world thought that CEOs were very credible.[270] Be honest: how credible do you think the typical CEO is?

A major study of public opinion for the Public Affairs Council in 2019 was even more discouraging.[271] Only 48 percent of Americans surveyed had a favorable view of major companies, and only six percent thought CEOs possess high honesty and ethical standards. Considering the results of that study, Public Affairs

---

[270] Edelman (2019). 19th Annual Edelman Trust Barometer
https://www.edelman.com/sites/g/files/aatuss191/files/2019-03/2019_Edelman_Trust_Barometer_Global_Report.pdf?utm

[271] *Public affairs pulse survey report: what Americans think about business* (2019). Washington DC Public Affairs Council. https://pac.org/wp-content/uploads/Pulse_2019_Report.pdf

Council President Doug Pinkham told me that companies might need to reconsider whether it's smart to use the CEO as spokesperson on all occasions, especially when trying to build trust with a suspicious public.

> *"If you're opening a chemical plant in a town that is worried about health and safety, you wouldn't want to send a CEO to a community meeting to face your critics. In such cases the best face for the company may need to come from the factory floor, not the corner office."*[272]

Mr. Pinkham may be right in some limited situations, though in a serious crisis the spokesperson must be able to speak for management.

Where to Go?

After considering whether the CEO should be the spokesperson, and before moving on to what they should say, you need to consider one other important question: "Should the CEO go to the scene to take charge?"

Here again conventional wisdom states the importance of the CEO being visible. In other words, the CEO must not only *do* the right thing, but must be *seen* to do the right thing. And in the fast-moving world of social media, where every phone is a camera, the answer is not only about being seen to do the right thing – but increasingly also about perception and reputation.

Whether your CEO should go to the scene of the crisis and take charge might seem like a tactical question for crisis planning, but it is one of the more contentious issues you may need to assess. In fact, the pioneering US crisis expert William Small once declared that no other issue has been debated so much as the role of the CEO in the first few hours of a crisis, and whether he or she should race to the scene.[273]

In some ways this question is almost unanswerable, and it links closely to the previous discussion about the CEO as spokesperson. At one level the solution

---

[272] pers comm December 2019

[273] Small, W. J. (1991). Exxon Valdez: How to spend billions and still get a black eye. *Public Relations Review*, 17(1), 9–25.

214

seems quite simple: your CEO should be where he or she can do the most good for the organization – perhaps out in the field comforting victims; perhaps in the board room directing recovery; or perhaps at external meetings to reassure your investors, regulators and other stakeholders, depending on the nature of the crisis.

The satirist H. L. Mencken, is supposed to have said: "For every complicated problem there is a solution which is clear, simple and wrong." That is certainly the case here. It's one of those questions which seems obvious... but isn't.

US President George W. Bush was famously attacked for failing to go to New Orleans soon enough after that city was ravaged by Hurricane Katrina, even though it was claimed he was in Washington with his experts closely monitoring and managing the situation.[274] Similarly, BP Chief Tony Hayward was bitterly criticized after being photographed at a yachting regatta in Britain during his company's Gulf of Mexico oil spill disaster, despite the fact that he had spent weeks constantly on call for the media.[275]

It's an easy criticism, particularly in politics. Take Russian President Vladimir Putin who came under attack for remaining on holiday on the Black Sea for four days during the crisis over the sinking of the submarine *Kursk*.[276] Or President Donald Trump criticized in May 2020 for playing at his private golf course in

---

[274] Bumiller, E. (2005, September 2). Bush criticised over storm response. *New York Times*. https://www.nytimes.com/2005/09/02/world/americas/bush-criticized-over-storm-response.html

[275] Kennedy, M. (2010, June 20). BP Chief's weekend sailing trip stokes anger at oil company. *The Guardian*. https://www.theguardian.com/business/2010/jun/20/tony-hayward-bp

[276] Wastell, D. (2000, September 10). Putin admits regrets over Kursk crisis. *Telegraph, UK*. https://www.telegraph.co.uk/news/worldnews/europe/russia/1354881/Putin-admits-regrets-over-Kursk-crisis.html

Northern Virginia instead of staying in Washington as US deaths in the COVID19 pandemic approached 100,000.[277]

Then of course there was CEO Lawrence Rawl of Exxon, who you will meet again elsewhere in this book. When the tanker *Exxon Valdez* ran aground off Alaska, causing one of the worst oil spills in the United States, he didn't fly to the scene but stayed unseen in his office for six days. He then emerged to give a disastrous TV interview in which he blamed the captain for being drunk and blamed the US Coast Guard and Alaska state officials for delays in the cleanup.[278]

Three weeks after the spill, the CEO finally went to Alaska, where he was asked why he didn't go sooner. The hapless Mr. Rawl told a news conference:

> *"I'm technologically obsolete. Getting me up there would have diverted our own people's attention. I couldn't help with the spill; I couldn't do anything about getting the ship off the rocks."* [279]

This tone-deaf statement demonstrated that the CEO had no real understanding of his role. Of course he wasn't expected to help get the ship off the rocks. But he did need to be there to show a personal commitment to the people of Alaska.

Australian Prime Minister Scott Morrison took a similar ill-advised approach in December 2019 when he went on a family holiday in Hawaii while the country was experiencing catastrophic bushfires. Public outcry forced him to return home, but his "explanation" damaged his reputation even further.

He started off well, saying he accepted that in the circumstances his absence had "understandably caused a lot of anxiety and I deeply regret that." Then he added:

---

[277] Sternlicht, A. (2020, May 24). After Biden Attacks Trump For Golfing Amid Pandemic, Trump Golfs Again. *Forbes.* https://www.forbes.com/sites/alexandrasternlicht/2020/05/24/after-biden-attacks-trump-for-golfing-amid-pandemic-trump-golfs-again/#ab90d843f802

[278] Some experts have argued that Rawl was right to remain at headquarters but wrong to stay silent.

[279] Holusha, J. (1989, April 21). Exxon's public relations problems. *New York Times.* https://www.nytimes.com/1989/04/21/business/exxon-s-public-relations-problem.html

"I know Australians understand this and they'll be pleased I'm coming back, I'm sure. But they know I don't hold a hose. I don't sit in a control room."[280]

Like Mr. Rawl of Exxon, he seemed to misunderstand his leadership role in a crisis and his unfortunate statement appeared in critical news reports around the world. Contrast this with Warren Anderson, Chairman and CEO of Union Carbide, who was praised for flying to India immediately after the notorious chemical leak at Bhopal in 1984 to take charge on the scene. However, he was briefly arrested on arrival and spent time cut off from proper communication, leaving the company leaderless at a critical time.[281] Right intention, wrong outcome.

Or Tony Fernandes, owner and CEO of AirAsia, who was similarly praised for flying immediately to Indonesia to personally take charge after flight QZ8501 crashed into the Java Sea in December 2014.[282]

It's not easy, and the window of opportunity for your CEO to do the right thing in a crisis is narrow. Moreover, it's sometimes extremely hard to know what *is* the right thing to do. However, from my research, you are much more likely to be criticized for *not* going to the scene than be criticized for going when it may prove to be the wrong decision. Broadly, I believe there are good grounds to argue that the CEO *should* go to the scene of a crisis, even if for no reason other than to be visible and to show that the organization cares.

---

[280] Karp, S. (2020, December 20). Scott Morrison apologises for taking holiday during Australia's bushfire crisis. *The Guardian.* https://www.theguardian.com/australia-news/2019/dec/20/scott-morrison-apologises-for-taking-holiday-during-australias-bushfire-crisis

[281] Claiborne, W. (1984, December 8). American detained in India. *Washington Post.* https://www.washingtonpost.com/archive/politics/1984/12/08/american-detained-in-india/48b70d46-b3e7-4583-9cf5-202249d838b6/

[282] Stevenson, A. and Gough, N. (2015, January 1). AirAsia's Tony Fernandes responds to crisis with quick compassion. *Sydney Morning Herald.* https://www.smh.com.au/business/companies/airasias-chief-tony-fernandes-responds-to-crisis-with-quick-compassion-20150101-12gb9k.html

Getting Ready to Speak

No sportsperson would go onto the field without a game plan, and no musician would stride onto the stage without having memorized the score. So it seems logical to have a plan before dealing with the media rather than trying to "wing it."

Too often that "plan" turns out to be over-reliance on a list of Frequently Asked Questions (FAQ), which I suggest is one of the most misunderstood and misapplied instruments in crisis communication.

> "Everyone has a plan until they get punched in the mouth."
>
> Mike Tyson

The problem is that how the FAQ is used in theory differs so greatly from its use in practice. In theory a formal FAQ provides you with the opportunity to predict and prepare for the likely questions in an interview. But I have seen FAQs which extend to six or eight pages, making them virtually useless in a real interview situation where the pace of questioning can easily outrun the interviewee's ability to keep up.

Imagine the journalist asks you a question and you said "Just a minute. Let me just check for the answer on page five... or was it page six." In reality the conventional detailed FAQ – even if it does not extend to multiple pages – is of limited practical use during an interview in response to a crisis.

The key reason, I have found, is that my clients sometimes want to prepare a list of questions they would *like* to answer, and not necessarily the questions any smart journalist is likely to ask. In other words, they typically try to avoid the difficult questions.

When I insist we need to include this or that difficult question a common answer is: "Oh no, we don't want to talk about that" or "Our lawyers would never let us talk about that."

That's the heart of the problem. The hard questions in a crisis are exactly the ones you are likely to be asked. Without them your FAQ becomes more of a statement of policy than a practical media tool.

Is the conventional FAQ a total waste of time? My answer is no. It does have a real value, which the lawyers tend to appreciate.

The value is that simply preparing the FAQ forces your organization to think about a range of important issues relating to the crisis; to record and agree upon answers which come to represent the corporate viewpoint; and to secure clearance from the lawyers.

It might not be a very useful document in a live media interview situation, but it's often a very powerful resource for developing other types of communication.

Specifically, you can use it to help develop the main alternative to an FAQ in dealing with the media in a crisis, namely a concise list of key messages or talking points.

I know that over-use of talking points by politicians has given them a bad name, but key messages are simply pre-agreed statements the spokesperson would like to convey in an interview. They are easy to remember and you try to "bridge" to them if the right questions are not asked. Focusing on your key messages does *not* mean refusing to answer legitimate questions. That irritates the journalist and also the public. I'm sure you've seen politicians constantly repeating some talking point and you've shouted at the TV screen "just answer the question."

When properly used, sticking to your key messages does help keep the interview focused where you want. There is nothing more annoying than the interview ending and you suddenly realize you forgot to make your most important point.

Getting Your Message Across

The purpose of a media interview, *from your perspective*, is to communicate your key points. The journalist's questions may or may not help you achieve that purpose. And in a crisis situation you will likely be facing highly emotional or sensitive issues.

To help get to your message across, the common technique is bridging. For example:

- "That's a good question but I think what's important here is..."
- "I think that's a question for another day. Right now we are dealing with the crisis and what we need to focus on is..."

- "You've raised a really important issue with that question because..."
- "I have been speaking to the people affected and what they've told me they want to know is..."
- "Before we finish it's important to mention that..."

Use these techniques sparingly. In a crisis you need to be seen as compassionate and responsive, not an uncaring robot.

There is one other useful technique you can use at the start of an interview to pre-empt the likelihood that the journalist has already started to "construct" the story in their own mind. If the opening question suggests that construction is negative, you might consider saying: "Before I respond to that I would like to clarify that this situation was one we couldn't control because..." That can help you to frame the interview in a way which is aligned to your key messages.

So what is my recommended approach? I generally advise a well-planned combination of both methods. First, a *brief* list of key messages – no more than five or six depending on the format of the interview. In a face to face interview without notes – such as on television – it's not easy to remember more than three messages you want to convey. Plus a *very brief* FAQ of prepared answers for particularly important or sensitive issues, typically no more than three or four. Any experienced journalist will respect the fact that you may need to refer to notes.

Remember, when it comes to getting ready to speak to the media in a crisis think of the sportsperson going onto the field or the musician striding on stage. Practice, practice, practice.

What to Say... and Not Say

Finally, there is the question of what you should say in a crisis. As I mentioned earlier, while effective crisis management involves much more than just media relations, doing it well may be critical to public perception, reputation recovery and legal liability.

At the most basic level, when you need to speak to the media in a crisis situation there are some common dos and don'ts, which set a basic framework for success.

Dos and Don'ts of Crisis Communication	
Do	**Don't**
Respond quickly	Speculate about cause or effect
Be informed and accurate	Lie or stonewall
Admit what you don't know	Be "unavailable"
Demonstrate empathy and caring	Treat media as the enemy
Correct misinformation	Say "no comment"
Focus on what you're going to say	Apportion blame or point fingers
State when more information will be available	Use jargon or acronyms

Naturally, there is much more to it than that. Yet these "golden rules" will serve you well. Are these Dos and Don'ts new or original or revolutionary? Absolutely not. Are they fairly obvious? Yes. But, as I like to say, the obvious is always obvious when someone else points it out to you.

The news media often report stories of bad crisis communication, and I'll warrant that in just about every case you'll see failure to comply with at least one of these basics.

Beyond these guidelines, this chapter has already discussed topics such as who should speak, the true meaning of speaking with one voice, and the desired qualities of a spokesperson.

However, there are two other areas I want to touch on which often attract disagreement between legal and communications advisors – namely whether the organization should speak at all, and the related issue of when and how to offer no comment.

A lot of expert advice I've read about responding to reporters starts with the question: "What shall we say to the media?" I believe there is an important question you need to consider first: "Should we say anything at all?"

It's a common misapprehension that an organization *must* speak to the media – and right away. That you somehow have a duty or obligation to do so.

This is simply not true. Your principal obligation is to your organization, your investors and other stakeholders. The journalist's urgent media deadline is their problem, not yours. Although it may be unpopular advice, sometimes it *is* better for the media to report that you were asked for comment but were unavailable. Or were unavailable at this time. It's certainly a much better option than making a premature comment you come to regret.

The same regret can arise when you give an interview you didn't need to. I have already mentioned in this chapter the outcome when Chip Wilson of Lululemon chose to go on TV to "explain" about the company's faulty yoga pants – and finished up losing his job.

But there can be no better example of a voluntary interview turning into a total disaster than when Britain's Prince Andrew made the decision to go on TV in late 2019 to discuss his involvement with sex-offender Jeffrey Epstein. [283] He reportedly expected it would "draw a line" under the controversy, but he was demonstrably ill-prepared for the most obvious questions and the predictable outcry after the interview forced him to withdraw from all royal duties. One respected industry publication called it "a master class in PR disasters."[284]

We don't know what legal advice the Prince received beforehand, if any, but we do know that his communications advisor warned him against this folly and resigned when his counsel was ignored.

---

[283] Maltby, K. (2019, November 19). Prince Andrew interview is a PR nightmare and a national joke. *CNN*. https://edition.cnn.com/2019/11/18/opinions/prince-andrew-bbc-interview-disaster-maltby/index.html

[284] Hickman, A. (2019. November 18). 'Prince Andrew interview will reign as a masterclass in PR disasters for some time' - industry reaction. *PR Week*. https://www.prweek.com/article/1666041/prince-andrew-interview-will-reign-masterclass-pr-disasters-time-industry-reaction

While the ill-advised interview and its fallout received massive media coverage around the world, the point I want to make here is that the Prince had no urgent reason to give the interview at all. Certainly, he had got himself into a controversy, but agreeing to this interview with a journalist known to be a tough interrogator was a life-changing error of judgement. The lesson for you is to never lose sight of your strategic objective.

Crisis guru James Lukaszewski has expressed this bluntly:

> *"Respond to the media only when your message goals are served. There is nothing in the US Constitution which says you have to call the press back."*[285]

However – and this is a crucial distinction – being "unavailable for comment" in the face of a crisis is almost *never* the right answer.

In an organizational crisis you have very little choice and there is *almost always* something to say which is useful and legally appropriate. Media reports around the world show that saying nothing in response to a crisis can very easily make the crisis much, much worse and entrench reputational and legal damage.

Certainly, every crisis is different and I've heard that fact used as a "reason" not to commit resources to detailed crisis planning. Yet while specific circumstances vary for every crisis, you can build effective crisis communication around my five key *initial* steps, which apply in just about every crisis situation.

---

[285] Lukaszewski, J. E. (1997). The Other Prosecutors. *Public Relations Quarterly* *42*(1), 23-20.

	Five Initial Steps for Effective Crisis Communication
1	**Briefly state the facts as currently known**. Don't speculate and don't guess but be active to address false rumors and perceptions as well as clarifying what actually happened.
2	**Apologize**. To be effective, any apology must be swift and sincere. Your apology does not need to accept liability yet can honestly acknowledge the impact of the crisis.
3	**Express sympathy.** Those affected by a crisis not only need to hear that you are sorry for the crisis, but also that you are sorry for how it has affected them personally. As the old maxim goes: "People don't care what you know – they want to know that you care."
4	**Express empathy**. You need to show those affected that you know how they feel. Crises are about feelings as well as facts. Demonstrating empathy shows you are human, not just a brand or organizational figurehead.
5	**Focus on actions.** Describe what actions you have already taken and what actions. you plan to take to deal with the problem and prevent it happening again

Importantly, you will note that these five initial steps do not include blaming, justification, explanation or recovery. There will be plenty of time for that later. But cover these five basic communication requirements right at the beginning and you will go a long way towards managing the crisis and avoiding disaster.

Yet, having said this, there may be some aspects of the crisis you legitimately don't want to comment on. Or which you are not ready to comment on. Or which you are legally constrained from commenting on.

How to Make No Comment

The first important point here is that *making* no comment is entirely different from *saying* "no comment." Simply saying "no comment" is the verbal equivalent of putting your hand over the lens of the TV camera, and you know that nearly always ends badly. Indeed, one expert has written that using those fateful words can be compared to admitting guilt or waving a red flag in front of a bull.[286]

An American survey found that when a large company is accused of wrongdoing in a lawsuit more than one third of the population believe that company is "probably guilty" and 58 percent believe a large company charged with wrongdoing is guilty when its spokesperson responds with "no comment." [287] As California-based security advisor Robert Gardner wrote for a risk management magazine:

> *"Those two words are deadly because they imply you have something to hide. There are other ways to convey the same message. Be creative."*[288]

So follow his advice and be creative. There are effective and appropriate ways you can avoid answering specific questions *when there are good reasons not to comment*. However, before proceeding, be very clear that this is not about simply stalling or stonewalling. It's not about declining to speak, but about declining to address specific subjects. Or as it is sometimes called, commenting without commenting.

This is where sensible legal and communications advice is essential. It's about properly balancing the communicator's natural desire to communicate and the lawyer's natural inclination towards caution and saying as little as possible.

---

[286] Comcowich, W. (2018, September 5). 5 Ways to avoid saying "no comment" to reporters. *Glean.info Blog*. https://glean.info/5-ways-to-avoid-saying-no-comment/

[287] DeMartino, T. (1997, February 17). How to do litigation public relations. *Inside PR*.

[288] Gardner, R. A. (1996). No comment. *Crimewise.com*. http://www.crimewise.com/library/comment.html

In addition, it's one area where legal considerations can legitimately override communications advice, because a crisis situation may genuinely involve a range of complex and sensitive legal concerns.

> "Whereas we will advocate telling it all, telling it fast, and telling it truthfully, lawyers will often advocate saying nothing, doing nothing and admitting nothing."
>
> Michael Regester and Judy Larkin[289]

Assuming you have made an informed decision that certain information should *not* be made public at this stage – for good legal or business reasons – what's the best way to *make* no comment without *saying* "no comment?"

There are many ways to skin this cat, and these are some of the suggested approaches (remember such approaches should be used only when the facts justify them, not simply to evade questions which might be awkward or embarrassing.)

- It's premature to comment right now because...

- We are constrained by law from commenting.

- We can't prejudge a situation that's still under investigation.

- I'm not in a position to talk about this specific instance, but here's the general rule.

- I wish I could comment on that but let me explain...

- I won't be able to answer that until the independent experts have finished their work.

- I can't give you a yes or no answer to that question right now.

- It would be improper to comment on a matter before the courts.

- I hope to have an answer for you very soon.

---

[289] Register, M. and Larkin, J. (2008). Risk issues and crisis management (4th edtn). London: Kogan Page.

- That's not something I can answer at the moment, but what we do know is...

- We don't yet have all the facts, but we have launched a formal investigation.

- We are assessing the situation and will have more to say once all the facts are known.

None of these responses are likely to make a reporter happy. But it is important that you acknowledge the question and, where appropriate, provide an explanation and/or commit to a response at a future time.

Moreover, it is important to decide who is giving these responses. From reading the suggestions above you will recognize that some of these statements may be better coming from the mouth of the lawyer rather than the CEO or a public relations professional.

Before concluding this topic, I want to share an instructive real-life example of what can happen when a company unwisely says "no comment."

In a classic case from the late 1990s, a reporter from the *Corning (NY) Leader* asked management at Corning Inc. to respond to his information from inside the company that they had seriously overestimated demand for optical fiber.[290] The company said "no comment" and the reporter wrote his conclusion that Corning was "in a state of emergency."

The story was picked up by *Bloomberg Business News*, the *Associated Press* and *CNBC*, and in a single day the company's stock dropped in value by 8.4 per cent, or just over $1 billion. The company responded by claiming the story was "filled with inaccuracies." They also removed the local paper's coin boxes and display racks from its halls and canteens and dumped them in the newspaper's carpark.

---

[290] Henry, R. (2000). Who said silence is golden? Chapter Four in *You'd better have a hose if you want to put the fire out*. Windsor, CA.: Gollywobbler, pp 50-71

But the next day the stock kept dropping, and then the company confirmed falling sales of optical fiber and lowered its earnings forecast. Corning stock plunged again, reportedly losing $3 billion in value before beginning to recover.[291]

Was the "no comment" answer solely responsible for crash in share value? Probably not. But it certainly helped trigger the crisis, which might have been minimized by a timely and honest answer.

[291] Corning Blames newspaper report for huge stock drop. (1997, September 13). *The Spokesman-Review*.
https://www.spokesman.com/stories/1997/sep/13/corning-blames-newspaper-report-for-huge-stock/

Key Takeaways

- Choice of spokesperson can make or break effective crisis response.
- Speaking with one voice does not mean you have only one spokesperson.
- The CEO may not be the best choice to deal with the media.
- *Making* no comment is entirely different from *saying* "no comment."
- You don't have to answer just because a journalist asks.
- Failed media communication in a crisis can have a devastating and prolonged effect.

Questions for Discussion

1. *Does a bad relationship with the media in crises arise mainly from ignorance or arrogance?*
2. *How has blurring between hard news and comment in the media affected the way crises are reported?*
3. *Has the rise of social media led to more or less openness with mainstream reporters?*
4. *Why do reporters (and the public) tend to assume that a company in a crisis situation is trying to hide something? What can be done about it?*
5. *How would organizations benefit from making more use of lawyers as spokespersons?*

Chapter Eight

Doing What's Right – Liability Versus Responsibility

The time is always right to do what is right.
Martin Luther King Jr.

Liability and responsibility are certainly not the same. However, the two words often appear together in crisis response. Liability is primarily about legal obligation. Responsibility is more about reputation and human behavior.

The challenge is that lawyers sometimes frame their advice as trying to minimize liability, or to avoid exposing the organization to fresh legal liability; that's a legitimate role for lawyers.

At the same time communications advisors may recommend that the organization should step forward and accept responsibility, despite recognizing that this might increase legal liability as the price of protecting reputation.

This is a management conundrum at the heart of how to respond in the face of a crisis and how you determine questions such as when to take responsibility and when to apologize.

This chapter will help you to:

- Distinguish the essential difference between corporate responsibility and legal liability... and why it's important.
- Respond effectively to protect reputation after a crisis.
- Learn from real-world examples to take the lead and "do the right thing" in the face of potential legal risk.
- Determine the tone from the top about the relationship with lawyers.
- Apologize without increasing liability.

While I seldom see much value in arguing about semantics, we do need to agree on some clear meanings here.

I guess you won't have much doubt about interpretation of the word *liable*. It has a distinct legal meaning – namely that a liability is a legal obligation. For example

- The business owner was held personally liable for the company's debts.
- The insurance company admitted liability under the policy but was challenging the amount of the claim.

So, it's no surprise that the financial obligations entered into the balance sheet of your organization are formally referred to as Liabilities.

Dictionary definitions:

Liable

(i) obligated according to law or equity (ii) exposed or subject to some usually adverse contingency or action.

Responsible

(i) being the cause or explanation (ii) able to answer for one's conduct and obligations, trustworthy (iii) able to choose for oneself between right and wrong.

Source: www.merriam-webster.com

By contrast the word *responsible* is not quite as clear. For example:
- Think about if you got seriously ill from eating your favorite peanut butter. This is what happened to hundreds of consumers when the Peter Pan brand was contaminated with salmonella. Your local supermarket may have been responsible for selling peanut butter which was unfit for consumption, but it was probably not legally liable because they could show it was supplied by someone else and they took all reasonable steps to ensure it was good quality. Meanwhile the manufacturer admitted liability,

and in 2016 was hit with the largest criminal fine ever in a US food safety case.[292]

- The manufacturer of your blender is liable if it can't be operated safely. But you are responsible if you override safety features. Think no further than local TV personality Emma Alberici who nearly lost her fingers in October 2019 when trying to clean her blender while it was still plugged in.[293]
- Similarly, your local railway is responsible to ensure the level crossing is closed when a train is passing. But it is not liable if a commuter running late jumps over the barrier and is killed.

The word *responsible* has several meanings. The first and most obvious is being answerable for an act or its consequences, as in:

- The CEO was responsible to the board for a marketing plan which would deliver consistent profits.

It can also relate to governance over others, as in:

- Management was responsible for preventing bullying in the workplace.

But there is also another application of the word responsible which you will find has particular relevance when it comes to crisis response and reputation, namely responsible meaning trustworthy and reliable, as in:

- I wouldn't hire a salesperson who didn't seem responsible.
- We wouldn't buy product from a supplier which didn't have responsible sourcing.

---

[292] Tainted peanut butter case ends in $11.2 million penalty (2016, December 14). *CBS News* https://www.cbsnews.com/news/peter-pan-peanut-butter-tainted-with-salmonella-case-11-million-penalty/

[293] ABC reporter Emma Alberici suffers horrific kitchen injury (2019, June 17).*News.com.* https://www.news.com.au/entertainment/celebrity-life/celebrity-selfies/abc-reporter-emma-alberici-suffers-horrific-kitchen-injury/news-story/567db9c0ac30185ad41d4c6d350fc2b2

It's this last meaning communicators are typically thinking of when they talk about potential impact on reputation. And this is the meaning I will be focusing on in this chapter. If there is any doubt about that meaning, you can understand it even more easily by thinking about the opposite, namely *irresponsible*. Try imagining any company or executive being happy to be labelled irresponsible?

Stepping Up to Do What's Right

One critical area where lawyers and professional communicators may come into conflict over liability versus responsibility is when deciding what to do after a crisis, when taking particular actions may be interpreted by others as accepting liability. This is a true test of executive leadership, which can best be illustrated by some real-life cases.

Consider the response by BHP Billiton when an iron ore tailings dam at a mine in Brazil suffered a catastrophic failure in November 2015, killing 19 people and destroying at least 200 homes. It caused extensive flooding and environmental contamination.[294]

The dam is owned and operated by Samarco, a standalone 50/50 joint venture between the Brazilian company Vale and the Anglo-Australian conglomerate BHP Billiton.

In the face of likely investigations, prosecutions, fines, compensation costs and class actions it would have been very easy for BHP Billiton to try to distance itself from the disaster, maintaining that Samarco was a standalone, self-operated, joint venture. Instead it chose from the outset to adopt a "do the right thing" approach which it appears to have sustained throughout, irrespective of the legal structure or potential exposure and even though its response might weaken future legal defenses.

---

[294] Samarco Dam disaster: Dealing with the fallout of a tragedy (2018, July 30). *Mining technology*. https://www.mining-technology.com/mining-safety/samarco-dam-disaster-dealing-fallout-tragedy

The subsequent monetary costs have been enormous, and legal action is still ongoing, but four years after the disaster the Brazilian Government gave approval for the mine to resume operation.[295]

Structural failures and building collapses are never far away from the headlines. For example, a single week in 2019 saw two people killed in the partial collapse of the new Hard Rock Casino in New Orleans,[296] and just days later, the media reported three companies fined following a crane collapse which killed four people on the new Google office building under construction in Seattle.[297]

Such crises are often badly handled, perhaps as a result of typically complex lines of shared responsibility in the building industry or some companies being ill-equipped to respond effectively.

In this respect, I believe there is no clearer statement of the principle of doing what's right than what occurred in Austin, Texas, in June 2011, when glass panels started falling from balconies of the newly opened 37-storey W Hotel.

Although the cause of the failure was not yet known, Beau Armstrong, CEO of the hotel owner, immediately held a press conference in front of the building, describing what happened and announcing that he was closing the hotel and relocating all guests.

[295] Nogueira, M. (2019, October 26). Vale, BHP's Samarco gets license to resume operations after dam burst. *Reuters Business News*. https://www.reuters.com/article/us-vale-sa-bhp-group-au-samarco/vale-bhps-samarco-gets-license-to-resume-operations-after-dam-burst-idUSKBN1X42GW

[296] Carlisle, M. (2019, October 12). Construction Partially Collapses in New Orleans, killing at Least Two. *Time*. https://time.com/5699136/new-orleans-building-collapse-hard-rock-hotel/

[297] Lam, K. (2019, October 17). 'Totally avoidable': Three construction companies fined for deadly Seattle crane collapse. *USA Today* https://www.usatoday.com/story/news/nation/2019/10/17/seattle-crane-collapse-investigation-companies-fined-avoidable-accident/4018256002/

"The entire team here at the W couldn't be more devastated that this has occurred but unfortunately, after consulting with numerous experts, we still do not know why this has happened. So here's what we're doing. We are replacing every piece of balcony glass on the building.

"We have experts and the City of Austin on site to ensure this work is done safely and as expeditiously as possible. Safety is our top priority.

"We apologize to our hotel guests, our residents, our neighbors, and to the City. We will make this right."[298]

It was undoubtedly a forthright statement, though it may well have made the company lawyers nervous. As local communications consultant Don Martin later commented:

"You can bet that some of his lawyers advised against taking responsibility when contractors, subcontractors and suppliers were ultimately at fault. But it was the right thing to do, calmed fears, created empathy for the company, and won his company praise and public support."[299]

"If you don't stick to your values when they're being tested, they're not values – they're hobbies."

Jon Stewart

---

[298] Forbes, P. (2011, June 29). Falling glass at the shuttered W. *The Austin Eater.* https://austin.eater.com/2011/6/29/6672371/falling-glass-and-a-missing-hostess-at-the-shuttered-w

[299] Martin, D. (2013, March 6). Attorneys and PR together in crisis communication. *Bernstein Crisis Blog.* https://managementhelp.org/blogs/crisis-management/2013/03/06/attorneys-and-pr-together-in-crisis-communications-guest-post-by-don-martin/

Another CEO who stepped up to do the right thing when the facts were still unclear was Nick Varney of Merlin Entertainment, owners of Alton Towers theme park in Staffordshire, England, where disaster struck a featured roller-coaster in June 2015.

One of the carriages on the 14-loop "Smiler" ride crashed into a stalled empty carriage, injuring 16 people, including two teenage girls who each needed a leg amputation.

Nick Varney immediately went to the scene and took the lead in all communication as the spokesperson, stating without hesitation on the day that the company took full responsibility.

After the company was fined £5 million (about US$6 million) for health and safety breaches Varney said:

> *"From the beginning the company has accepted full responsibility for the terrible accident at Alton Towers and has made sincere and heartfelt apologies to those who were injured.*
>
> *"In accepting responsibility and liability very early on we have tried to make the healing and compensation process as trouble free as possible for all of those involved.*
>
> *"We have strived to fulfil our promise to support them in every way and I promise that this support will continue as long as they need it.*
>
> *"We were always aware that we would end up here today facing a substantial penalty, as has been delivered by the court today. But the far greater punishment for all of us is knowing that on this occasion we let people down with devastating consequences.*

> *"It is something we will never forget and it is something we are utterly determined will never be repeated."[300]*

It was sincere, heartfelt and focused entirely on the victims. In fact, Merlin even paid for the families' injury lawyers.

You might question the legal implications of such an early admission of liability. When it was all over, the company's Corporate Affairs Director, James Crampton, told the BBC they never underestimated the severity of the incident and chose not to have a long consultation with lawyers and other advisors.

> *"Our immediate response and subsequent actions were driven by a desire to do what we believed was the right thing by all those affected by the accident. We didn't try to hide behind lawyers."[301]*

Lessons learned

Following the Samarco dam collapse in Brazil, BHP Billiton committed to doing the right thing and, despite massive financial penalties, within four years had secured permission to reopen the iron ore mine. And at the time of writing, no executive has been convicted or imprisoned.

Contrast this with another tailings dam collapse in January 2019 at Brumadinho, Brazil, which killed 270 people. This mine was operated by Vale, BHP's JV partner at Samarco, and in January 2020 16 people were charged with murder and environmental

---

[300] Merlin boss: We 'let people down' over Smiler crash (2016, September 27). *ITV News.* https://www.itv.com/news/update/2016-09-27/merlin-boss-we-let-people-down-over-smiler-crash/
[301] Shadbolt, P. (2016, October 13). How can a company repair a damaged reputation? *BBC News.* http://www.bbc.com/news/business-37630983

crimes, including the former CEO of Vale.[302] *It would be unwise to over-interpret the difference, but this does seem to contain a lesson.*

With regard to the building failure in Texas and the roller-coaster fatalities in Britain, despite not knowing why these crises happened, both CEOs took responsibility, set out clearly what would be done, and committed to fixing the situation.

In truth they both tracked precisely what I have developed as the five key initial steps for any crisis communication (which you will have seen set out in detail in Chapter Seven on Dealing with the Media). They briefly stated the facts as currently known; apologized; expressed sympathy; conveyed empathy; and focused on actions to deal with the problem and prevent it happening again.

These five communication steps are not all you need to say, but they provide a solid foundation to regain control and set the framework for crisis management over the coming days.

Take note also that the hotel CEO used language which was simple, direct and unambiguous. For example, "Safety is our top priority" and "We will make this right."

Crises by definition create high levels of stress, where people's ability to receive and process information may be compromised. Beau Armstrong's choice of words provided clarity and certainty in an uncertain situation.

The same applied to Nick Varney after the roller-coaster accident. His statement on the courthouse steps was not read from a prepared statement, even though it may have been rehearsed. During his many statements following the accident he showed humanity,

---

[302] Phillips, D. (2020, January 22). Brazil prosecutors charge 16 people with murder in dam collapse that killed 270. *The Guardian.* https://www.theguardian.com/world/2020/jan/21/brazil-dam-collapse-mining-disaster-charges

humility and authenticity, not always qualities you might expect from a CEO.

One commentator called it a shining example of how to limit the reputation damage from a high-profile event, and its legal outcomes. I think you'd find that hard to dispute.

San Ysidro Massacre

Although the CEO of the hotel in Austin, Texas, and the CEO of the theme park in the British Midlands may have made their lawyers nervous, they were individuals following the tradition of executives who are prepared to deal with the crisis first and the legal implications later.

One of the best modern examples was seen in the early 1980s following a terrible mass shooting at the McDonald's restaurant in San Ysidro, California, outside San Diego.

The case is significant today because not only did the company deal with the crisis first and the legal implications later, but it was one of the extremely rare occasions when the company's own lawyer set that priority and did so "on the record."

Gunman James Huberty entered the store in July 1984, where he shot and killed 19 customers and wounded more than 20 others before he was killed by a police sniper.

Richard Starmann, McDonald's Senior Vice-President of Communication, later wrote that the day after the incident, with communication staff fielding more than 1,000 media calls, Don Horwitz, the company's then Executive Vice president and General Legal Counsel, told them:

"I don't want you people to worry or care about the legal implications of what you might say. We are going to do what's right for the survivors and families of the victims and we'll worry about the lawsuits later."[303]

Starmann says that "We're going to do what's right" became known as the "Horwitz rule" and it governed the company's response. They paid hospital bills of the wounded; flew in relatives of victims for the funerals; provided counseling for families of victims; and gave $1 million to the survivors' fund; actions which Starmann conceded could have been taken into a court of law at a later date and misconstrued as evidence that McDonald's was at fault for the tragedy.

The company also made the extraordinary decision to bulldoze the store to the ground to foil souvenir hunters and to prevent gun-control protesters using the location for political purposes. McDonald's then donated the valuable site to the city for the benefit of citizens on the provision it would never be used as a commercial establishment. Meantime they quietly opened a new restaurant three blocks away. The decision to bulldoze the site was a controversial one, but I believe it was correct and it proved effective.

Some media outlets thought it would be clever to use headlines such as "McMurder" and "McMassacre" and "Big Mac Attack." But overall the response was respectful. Three months after the shooting, CBC News of Raleigh, North Carolina, ran an editorial which concluded:

---

[303] Starmann, R. G. (1993). Tragedy at McDonalds. In J.Gottschalk (ed) Crisis Response: Inside stories on managing image under siege. (pp 309-321) Detroit: Visible Ink Press,

"Many in the news media unfairly dubbed this tragedy the 'McDonald's Massacre.' It was not the McDonald's Massacre. It was the Huberty massacre, and McDonald's restaurant was victimized along with the others. The McDonald's Corporation response to that San Diego community is laudable and worthy of our respect and appreciation nationwide."[304]

Lessons learned

While a commitment to doing the right thing is highly desirable in the face of a crisis, and shows genuine leadership, I would not recommend hoping for your own company's General Counsel to go on the record advising not to worry about the legal implications, as happened as San Ysidro. You might think it shows that not every lawyer fits the stereotype of "considered caution," but it also highlights how unusual the circumstances of this case were and that this is not what you can normally expect.

In addition, the San Ysidro massacre illustrates the critical value of the lawyer being an integral part of the crisis response and helping drive the action plan.

Another lesson arising – though it's not directly related to legal implications – is the challenge of dealing with an overwhelming volume of media calls. This aspect of crisis response is often underestimated. One of my friends was managing the media response to a leaking cross-town tunnel which shut down a major city access for days. She told me her major insight after the crisis was the need to have prearranged access to a source of "boots on the ground" to simply receive and record the calls and allow her to do her job of being spokesperson.

---

[304] Cited in Starmann, ibid, p 310

Did McDonald's make the right decision?

A major talking point from the San Ysidro case was the decision to demolish the store in order to foil souvenir hunters and gun-control protesters. I have tested this controversial decision at management workshops and seminars and it's surprising how many participants question the company's call, often on grounds of "overreacting to the tragedy" or "destroying evidence" or "contaminating a crime scene" (though we have to assume it was done with the agreement of local law enforcement). They also point out that the crisis took place at a time when mass shootings were less common than they have become today.

If you had been McDonald's management, would you have made the same decision?

The Ashland Oil Spill

While it's not easy doing what's right in the face of uncertainty about the facts, in some ways it's even harder when the facts are glaringly obvious and there is no doubt at all about who's responsible.

That's usually the case with an oil spill, where the facts are pretty clear and where media attention is high. I want to briefly delve into history to discuss four notorious oil spills and share what we can learn from them.

The first instructive case began on a cold Saturday afternoon just after New Year of 1988 in the small town of Floreffe, Pennsylvania, just southeast of Pittsburgh, where a storage tank at the Ashland Corporation plant collapsed. Four million gallons of diesel fuel was released and about 700,000 gallons escaped into the nearby Monongahela River. It was one of America's worst inland oil spills and the toxic slick flowed down icy rivers into West Virginia, Kentucky, Ohio and Indiana, endangering the drinking water supply for up to a million residents.

The tank which collapsed was old and had been moved from another site and rebuilt. Subsequent investigations revealed faulty welds and a defect in the steel, as well as dispute over whether there was a valid construction permit

There was no question about legal liability. Yet the response by Ashland CEO John Hall is significant today because it emphasizes the importance of balancing responsibility against potential legal risks.

In a series of what became twice a day media conferences, Hall was honest, believable and contrite. And he turned his candor into action. The company hired two Air Force C-130 transport planes to fly in Coast Guard oil pollution clean-up specialists. Within a week Ashland presented Allegheny County with its first cheque for over $200,000 towards cleanup expenses. Furthermore, the company knew they faced legal action, so *encouraged* people to submit claims so that they could make advance payments, and they set up a toll-free 800 claims line.[305]

The company also decided to publicly admit every mistake. "What we didn't want to happen," they said, "was for some outside investigation to reveal unpleasant information. Then, charges of coverup could undermine the company's credibility."[306]

In addition, the company commissioned the Battelle Institute – a large private research organization – to conduct an independent investigation, and they also made a grant to the University of Pittsburgh to fund a study assessing the spill's long-term environmental impact.

CEO Hall later said: "Our attitude was: Hey guys, we've made a mess here. We've got to clean this thing up and we've got to try to do anything we can to help the people who have been inconvenienced."[307] He told the media: "If we made mistakes we need to stand up and admit them"[308] When asked about the cost

[305] Henry, R. (2000). Do the right thing – take responsibility and win public support. In *You'd better have a hose if you want to put the fire out* pp 165-188. Windsor, CA.: Gollywobbler Press.
[306] Holmes, P. (1992, October 5). Ashland: The Anti-Exxon. *The Holmes Report.* https://www.holmesreport.com/latest/article/ashland-the-anti-exxon-(1992)
[307] Holmes, ibid
[308] Ansberry, C. (1988, January 8). Oil spill in the midwest provides case study in crisis management. *Wall Street Journal.*

of the clean-up, Hall told reporters; "The company is assuming all costs associated with the spill."[309] Just a few weeks later, Hall was called to Washington to testify before Congress and found himself being praised by his questioners. And on Wall Street, the company stock quickly recovered its initial loss, and was substantially up by year's end.

> "Our attitude was: Hey guys, we've made a mess here. We've got to clean this thing up and we've got to try to do anything we can to help the people who have been inconvenienced."[310]

The crisis generated enormous media coverage, much of which focused on the company's response. Typical newspaper headlines were "Ashland Chief's honesty wins praise" *(The Cincinnati Inquirer)*; "Ashland getting praise for candor" *(Louisville Courier-Journal)* and "For Ashland's Hall, honesty was the best policy" *(Akron Beacon-Journal)*.

Media editorials were similarly full of praise:

> *"We can't help but say 'well done' to John Hall, Ashland's no-nonsense Chairman and CEO . . . Hall's unusual candor has gone a long way toward making the best of a bad situation."* The Herald-Dispatch.[311]

> *"Ashland Oil and John R. Hall are to be congratulated on their honesty and willingness to accept the blame."* The Ironton Tribune.[312]

> *"Many companies' first reaction would have been to stonewall in the face of such an incident. Ashland's*

---

[309] Ansberry ibid.

[310] Holmes op cit

[311] Ashland doesn't try to duck the blame. (1988, January 9). *The Herald-Dispatch*, Huntington, West Virginia.

[312] Ashland oil cleanup sign of good neighbour (1988, January 9). *Ironton Tribune,* Ironton, Ohio.

open and honest approach should help the oil and
chemical industries come to some conclusions about
how to avoid a repeat performance" WTVN Radio,
Columbus, Ohio[313]

At the same time, the legal risk of the company strategy was clearly understood. Ashland's VP of Corporate Communication, Dan Lacy, admitted that the company's attorneys "may have winced" out of fear the CEOs comments would haunt him any future lawsuits.[314]

Pittsburgh Post-Gazette reporter Jim Gallagher wrote: "That kind of openness can give ulcers to corporate lawyers."[315]

Gerald Meyers, Professor of Crisis Management at Carnegie-Mellon University went even further:

> *"The lawyers are turning over in the classrooms at*
> *Yale and Harvard. Apologizing, that's an admission*
> *of guilt... The alternative is to stonewall and be*
> *accused of three things – ignorance, indifference or,*
> *worst of all, guilt... Honesty during a crisis is in*
> *vogue in management these days... Ashland has to be*
> *congratulated on how well they're executing it."[316]*

Concerns over the legal risk of accepting liability appear not to have damaged the company's reputation. A month after the spill, as the inevitable investigations and lawsuits began to play out, Pennsylvania Lieutenant-Governor Mark Singel wrote in the *Pittsburgh Post-Gazette*:

---

[313] Editorial. (1988, January 12). WTVN Radio, Great American TV and radio company. cited in Henry, op cit. p 173.

[314] Crisis Control: Ashland Chairman's conduct on oil spill wins public support. (1988, January 8). *Los Angeles Times.* https://www.latimes.com/archives/la-xpm-1988-01-08-fi-23221-story.html

[315] Gallagher, J. (1988, January 8). Ashland scores high in public relations. *Pittsburgh Post-Gazette*.

[316] Bohn, E. (1988, January 8) What price honesty: Industry experts assess Hall's performance. *The Daily Independent,* Ashland, Kentucky.

"Litigation is a fact of life, and it is likely that Ashland Oil will be in court for years. Ashland taught us, however, how a company should respond to an obvious error and its aftermath. Official and early statements from the company expressed more than regret – they assumed responsibility."[317]

Ashland was eventually fined $2.5 million for the spill and spent about $18 million in clean-up costs and civil lawsuits.

Lessons learned

This case remains significant because it demonstrates that even when the crisis is entirely your fault, you can still protect your reputation. In fact, PR expert Paul Holmes concluded at the time: "Ashland came through the crisis better-known and better-respected than it went in."[318]

While that may be true, very few modern companies could reasonably hope for such an outcome. I doubt you can think of any company today which has caused such widespread pollution and still came out with an enhanced reputation.

Moreover, the case shows very clearly that even when lawsuits are sure to follow, a deliberate strategy of candor and honesty can pay dividends and create a positive perception of both the CEO and the company.

The role of the CEO in this case also gives you a further valuable insight, which is the central role of strong leadership. Although the company's VP of Communications admitted that the CEO's candor may have caused their attorneys to wince, there is no evidence that he acted counter to their advice. I believe that more likely what you can draw from the case is that the executive and his legal advisors worked closely together to shape their response.

---

[317] Singel, M.S. (1988, March 4). Good grades for crisis reaction, *Pittsburgh Post-Gazette*.

[318] Holmes. op cit.

Hall also made himself extraordinarily available during the crisis, personally contacting the State Governor and other officials as well as holding regular media conferences. While the company decided against press releases because the situation was evolving so rapidly, I am sure that in today's environment the CEO would have maintained a high social media presence.

Although the evolution of social media has dramatically altered the method of communication in a crisis, the basics remain the same and lessons about liability and responsibility are virtually unchanged.

Sadly, one other thing also remains unchanged in some cases. Take the Lieutenant-Governor's hopeful optimism about the oil industry learning a lesson from the Ashland example. This proved to be not entirely warranted. Just over a year later, in March 1989, came the notorious Exxon Valdez oil spill disaster which suggested even the most fundamental lessons about responsibility had not been learned. After the oil tanker Exxon Valdez crashed into rocks in Prince William Sound, on the southeast coast of Alaska, polluting miles of sensitive coastline, the Justice Department indicted Exxon on criminal charges. CEO Lawrence Rawl responded:

> *"They almost act as if it was some conspiracy of ours to foul up that Sound. In the future, corporations are going to conclude that it just doesn't pay to take responsibility and make restitution. Instead companies will say, 'Let everyone else clean it up and sue us and see if they can collect'."* [319]

Fortunately, most corporations have not reached that conclusion and do not say that. However Exxon itself spent almost 20 years resisting compensation litigation (You can read more details of this famous case in Chapter Nine).

---

[319] Behar, R. (1990, March 26). Exxon strikes back. *Time*
http://content.time.com/time/magazine/article/0,9171,969673,00.html

The Huntington Beach Disaster

While the *Exxon Valdez* spill in Alaska still appears in textbooks and journal articles everywhere as an example of what not to do, there is another notable spill which you likely may not even have heard of. When it comes to discussion about liability and responsibility in the face of a crisis, there are few better examples of how to do the right thing than the Huntington Beach oil spill, which massively polluted part of the coast of Southern California.

It deserves to be remembered because it's a case which gives you truly valuable lessons in how a company should respond.

In February 1990, the vessel *American Trader,* chartered to BP, was attempting to dock at an offshore terminal when it ran over its own anchor, rupturing the hull and leaking almost half a million gallons of crude oil onto the popular Huntington Beach, in Orange County, causing heavy pollution along 15 miles of the coast.

In a true display of executive leadership, BP America Chairman James Ross flew straight to the scene. At a memorable media conference, standing on the polluted beach, Ross told reporters:

> *"Our lawyers tell us it's not our fault, but we feel like it's our fault and we are going to act like it's our fault."*[320]

Risk expert Peter Sandman described this answer as superb.

> *"The lawyers went home saying, 'Thank God he said it's not our fault.' The defense was preserved. But millions of viewers who saw the sound bite on television said to themselves, 'I can't believe the CEO of an oil company is taking moral responsibility for a spill.' Most importantly, residents of the Huntington Beach area were inclined to forgive the company – and six months after the spill BP's*

---

[320] Cited in Sandman, P. M. (2002, July 11). *Lawyers and outrage management.* Column published at https://www.psandman.com/col/lawyers.htm

reputation in Southern California had rebounded to better than pre-spill levels."[321]

It was certainly an unexpected statement from the leader of any major company. Yet by his words CEO Ross unambiguously set the tone for the company's response. In just over two hours, oil skimming vessels were on the scene and the company's crisis team was in the air. Within 24 hours, there were 36 BP technical specialists on-site. In addition, more than 100 people from other big oil companies took part in the spill response, and BP trained and equipped volunteer bird-rescuers who became some of the company's strongest supporters in the community.[322]

It was later reported that BP spent $35 million removing foamy oil and tar balls in a five-week clean-up of beaches which was "considered one of the most successful clean-ups in history."[323]

The outcome was strikingly evident. The *Los Angeles Times* ran a story praising the company's efforts under the headline; "After spill, BP soaks up oil and good press."[324] It later ran a front-page photograph of the company's crisis manager fulfilling his promise to be the first to swim at the cleaned-up beach.

But it could have been very different. Ross later told an oil industry conference in Texas:

[321] Sandman ibid

[322] Jaques, T. (2015, April 23). Lessons from an oil spill: How BP gained - and then lost - our trust. *The Conversation.* https://theconversation.com/lessons-from-an-oil-spill-how-bp-gained-then-lost-our-trust-40307

[323] Cone, M. (1993, February 7). 3 years later no-one has taken blame for oil spill. *Los Angeles Times.* https://www.latimes.com/archives/la-xpm-1993-02-07-me-1646-story.html

[324] Woodyard, C. (1990, February 20). After spill, BP soaks up oil and good press. *Los Angeles Times.* https://www.latimes.com/archives/la-xpm-1990-02-20-fi-974-story.html

"Responsibility is not the same as liability. In the case of the Huntington Beach spill, BP was prepared from the outset to assume responsibility for a swift and well-supported response... We took the view that the early hours of the crisis were too precious to waste on bickering or waiting for someone else to be the 'responsible' party... You will not be surprised to hear that a company's public acceptance of responsibility where liability is unclear gives its legal counsel some concern. But in these circumstances, lawyers can be quick to focus on the immediate damage and too slow to perceive the larger political and regulatory costs."[325]

This was a brilliantly succinct assessment of the situation, which still resonates today. Responsibility is indeed not the same as liability. Time surely is too precious to be wasted on bickering, And his comment that such public acceptance of liability would give the lawyers "some concern" was a masterly understatement.

Contrast this outcome with another major spill involving the same company twenty years later, in April 2010, when fire destroyed the oil rig *Deepwater Horizon* and oil polluted the coast of the Gulf of Mexico. BP boss Tony Hayward's plea that he would "like to get his life back" came to personify that catastrophe and his name will likely remain for decades in the pantheon of bona fide management disasters.

Lessons learned

The Huntington Beach oil spill gives you a powerful example of doing the right thing, with CEO Ross showing outstanding leadership from the top, as well as courage and insight.

---

[325] Ross, J. (1993). Crisis management: Four lessons learned. In J. Fay (Ed.), *Encyclopaedia of Security Management* (pp. 207–211). Newton: Butterworth Heinemann. Mr. Ross' comments were reported from an address to the American Petroleum Institute in Dallas, Texas in September 1990.

He personally drove the response on the ground, which was rapid and comprehensive, and he also explained amazingly frankly his reasons for openly acting against legal advice, framing those reasons so as to keep everyone on-side.

But the critical lesson from the case is that he never lost sight of the big picture and he was able to balance the need to take action against the possibility of legal repercussions.

The reason the overall outcome was so positive was not primarily because BP handled the clean-up well, which it undoubtedly did, but because the company leadership handled the apology and communication so well – and did so without any apparent increase in liability.

A contrast in responses to a major oil spill				
Major oil spills are necessarily high profile, high risk crises. Sometimes they are best remembered not for what happened but for what was said by the CEO				
Company	**Location**	**Date**	**CEO**	**Statement**
Ashland	Floreffe, PA	1988	John Hall	"If we made mistakes we need to stand up and admit them." [326]
Exxon	Prince William Sound, AK	1989	Lawrence Rawl	"The thing that has bothered me most is not the castigation, the difficulties or the long hours; it's been the embarrassment. I hate to be embarrassed, and I am." [327]
BP	Huntington Beach, CA	1990	James Ross	"Our lawyers tell us it's not our fault, but we *feel like* it's our fault and we are going to *act like* it's our fault." [328]
BP	Deepwater Horizon, Gulf of Mexico	2010	Tony Hayward	"The Gulf of Mexico is a very big ocean. The amount of volume of oil and dispersant we are putting into it is tiny in relation to the total water volume." [329]

Setting the Tone

While these oil spill cases are not recent, they remain a valuable resource because they provide an unusual opportunity to compare similar events and to make your own judgement about how the respective CEOs responded.

However, it's not necessary to go so far back to find good examples of the CEO setting the right tone in a crisis. This critical management role has also been shown more recently, though not always reported to the same extent, and social media has shifted the frame for analysis.

For instance, consider the candid statement from Walmart boss Bill Simon after a Walmart truck crashed into the back of a limousine in early 2014, killing American comedian James McNair and seriously injuring comedy star Tracy Morgan:

> *"This is a tragedy and we are profoundly sorry that one of our trucks was involved. The facts are continuing to unfold. If it's determined that our truck caused the accident, Walmart will take full responsibility. We can't change what happened, but we will do what's right for the family of the victim and the survivors in the days and weeks ahead."[330]*

Simon was widely praised for his prompt and unequivocal response, though his leadership was somewhat undermined when Walmart lawyers lodged a statement

[326] Ansberry op cit

[327] Behar op cit

[328] Sandman op cit

[329] Webb, T. (2010, May 14). BP Boss admits job on the line after Gulf oil spill. *The Guardian.* https://www.theguardian.com/business/2010/may/13/bp-boss-admits-mistakes-gulf-oil-spill

[330] Wile, R. (2014, June 8). Walmart confirms one of its trucks was involved in the Tracy Morgan accident. *Business Insider.* https://www.businessinsider.com.au/walmat-statement-on-tracy-morgan-accident-2014-6

in court which unhelpfully argued the passengers' injuries were caused "in whole or in part by their failure to wear suitable seat belts."

A comparable response arc occurred following the fatal crash of a Delta airliner, after which high-ranking company employees showed great respect for the survivors and families of victims, sending flowers, visiting and attending funerals. Their response was similarly widely praised and was said to have avoided many lawsuits. But when cases reached court, cross-examination of some plaintiffs was so brutally personal, one paper called the company a Jekyll and Hyde monster. Airline executives were understandably upset over the negative publicity, but their lawyers insisted they had to introduce relevant information "to fight money-hungry personal-injury lawyers."[331] It was a stark example of reputational achievement undone by subsequent legal strategy.

Another executive whose response exemplified the principle of doing what's right – also following an air disaster – was Tony Fernandes, owner and CEO of AirAsia, after flight QZ8501 crashed into the Java Sea in December 2014 during a flight from Surabaya in Indonesia to Singapore, killing all 162 souls aboard.

Speaking to reporters after meeting relatives of the passengers and crew of the downed plane he said:

> *"I am the leader of this company, and I have to take responsibility. That is why I am here. I am not running away from my obligations. Even though we don't know what's wrong, the passengers were on my aircraft and I have to take responsibility for that."[332]*

He also declared that compensation to victims' families would be at the industry standard, which is higher than the level legally required by an airline based in Malaysia and a flight operating out of Indonesia.

---

[331] Cited in Fearn-Banks, K. (2016). *Crisis Communications: A Casebook Approach*. (5th edtn) New York: Routledge, Taylor and Francis.
[332] Stevenson, A. and Gough, N. (2014, December 31). Air Asia's Chief responds to crisis with quick compassion. *New York Times*.
https://www.nytimes.com/2015/01/01/business/international/airasia-tony-fernandes-responds-to-crisis-with-quick-compassion.html

Like the previous generation of executives, Simon at Walmart and Fernandes at AirAsia help demonstrate that a strong leader *can* balance the legal and communication needs to help Crisis Proof the organization. However, one of my first experiences with a genuine crisis involved another airline, and that turned into a legal nightmare.

As a very young reporter I was on duty in the newsroom on the night in November 1979 when an Air New Zealand aircraft on a sightseeing flight over Antarctica lost radio contact. It had crashed into Mount Erebus, the world's southernmost active volcano, killing all 257 aboard, including the mother of one of my best friends.[333]

The detail of this disaster is beyond our scope here, except to say that the airline was accused of being less than open with the subsequent official inquiry. Today I always advise executives that one of the most obvious statements to make after a crisis is "We are cooperating fully with the authorities." It conveys responsibility and reassurance, even though you typically don't have much choice.

But in the case of the Mount Erebus Disaster, the Royal Commissioner heading the investigation controversially asserted that airline executives had engaged in a conspiracy to whitewash the inquiry, covered up evidence and lied to investigators, and he famously claimed they had told "an orchestrated litany of lies." The Commissioner's damning conclusions were later challenged legally, but the CEO's reputation was destroyed. It might all seem like a long time ago, but it's a stark reminder to current managers that the greatest reputational risk from a crisis is not necessarily the event itself but the way it is handled.

It's also a reminder that the tone set from the top in a crisis is not always positive. In November 2019, Westpac, the second largest bank in Australia, was accused by regulators of failing to report more than 23 million transactions which may have breached anti-money-laundering laws, including some which allegedly facilitated child sex exploitation in the Philippines.

---

[333] Brettkelly, S. (2019, November 27). Erebus and the "orchestrated litany of lies." *Stuff.com*. https://www.stuff.co.nz/national/the-detail/117731099/the-detail-legal-clarification-over-the-orchestrated-litany-of-lies-phrase

It was a massive reputational crisis and Westpac Chairman Lindsay Maxsted issued what one media outlet called a groveling apology:

> *"As a board, and as individuals, we are devastated by the issues raised by AUSTRAC in its recent statement of claim. The notion that any child has been hurt as a result of any failings by Westpac is deeply distressing and we are truly sorry. The board unreservedly apologises."*[334]

However, it was then reported that bank CEO Brian Hartzer held a private meeting with his senior managers and told them the scandal "was not playing out as a high street issue." It was claimed he said: "For people in mainstream Australia going about their daily lives, this is not a major issue so we don't need to overcook this."[335]

He added that he was "very sorry" that they would have to cancel staff Christmas parties. Next day CEO and Chairman both lost their jobs.

Given that the company lost NZ$8 billion (about US$5 billion) in share value and faced up to NZ$1 billion (about US$600 million) in fines, it was extraordinary that the CEO should privately tell his managers that it was not a major issue and urge them to concentrate on achieving their mortgage targets.

As Denny Lynch, Senior Vice President of Communications at Wendy's, once said:

---

[334] Carey, A. (2019, November 22). Banking board issues grovelling apology to Australians, vowing change. *News.com.*
https://www.news.com.au/finance/business/banking/banking-board-issues-grovelling-apology-to-australians-vowing-change/news-story/05637c000b410a227799c310077eeafe

[335] Moore, C. (2019, November 26). Tone-deaf $5million-a-year Westpac boss resigns. *Daily Mail.*
https://www.dailymail.co.uk/news/article-7724711/Embattled-Westpac-boss-Brian-Hartzer-QUITS.html

"If it's not important to senior management, it will not be important to middle management or line management at all."[336]

Could you do the right thing?

Imagine this: A worker in your factory has been killed when he was dragged into a machine. The corporate lawyer says the accident occurred after the man removed a safety guard because he found that made the process easier. He had been verbally warned not to remove the guard and a notice was posted which said the safety guard must be in place at all times. The lawyer recommends that you express regret about the loss of life but state that it would be inappropriate to comment further until after the official investigation.

The communications advisor says the man had an unblemished 20-year work record and leaves behind a widow and three young children. The communicator says the union claims there are reports that the man removed the safety guard to work quicker in an effort to meet management demands for faster production. The communications advisor also recommends you do not mention the safety guard but immediately express sincere sorrow for the fatal accident; say that you take responsibility for the safety of your workers; that you will take whatever action is necessary to prevent it happening again; and that you will

---

[336] Cited in Wheeler, A. (2013), *Designing brand identity.* Hoboken NJ, John Wiley. pg 88.

do everything possible to support the man's
family.

As the CEO how would you judge what's the
right thing do?

Apologizing Without Admitting Liability

Another common area where responsibility and liability can come into conflict in
a crisis is the seemingly simple question: Should we apologize and will
apologizing admit liability? In Chapter Four you read about situations where
apologizing can actually *reduce* liability. Yet those occasions are generally the
exception rather than the rule.

In reality the more likely scenario is where the lawyer is saying: "Let's not
apologize so we can avoid admitting liability," and the communicator is asking:
"Is there a way we can apologize to protect our reputation and not jeopardize our
legal position?" Sadly, this particular discussion can lead to the insincere,
grudging, qualified and often damaging non-apologies I describe in Chapter Five.
For example, "I'm sorry if you were offended" or "I'm sorry you misunderstood
what I said." Of course, the lawyers are not always to blame for such statements,
though it often looks that way. As the Washington DC crisis-legal expert Richard
Levick has said:

> *"A lawyerly press release or public statement is often
> as dangerous as no statement at all. Legal language,
> so vital and appropriate in the court room or in
> contract negotiations, won't help you win cases in
> the court of public opinion during a crisis."[337]*

Before proceeding on this topic, I need to introduce an important distinction.
Apologizing without creating a legal liability is very different from using "weasel
words" to craft a damaging non-apology.

In the first instance the organization involved is genuinely apologetic and trying
to find a way to express that feeling. One commentator described it as:

---

[337] Levick, R. S. (2010). *The Communicators: Leadership in the age of crisis.*
Washington DC: Watershed Press.

260

". . . the conflict between trying to be nice and trying not to incur liability, which occurs in crisis communication in magnified form."[338]

By contrast a typical non-apology often indicates that the organization is not truly apologetic and is not "trying to be nice." (Chapter Five presented some real-life examples to help you learn what not to say in an apology).

"WEASEL WORDS" refers to words used with the intention to mislead or misinform. The term was coined by author Stewart Chaplin in 1900 in the *Century Magazine.*

"Weasel words are words that suck all the life out of the words next to them, just as a weasel sucks an egg and leaves the shell. If you heft the egg afterward it's as light as a feather, and not very filling when you're hungry, but a basketful of them would make quite a show and would bamboozle the unwary."

The term was popularized in 1916 by Colonel (later President) Theodore Roosevelt.[339]

I acknowledge that legal practice varies greatly between countries and jurisdictions, which may have widely different laws and precedent about whether an apology can be admitted as evidence for the plaintiff.

But that discussion is best left to legal textbooks. My focus here is not on courtroom procedure but on how best you can communicate in the aftermath of a crisis.

---

[338] McCord, E. A. (1991). The business writer, the law, and routine business communication: A legal and rhetorical analysis. *Journal of Business and Technical Communication*, 5(2), 173-199

[339] Nordquist, R. (2019, November 4). What is a weasel word? https://www.thoughtco.com/weasel-word-1692604. See also Don Watson's brilliantly funny book *Watson's Dictionary of Weasel Words* (2005, Sydney:Vintage)

For executives it's a classic quandary between legal and communications advice. Your apology may risk incurring a legal liability, while not apologizing may incur public anger and consequent damage to reputation. In fact, the damage may be much greater than just to reputation.

Apologizing without creating liability also poses a challenge in terms of corporate governance. As a company officer you have a legal obligation to act in the interests of creditors and stockholders, not just those who are (or claim to be) adversely affected by the crisis. In other words, while the media and the general public may clamor for an outright apology and admission of guilt, you have a very clear fiduciary responsibility to stockholders.

Navigating this dilemma has led to the concept of the "safe apology" or "partial apology" or the "no-admission apology," where you may deny guilt while nevertheless expressing remorse that an incident occurred. The basic idea was well expressed by Kathy Fitzpatrick, who is both a qualified attorney and a Professor of Communications in Washington DC:

> *"Before accepting responsibility for a particular act or admitting fault, the spokesperson should consider the potential legal liability attached to such admissions. Regret for the occurrence and consequences of a particular event can be expressed without accepting responsibility for causing it."* [340]

However, I do need to tell you upfront that the whole concept of the safe apology has been controversial, and some critics assert that it's just an easy way out. In fact one legal expert, writing about apologizing to avoid liability, posed the question "Cynical civility or practical morality?" [341]

The American Jonathan Cohen, (then at Harvard Law School) was an early champion of the concept of a safe apology, which he said offers an avenue for decoupling the issue of apology from the issue of liability, and as such helps to

---

[340] Fitzpatrick, K. R. (1995). Ten guidelines for reducing legal risks in crisis management. *Public Relations Quarterly, 40*(2), 35-38.
[341] Vines,P. (2005). Apologising to avoid liability: Cynical civility or practical morality. *Sydney Law Review, 27*(3).

avoid needless conflict. [342] He added that it also helps to prevent the added insult of refusing to apologize or offering a non-apology, which makes the recipient even more angry.

Cohen suggests, for example, that a linguistic shift from the active to the passive voice – from "I'm sorry for hurting you" to "I'm sorry you were hurt" – can produce very different legal consequences. The former admits one's fault. The other does not.

Examples of safe apologies could include:

- "I'm sorry your leg is broken and I hope you feel better soon" – an expression of sympathy and caring, and not an admission of wrongdoing.
- "I won't do it again" – a commitment simply not to repeat the offending behavior.
- "If I could turn back the clock, I would do things differently" – an admission only that other choices could have been made.

But most importantly for executives responding to a crisis, an apology has to be regarded by *both* sides as sincere and genuine.

Have you ever received a "safe apology?"

Safe apologies have their place, but their effectiveness relies entirely on motivation. Can you remember a personal situation where someone said sorry, but it didn't ring true? Was it an honest attempt to apologize or an effort to avoid a real apology? How did it make you feel? That's what you need to think about before attempting a safe apology after an organizational crisis.

Of course, it's critical to remember that the safe apology doesn't make the issue of liability disappear, and the apology is not an end in itself but is usually part of a broader strategy.

---

[342] Cohen, J. R. (1999). Advising clients to apologize. *Southern California Law Review*, 72, pp 1009-1069

However, a safe apology lets parties talk to one another without the specter of liability overshadowing open discussion. The record shows that far more cases are settled or go nowhere than are litigated. One reason is that lawyers and managers are increasingly likely to have experience with alternative dispute resolution and understand that this is often a wiser course than litigation. Moreover, they increasingly recognize that, when a matter does go to court, the legal system focuses on adjudicating rights rather than on repairing relationships.

On the subject of apologies and liability I was recently struck by a comment from two usually reliable writers: "The risks of making an apology are low and the potential reward is high."[343]

It's a rather bold assertion which oversimplifies the reality, and I suspect would not be very popular in an organization's legal department.

First, no apology is without risk and, if not properly managed, that risk is certainly not low.

Second, I can't simply accept that the potential reward of an apology is high. Apologies are most often used to make the best of a bad situation, to minimize damage, and to recover whatever reputation remains. It's a mistake to think of that as a reward.

But this questionable statement does bring me back to the challenge the top executive faces when having to judge when and how to apologize; how to seek and weigh well-informed communications and legal advice; and how to balance the legitimate needs of all parties.

It's not about being popular or "trying to be nice." It's about doing the right thing in the overall best interests of the organization and at the same time protecting and maintaining relationships with your many stakeholders, including creditors, stockholders, staff, customers and regulators as well as the perceived victims of whatever has gone wrong.

---

[343] Patel, A. and Reinsch, L. (2003). Companies can apologize: Corporate apologies and legal liability. *Business Communication Quarterly*, 66(1) 9-25.

> It's not about being popular or "trying to be nice." It's about doing the right thing.

Can you apologize on behalf of a brand or an organization without courting fresh legal liability? My answer is absolutely yes. This challenging question has been exhaustively analyzed both by legal and communication experts, and it's very clear that an appropriate apology can not only minimize fresh liability but can in fact reduce claims and reduce the likelihood of being sued.

The overall subject of liability versus responsibility is controversial, and some of the expert opinion is contradictory. Yet I believe it's clear that while apologizing *may* increase legal liability, not apologizing is just about *guaranteed* to increase public anger, victim resolve and even regulatory concern.

Key Takeaways

- Liability and responsibility are not the same and it's crucial to understand the difference.
- "Doing the right thing" doesn't make legal liability go away, but it can protect your reputation.
- To successfully survive a crisis you need to manage all stakeholders, including legal advisors.
- It's okay to make your lawyers nervous, but that's very different from taking unwarranted legal risks.
- Expressing regret for what has happened does not constitute an admission of liability.
- You do have the option of making a "safe" apology but it must be done for the right reasons.
- Apologizing *may* increase your legal liability, but not apologizing is just about *guaranteed* to increase reputational damage.

Questions for Discussion

1. *Doing what's right seems a worthy goal, but who should decide what's right?*
2. *Is the "safe apology" just a way to avoid a genuine apology?*
3. *Was McDonald's right to demolish the store where a mass-shooting took place? Or was it an over-reaction?*
4. *Why is "doing the right thing" in a crisis not the same as "trying to be nice"?*
5. *What's important about the difference between being liable in a crisis and being responsible?*

Chapter Nine

Marathon Cases:

In for the Long Haul

*Lawsuit: A machine which you go into as a pig
and come out of as a sausage.*

Ambrose Bierce

One of the best-known court cases in literature is *Jarndyce v Jarndyce*, which is central to the Charles Dickens classic novel *Bleak House*. This fictional case has come to be a byword for seemingly interminable legal proceedings which last for years until the parties become exhausted or the funds run out. As Dickens wrote:

> *"Jarndyce and Jarndyce drones on. This scarecrow
> of a case has, over the course of time, become so
> complicated that no man alive knows what it means.
> The parties to it understand it least."*

A similar reality applies to some modern marathon lawsuits where a high-profile brand name gets involved in a legal dispute which seems to go on forever.

Unlike in Jarndyce v Jarndyce the parties involved typically *do* understand the case. Yet the public and the news media scarcely remember exactly what it was all about. However they do remember the name of the brand or the big corporation... and they are hardly ever cheering for the corporate giant to win. As a result, marathon cases make reputation particularly vulnerable.

This is the third chapter devoted to more in-depth review of situations where lawyers and communicators often come into conflict, in this case focusing on crises involving prolonged legal proceedings

This chapter will help you to:

- Identify the behavioral bias which encourages individuals and companies to persist in the face of likely failure.
- Avoid litigation by exhaustion, where organizations try to use their legal muscle to prevail.
- Learn from "the most expensive and disastrous public relations exercise ever mounted by a multinational company."
- Communicate the rising importance of social media to your organization with a case where online intervention took just days to resolve a seven-year dispute.
- Persuade others that the courts are generally no place to resolve community issues.

Marathon court cases are often about complex matters involving fraud, or financial disputes, or family arguments – like the record-breaking child custody case in Britain which was finally resolved in 2014 after 13 years of legal proceedings.[344] Or the Australian inheritance dispute which was eventually resolved in 2010 an extraordinary 42 years after the person died without a will.[345]

Such cases remind you that the legal system is basically designed to protect the public and advocate for victims. But when it comes to big corporate cases, the public belief is that most companies and large organizations are not victims, even though management might tend to feel, think and attempt to act like victims. The simple truth is that corporations generally have the power, the money, the resources and the influence, and public perception is that corporations probably caused the problem in the first place. [346]

It's no surprise that most often the public and other stakeholders – whose opinions and impressions drive reputation – remember the headline-grabbing initial accusations at the outset of proceedings involving some big corporation, but don't know or much care about the ultimate outcome.

Take the case of alleged quality issues in Toyota vehicles which dragged on through 2009-2011, temporarily damaging Toyota's brand and even diminishing the sales of *other* Japanese carmakers.

After a veritable news media frenzy over "unintended sudden acceleration" of Toyota vehicles – which forced the Japanese CEO to apologize – came the official report that it wasn't a vehicle fault after all.

As I mentioned in Chapter Four about why you need to apologize, a ten-month investigation by The National Highway Traffic Safety Administration (NHTSA),

---

[344] Carter, C. (2014, June 13). Family court case spanning 13 years is 'longest case' in history, judge says. *Telegraph*. https://www.telegraph.co.uk/news/uknews/law-and-order/10898906/Family-court-case-spanning-13-years-is-longest-case-in-history-judge-says.html

[345] Arlington, K. (2010, June 28). Justice after 42 years in court marathon. *Sydney Morning Herald*. https://www.smh.com.au/national/justice-after-42-years-in-court-marathon-20100627-zc27.html

[346] Lukaszewski, J. E. (1995). Managing litigation visibility: How to avoid lousy trial publicity. *Public Relations Quarterly, 40*(1), 18-24.

with help from NASA, cleared Toyota by announcing that the company's electronic throttle system was not to blame for reported episodes of runaway acceleration, as alleged by safety advocates and some members of Congress.[347]

The Federal safety agency looked at the "black boxes" in dozens of Toyotas and Lexuses whose drivers blamed their crash on unresponsive brakes and runaway acceleration, and found that in nearly all cases the accelerator was at full throttle and the brakes weren't engaged. NHTSA coyly referred to the problem as "pedal misapplication" – in other words the drivers pressed the accelerator and not the brake.

This outcome mirrored work by Toyota's own engineers on over 2,000 cars, which similarly found human error in most cases. Meantime, Toyota had recalled millions of cars at a cost of billions of dollars, paid nearly $50 million in fines and suffered a massive fall in its share price.

It's true that the NHTSA report came under attack in some subsequent court cases, but the lesson for lawyers and communicators alike is that being right – and proven right long after the event – is little defense against a high-profile allegation of wrongdoing.

A report I wrote at the time was headlined: "Toyota was right. But who cares?"[348]

When the evidence changes

After six years of legal proceedings, Dow Corning agreed to a settlement of $3.4 billion to women who claimed ill heath as result of having silicone-gel breast implants. Soon after the decision in 1998 – the largest ever class action settlement at the time – new scientific

---

347 Abdel-Razzaq, L. (2011, February 7). U.S. Transportation Department says no defect found in Toyota's electronic throttles. *Automotive News*. https://autoweek.com/article/car-news/us-transportation-department-says-no-defect-found-toyotas-electronic-throttles
348 Jaques, T. (2011, March 1). Toyota was right. But who cares? *Managing Outcomes Blog*. https://managingoutcomes.wordpress.com/2011/03/01/toyota-was-right-but-who-cares/

reports began to emerge questioning the basis of the case. By 2010 the AMA Journal of Ethics concluded: "The wave of silicone breast implant lawsuits was largely a result of public opinion and aggressive pursuit of lawsuits by plaintiffs' attorneys – not medical evidence."[349] While the issue remains controversial to this day, a major medical review in 2019 concluded that there is no concrete or evidence-based studies or peer-reviewed data to support the existence of "silicone implant illness."[350]

Considering the Toyota recall and the Dow Corning settlement – both undertaken in the face of massive adverse publicity before the results of new research – do you think the companies made the right decision?

While the Toyota recall provides an important lesson, my focus here is not just on cases where companies found themselves dragged unwillingly into court, but also where lawyers apparently persuaded management to go to court, and then to keep fighting, despite the ongoing cost to reputation.

Behavioral psychologists talk about cognitive biases, which affect the way we think and act. The best known such behaviors are Confirmation Bias – where you look for ways to justify your existing beliefs – and the Placebo Effect – where you believe your health is improving even if your treatment is fake.

Less well known is the Sunk Cost Fallacy, where you irrationally cling to things that have already cost you, not necessarily just money. When you have invested time, money, resources or emotion, it hurts to let go. This aversion to pain can distort better judgement and lead to unwise decisions.

---

[349] Schleiter, K. E. (2010). Silicone Breast Implant Litigation. *AMA Journal of Ethics – Virtual Mentor*. https://journalofethics.ama-assn.org/article/silicone-breast-implant-litigation/2010-05

[350] Rohrich, R.J., Kaplan, J. and Dayan, E. (2019). Silicone Implant Illness: Science versus Myth?. *Plastic Reconstructive Surgery,* 144(1), 98-109.

While this is true of individuals, it's also true of organizations, which may for example persist in spending money to market a product which is known to be uncompetitive, or persist in developing a new product when every test so far shows it doesn't always work.

Imagine a software developer which spends $100 million developing a new platform and it doesn't perform as required. It's too easy to say: "We've spent all this money. If we just invest another $10 million, I'm sure we can get it right."

This same Sunk Cost Fallacy can apply to long-running legal proceedings, where false or misguided optimism in the face of contrary evidence can lead an organization to continue a case even when it is clear to most observers they can never win. Or when the cost of winning will likely far exceed any possible benefit. Or, as in the case of Toyota and Dow Corning, when "winning" comes too late to matter.

I have chosen a handful of cases to help illustrate what happens when organizations find themselves caught up in a prolonged legal strategy where common sense might suggest it's time to back off. Or put another way, when management and lawyers think the case is worth sustaining "for legal reasons" while their communication and marketing professionals are likely arguing that the longer the case continues the greater damage to reputation.

Crisis guru James Lukaszewski asserts that the most significant effect of intense litigation is the combative attitude most senior executives tend to adopt, encouraged, he says, by their litigation counsel. It leads to a mindset of confrontation – "Let's not give in or give up anything" – which he calls *testosterosis*, a fear caused by the realization that not responding to a problem immediately has only made it worse. In turn this causes stalling, a search to find who's really guilty, and refusal to consider all offers of settlement, mediation or negotiation.[351]

This attitude of combativeness, Lukaszewksi warns, causes long-term publicity problems and costly settlements. And every first-year law student learns that when you go to court you get the law, but you don't necessarily get justice. So if you are concerned about your reputation rather than winning, legal action may be the last resort rather than the first option. Consequent long-term publicity

---

[351] Lukaszewski, op cit

problems are never more evident than in marathon cases where so-called "warrior lawyers" persuade management to keep fighting.

Such cases are not common, and I have to go back a few years, but these examples reveal what happens when enthusiasm for litigation outweighs what might be a less risky strategy.

Litigation by Exhaustion

One such marathon case – settled in 2015 after six years and over $1 million in legal fees – was the aftermath of the tragic death of an employee at a Walmart store in Valley Stream, New York, when a surging crowd trying to get into a Black Friday sale crushed the unfortunate man to death.

The following year Walmart agreed to a nearly $2 million settlement with Nassau County to avoid criminal prosecution and to compensate customers injured in the stampede. They also agreed to adopt new crowd management controls in all Walmart stores in New York State.

But the company elected to fight a $7,000 fine levied by the Federal Occupational Safety and Health Administration (OHSA) for failing to take adequate steps to protect employees from danger because of crowd trampling.

Walmart said it was committed to learning from the incident and making stores safe for staff and customers but argued they should not be held accountable for a standard which didn't exist at the time. Company spokesman David Tovar explained:

> *"The citation has far-reaching implications for the retail industry that could subject retailers to unfairly harsh penalties on future sales promotions."*[352]

It's always risky when companies claim to be acting on a matter of principle, and Walmart dug in for what became a marathon of court proceedings and endless appeals. It was reported that Walmart filed 20 motions and responses totaling nearly 400 pages, and made so many demands on OHSA officials that over one

---

[352] Greenhouse, S. (2010, July 6). Walmart fighting $7,000 fine in trampling case. *New York Times*. https://www.nytimes.com/2010/07/07/business/07walmart.html

five month period the case took up 17 per cent of available attorney hours in the Department's New York office, consuming the equivalent of five full-time lawyers.[353]

All over a $7,000 citation and a claimed legal principle.

Finally, after nearly six years, and more than $1 million spent in attorney fees, in March 2015 Walmart agreed to pay the $7,000 fine.

With no apparent sense of irony, spokesman Randy Hargrove said Walmart didn't want the matter to continue to drag on.

> *"With the likelihood that this matter would not conclude for a long time, we've decided to put it behind us and withdraw our appeal."[354]*

I presume this statement was a case of putting the best possible complexion on a given set of not-so-good facts, though saying they didn't want the case to drag on after it had already taken nearly six years does seem to stretch credulity.

Another example of litigation by exhaustion – though on a much larger scale – is the notorious Exxon Valdez compensation case.

There's scarcely a crisis management book in the last 30 years which doesn't reference the Exxon Valdez oil spill disaster. The focus is typically on Exxon's tardy media relations; the CEO's lack of visibility; or the natural beauty of Prince William Sound on the southeast coast of Alaska, where 11 million gallons of crude oil spilled when the giant tanker ran aground in March 1989.

However, much less attention is paid to the prolonged and painful legal process to secure compensation for the local fishermen, Alaska natives, local businesses and others whose livelihoods were destroyed by what was then the largest oil spill in American history.

---

[353] Greenhouse, ibid

[354] Mason-Draffen, C. (2015, March 19). Walmart drops $1 million fight against $7,000 fine in Valley Stream trampling death. *Newsday*. https://www.newsday.com/business/walmart-drops-1m-fight-in-trampling-death-of-jdimytai-damour-against-7-000-fine-in-valley-stream-1.10084693

Five years after the spill, a court in Alaska awarded more than 32,000 plaintiffs the sum of $5 billion, which was roughly equivalent to Exxon's annual profit at the time. Lawyers for Exxon then launched what one expert later called "scorched earth litigation" to reduce the company's liability, seemingly without regard for damage to Exxon's reputation.

Ten years after the spill the Ninth Circuit Court of Appeals reduced the award from $5 billion to $2.5 billion, but the fight was far from over. Exxon lawyers filed more than 60 petitions and appeals, sought 23 time-extensions and filed more than 1,000 motions, briefs, requests and demands.[355]

And in 2008, 19 years after the disaster, the US Supreme Court overturned the $2.5 billion award and reduced it to $507.5 million. By comparison Exxon had just reported a record-breaking profit of $40 billion, then the largest annual profit in US corporate history. The *Seattle Times* calculated that the reduced award was equivalent to about 12 hours of sales for Exxon. [356]

The Supreme Court decision brought an end to one of America's longest running class action lawsuits but it certainly wasn't the outcome many had hoped for. In fact more than 3,000 claimants had died while waiting.

The first payments to plaintiffs began to flow in November 2008, but Exxon did indeed keep fighting, appealing against a further $407 million in interest payments and $70 million in costs. It was only in December 2009 that the company finally abandoned their last appeal.

Lessons learned

Litigation by exhaustion is ugly – even when there is a principle at stake, as Walmart argued.

We'll never know whether it was the Walmart legal department or the communications people who finally got management to call it all off. And we'll never know whether the eventual decisive factor was

---

[355] Mapes, L.V. (2008, June 26). Supreme Court drastically cuts payments for plaintiffs in Exxon Valdez oil spill. *Seattle Times.* https://www.seattletimes.com/seattle-news/supreme-court-drastically-cuts-payouts-for-plaintiffs-in-exxon-valdez-oil-spill/

[356] Mapes, ibid.

the on-going reputational damage, or simply the endless drain on resources.

By contrast – from my perspective as a non-lawyer – the drawn-out Exxon campaign to limit its financial liability does not appear to turn on any specific legal principle.

I'd rather leave it to a genuine legal expert – Law Professor William Rodgers of the University of Washington – to draw a conclusion about the case. He told the Seattle Times:

"Crime pays, and environmental crime pays really well. I am sure they [Exxon] are sitting down and having a toast of the town. The other lesson they have learned is that scorched-earth litigation pays. Just keep fighting, making up issues."[357]

If Professor Rogers is correct that it shows crime pays, it seems like a sad reflection on the respective roles of lawyers and communicators that a giant corporation was able to use its muscle to minimize compensation for victims of its wrongdoing.

As Professor Rogers suggested, the company and its lawyers were most likely pleased at saving so much money over the course of the marathon case. But it came at the cost of 20 long years of continuous legal wrangling and damaging high profile publicity which I believe – combined with the oil spill crisis itself – will tarnish the Exxon brand for a generation.

And if you think I'm overstating that long-lasting impact, consider the fact that as recently as January 2020, Harvard law students staged on an-campus protest against the recruitment efforts of a legal firm which had represented ExxonMobil in a case about the oil company's environmental policies.[358]

---

[357] Mapes, ibid

[358] Holden, E. (2020, January 16). Harvard law students ramp up protest against ExxonMobil climate firm. *The Guardian.* https://www.theguardian.com/business/2020/jan/15/harvard-law-students-protest-firm-representing-exxon-climate-lawsuit

When Public Health and Profits Collide

A marathon case which involved much more than just money arose over the delivery of AIDS drugs in developing countries.

It would be naïve to believe that pharmaceutical companies exist solely to benefit mankind. Like all commercial organizations they have a legal obligation to act in the interests of shareholders.

At the same time this ground-breaking case vividly demonstrates what happens when profit and reputation clash in a very high-profile and very public way.

The British company GlaxoSmithKline (GSK) pioneered the development of anti-retroviral drugs to combat AIDS. But the drugs which came onto the market were expensive and out of the reach of many people in sub-Saharan Africa, where AIDS had reached epidemic proportions.

GSK and other companies agreed to reduce the cost in some countries, but it was a step too far when South African President Nelson Mandela (whose eldest son died from AIDS) signed a law allowing parallel imports of cheap copies – or what the big drug-makers call "bootleg generics."

Ultimately 40 drug companies launched a joint legal action to sue the South African Government, arguing that the new provision was unconstitutional.

From the industry point of view the case was about protecting patent rights and about the risk that the South African move could cause a "domino effect" in other countries or could spread to other classes of drugs.

For its part the South African perspective was simple and compelling. As Health Minister Dr Nkosazana Zuma said:

> *"I think the lives of our people override everything else. We are not intending to bust any patents. We're not intending to break any treaties. All we want to do is to give health services to the people who are poor in this country, and to the people who have been denied those health services for centuries."[359]*

While the various drug-makers were headquartered in a number of different countries, a leading supporter of legal action against South Africa was the US Government, which sided firmly with big business in support of patent rights, global trade treaties and the rule of law.

However, the case became a rallying point for AIDS activists, the civil rights movement and a range of critics aligned against what they characterized as greedy and immoral pharmaceutical companies making obscene profits from the misery of sick people.

Opposition to the lawsuit gathered support from the European Union, WHO, UNICEF, the World Bank, France's National AIDS Council and many others. And with an American national election looming, opposition also developed within the US Congress. Vice President Al Gore, for instance, who had been actively involved in trying to persuade South Africa to give in, faced noisy disruption of his election meetings. Finally, the US Government relented and switched its position, leaving the drug-makers virtually alone.

The *Wall Street Journal* then posed a particularly pertinent question:

> *"Can the pharmaceuticals industry inflict any more damage on its ailing public image? Well, how about suing Nelson Mandela?"[360]*

---

[359] Fisher, W. W. and Rigamonti, C. P. (2005, February 10). The South African AIDS Controversy: A case study in patent law and policy. *Harvard Law School*.
https://cyber.harvard.edu/people/tfisher/South%20Africa.pdf

[360] Cooper, H., Zimmerman, R. and McGinley L. (2001, March 2). Patents pending: AIDS epidemic traps drug firms in a vice, Treatment vs profits. *Wall Street Journal*.
https://www.wsj.com/articles/SB983487988418159849

While Mandela himself had by then retired, the classic conflict between the law and reputation remained.

Drug companies and reputation

A Gallup poll in late 2019 showed the pharmaceutical industry is now the most poorly regarded industry in Americans' eyes, ranking last on a list of 25 industries that Gallup tests annually.[361] Big Pharma pushed the US Federal government out of bottom place... with the Advertising and Public Relations industry just a few spots better.

A year earlier the Reputation Institute released the reputation scores of 22 international pharmaceutical companies, rated across products and services, innovation, workplace, governance, citizenship, leadership, and financial performance.[362] GSK came in second to last, just ahead of Pfizer. Sanofi topped the rankings.

As support ebbed away, and with the case heading to court after three years of reputational damage, the *Wall Street Journal* captured this management struggle.

---

[361] McCarthy, J. (2019, September 3). Big Pharma Sinks to the Bottom of U.S. Industry Rankings. *Gallup*.
https://news.gallup.com/poll/266060/big-pharma-sinks-bottom-industry-rankings.aspx?

[362] Hu, C. (2018, June 19). These are the most -- and least -- reputable drug companies in the world. *Business Insider*.
https://www.businessinsider.com.au/pharmaceutical-company-reputation-rankings-2018-6?r=US&IR=T

"Many drug-company executives privately say they wish the lawsuit – and the Scrooge-like picture it paints of their industry – would disappear. But publicly the companies say they're going forward because the South African law strikes at the heart of their most precious commodity: patents."[363]

Just weeks later, in April 2001, with their reputations plunging, GSK and the other companies dropped the lawsuit. Praise for the decision came from former President Mandela and UN Secretary General Kofi Annan, who had helped broker the deal. But it was undoubtedly a reputational disaster. GSK CEO Jean Pierre Garnier tried to explain the outcome:

"We don't live in a vacuum. We're a very major corporation. We're not insensitive to public opinion. That is a factor in our decision-making. We don't want the public to misunderstand the issues. We have never been opposed to wider access. We have discounted our drugs. We've done everything we could. Frankly, the legislation was the worst distraction. It did not allow us to communicate our message effectively."[364]

Lessons learned

I cannot accept the conclusion of the CEO of GSK that the litigation did not allow them to communicate their message effectively. To me that is not the real lesson of the case. The truth is that this was about corporate legal strategy, not about communicating more effectively.

Harvey Bale, Director General of the Geneva-based Pharmaceutical Trade group argued at the time: "It's never good

---

[363] Cooper et al, op cit.

[364] Swarns, R. L. (2001, April 20). Drug makers drop South Africa suit over AIDS medicine. *New York Times.*
https://www.nytimes.com/2001/04/20/world/drug-makers-drop-south-africa-suit-over-aids-medicine.html

to be embroiled in a suit with your customers."[365] However he insisted that, despite the bad press, the industry must protect its patents.

Bale was certainly right when he said you shouldn't get embroiled in lawsuits with your customers. And he was equally right when he said an industry should protect its patents. But at what cost and within what limits? That's the issue I have raised in several sections of this book.

Even big multinational corporations are not monolithic structures managed by robotic executives. They are made up of real people, who have personal morals and a personal ethical framework, and these people need to make proper judgements between legal and communication advice.

McDonald's and the Decision to Sue

No discussion of corporate legal strategies which backfired spectacularly for a consumer brand would be complete without the notorious McLibel case brought by McDonald's, which Britain's Channel 4 News dubbed "the most expensive and disastrous public relations exercise ever mounted by a multinational company."[366]

Given the rich catalogue of reputational disasters over the years that is a bold claim, but the case has special interest here because of the way it exposed corporate strategy and legal advice, plus the comparison with another case involving the same company 15 years later.[367]

The events and lessons from the McLibel case have featured in scores of articles and even books and documentaries. In brief it began after an activist group called London Greenpeace (not part of Greenpeace International) published a pamphlet

---

[365] Cooper et al, op cit.

[366] Cited in Kuszewski, J. (2010, July 6). McLibel: Reputation damage writ large. *Ethical Corporation*. http://www.ethicalcorp.com/supply-chains/mclibel-reputation-damage-writ-large

[367] Adapted from Jaques, T (2016). *Crisis proofing: How to save your company from disaster*. Melbourne: Oxford University Press.

titled "What's wrong with McDonald's? Everything they don't want you to know."

The pamphlet made some highly critical assertions about management practices at McDonald's and about its food. The fast-food giant threatened legal action against five individuals who were distributing it and three quickly buckled and apologized. But, to the company's apparent surprise, Helen Steel and David Morris (often referred to as "The *McLibel* Two") held firm.

McDonald's and its legal team made the fateful decision to file a lawsuit, and under Britain's famously strict libel laws, defendants are required to prove the truth of their allegations.

What ensued was the longest court trial in English history, which lasted for 313 days spread over two-and-a-half years – from July 1994 to December 1996 – during which the two virtually penniless defendants represented themselves against the legal might of the multinational. McDonald's executives spent months being forced to defend the company's practices in open court, with their sometimes painful explanations enthusiastically reported by news media around the world.

At the end of the marathon trial the judge upheld some of the statements made in the pamphlet, so the two activists claimed partial victory. But His Honour also found that other claims made were defamatory, so McDonald's also claimed victory.

When the judge ordered the two defendants to pay £60,000 in damages (about US$75,000), they promptly said they had no money – and even if they did have the money, they had no intention of paying. The damages were later reduced to £40,000 (about US$52,000) but McDonald's said it would not pursue payment and that the issue was never about the money.

From the perspective of protecting reputation it was the right decision not to pursue payment. But to claim the case was never about the money is a pretty remarkable statement given that McDonald's own legal costs were estimated at £10 million (about US$13 million).

From the public record it appears the company never admitted it was a disastrous mistake. However, more than a decade later the company's UK management conceded:

"It isn't a decision we would make today. We learnt from our experience and understand why it is so often used as a CSR case study." [368]

Would social media have made a difference?

While the McLibel case remains relevant today, it took place before the rise of the internet and digital communication.

Although the proceedings received massive publicity via traditional news sources, what difference might social media have made to the case? Do you think McDonald's would have pursued the same legal strategy?

A key question of course is whether McDonald's did in fact learn from their experience, as they claimed.

Fast forward about 15 years to the small settlement of Tecoma, 35km east of Melbourne, Australia, in the foothills of the Dandenong Ranges.

Local residents objected to the proposed construction of a McDonald's outlet in their town and picketed the site, later staging a sit-in on the roof of an old building which was due for demolition to make way for the store.

While community concern about a proposed local fast-food outlet is not unusual, in this case the company went to court to obtain an injunction to keep the protesters away so that work could proceed.

Significantly, McDonald's then decided to pursue legal action, not against the protest group, but against eight named individuals for "wrongly interfering with McDonald's use and enjoyment of the McDonald's land." The company demanded

---

[368] Kuszewski, op cit.

unspecified damages from the so-called "Tecoma Eight" for delays to the construction of the controversial development.[369]

In an affidavit filed with the court in 2013, McDonald's claimed that for each day the restaurant was not operating the company was losing an estimated $10,000 in sales, that "halted construction costs" of $13,000 a week were incurred when workers went out in sympathy, and that security guards at the site were costing $55,600 a week.

While community protests against the development had been continuing for years, this provocative legal action escalated the level of concern, and triggered headlines such as:

> *"McDonald's case against 'Tecoma Eight' is 'thuggish, bullying'." (The Age)[370]*

> *"David confronts Goliath in yellow overalls." (Red Flag)[371]*

> *"Maccas Tecoma stoush could slime brand, expert tells global HQ." (Crikey)[372]*

Four of the Tecoma Eight even flew to Chicago to present an online petition with more than 90,000 signatures to the company's chief executive, Don Thompson. They also took out a full-page protest advertisement in the company's hometown newspaper, the *Chicago Tribune*, and placed 30 inflatable kangaroos at the front of a McDonald's outlet in the city as a publicity stunt.

---

[369] Russell, M (2013, August 27). McDonald's case against 'Tecoma Eight' is 'thuggish, bullying'. *The Age*. https://www.theage.com.au/national/victoria/mcdonalds-case-against-tecoma-eight-is-thuggish-bullying-20130827-2sntu.html

[370] Russell, ibid

[371] Gibson, J. (2013, September 9). David confronts Goliath in yellow overalls (2013, September 9). *Red Flag*. https://redflag.org.au/article/david-confronts-goliath-yellow-overalls

[372] Crook, A. (2013, September 16). Maccas Tecoma stoush could slime brand, expert tells global HQ *Crikey*. https://www.crikey.com.au/2013/09/16/maccas-tecoma-stoush-could-slime-brand-expert-tells-global-hq/

Protest spokesman Garry Muratore was stating the blindingly obvious when he said: "This is a PR battle more than a legal battle."[373]

With the well-organized and well-financed protest intensifying, McDonald's apparently saw no option but to beat a retreat and agreed to "quietly drop" all charges against the Tecoma Eight.[374]

However, by the time the Tecoma McDonalds finally opened in April 2014 the brand had endured more than three years of hearings, protests, demonstrations and damaging headlines.

Lessons learned

The reason the McLibel case is important in assessing a legal strategy today is that the real impact had little to do with "winning the case" compared with the prolonged damage to McDonald's reputation.

New anti-McDonald's websites sprang up – some of which are still active – and the pamphlet which previously had been handed out in the thousands in the streets of London was reprinted and downloaded across the world in the millions. It's certainly clear that few people would have received – much less read – the pamphlet had McDonald's not taken the matter to court.

In fact, it was reported that two days after the trial ended, the two defendants were back outside a McDonald's store on London handing out pamphlets.

The McLibel trial's postscript came in 2005, when Steel and Morris won a judgment against the British government in the European

---

[373] Clark, H. (2013, July 19). McDonald's restaurant plan divides Melbourne Community. *The Guardian.*
https://www.theguardian.com/world/2013/jul/19/mcdonalds-melbourne-outlet-protesters-community

[374] Landy, S. (2013, October 30). McDonald's drops legal action against Tecoma protesters. *Herald Sun.*
https://www.heraldsun.com.au/news/law-order/mcdonalds-drops-legal-action-against-tecoma-protesters/news-story/94231196b9ab01492434d5a89779ad26

Court of Human Rights for denying the pair legal aid – as was government policy in libel cases – even though the defendants were of limited means. The court found the two were denied a fair trial and ordered the government to pay the pair £57,000 (about US$70,000) in damages and costs.

At that time McDonald's issued a statement:

> *"Although the so-called McLibel case came to court in 1994, the allegations related to practices in the 80s. The world has moved on since then and so has McDonald's."[375]*

There is no doubt that some McDonald's policies have "moved on," particularly in relation to environmental issues. For example McDonald's was a key player in a campaign spearheaded by Greenpeace to remove rainforest soya from chicken feed in the company's supply chain, and in 2018 the company announced major environmental goals for 2030.[376] These include reduction of greenhouse gases; more efficient use of water; a commitment to sustainable packaging; and minimizing the impacts of its supply chain on deforestation (ironically, addressing some of the issues raised in the contentious Greenpeace London pamphlet).

However, McDonald's seems not to have "moved on" from its willingness to actively exert their legal rights in other areas. Disputes and protests about the construction of fast-food restaurants in culturally or environmentally sensitive locations are not uncommon. Yet we still don't know the reasons behind the strategy they pursued to protect the proposed new outlet in Tecoma. Whether, for instance, McDonald's deliberately chose to "make a

---

[375] Kuszewski, op cit

[376] Siegal, R. (2018, March 22). McDonald's announces major environmental goals for 2030, sending a signal to the restaurant industry. *Washington Post*. https://www.washingtonpost.com/news/business/wp/2018/03/21/mcdonalds-announces-green-initiatives-for-2030-and-sends-a-signal-to-the-restaurant-industry/

stand" on this particular planning objection. And why they elected to take serious legal action against individual protesters.

In that case the legal charges were eventually dropped and the restaurant was built. But the truth is that the courts are generally no place to resolve community issues.

The high reputational and financial cost of a lawsuit which delivers very little legal benefit was equally well illustrated by the notorious case brought by the American supermarket chain Food Lion, which sought $2.4 billion in damages after two undercover ABC reporters got jobs at the company and secretly filmed unsavory food handling practice. A jury award of $5.5 million to the company was eventually reduced to $315,000, and in 1999 – seven years after the case was first launched – the verdict was overturned on appeal and the ABC was ordered to pay just $1 in damages for each reporter for trespass and breaching their duty to be loyal to Food Lion.[377]

Having spent millions of dollars on legal fees and failed public relations offensives in return for just $2 in damages, Food Lion was "left to sift through the remains of its image – arguably a wreckage it had, in large part, heaped on itself."[378]

A Canadian Soap Opera

Just in case you still need convincing of the power of reputation over legal strategy, consider finally a legal dispute which lasted seven years until 2012, when it was suddenly brought to an end in just days by the intervention of social media.

---

[377] Barringer, F. (1999, October 21). Appeals court rejects damages against ABC in Food Lion case. *New York Times.*
https://www.nytimes.com/1999/10/21/us/appeals-court-rejects-damages-against-abc-in-food-lion-case.html

[378] Richards, R. D. and Calvert, C. (2000). Counterspeech 2000: A new look at the old remedy for "bad" speech. *Brigham Young University Law Review*, 2000(2), 553-586.

Canadian Deborah Kudzman left a career in advertising to launch a line of boutique soap under the brand Olivia's Oasis, a name she chose because Olivia was her daughter's name and because her products contained olive oil.

She promptly received a legal letter from Quebec-based drinks giant Lassonde Industries, known for its Oasis brand fruit juices. Lassonde's lawyers demanded she immediately stop using the name, recall all her merchandise from stores, and hand over any profits she had made.

What followed was a nightmare of legal argument and costs for five years until the Quebec Superior Court ruled in favor of the fledgling businesswoman, finding that the trademark claim was groundless. Lassonde was ordered to pay her $25,000 in punitive damages and $100,000 to cover legal costs.[379]

I should point out that at that time Ms. Kudzman's annual revenue was about $250,000 and the juice maker's was more than $700 million.

Responding to the lower court defeat, Lassonde management then made a crucial legal decision which eventually brought them undone. The case had not attracted much media or public attention, and the company lawyers apparently believed they had good grounds to appeal.

And they were right. After a further two years of legal proceedings, in 2012 the Quebec Court of Appeal found in the company's favor, leaving Ms. Kudzman to pay her ballooning legal bills.

We can only assume the company was pretty satisfied with their victory. But when the court finding was reported in a local newspaper the following Saturday, it unleashed a social media storm of indignation that a major drinks manufacturer would go after a boutique soap maker on the grounds that consumers might confuse their products.

The weekend backlash reached a climax when popular TV host Guy Lepage tweeted to his 100,000 followers that he would boycott Oasis drinks to protest the company's treatment of Ms. Kudzman.

---

[379] Hamilton, G. (2012, April 9). Quebec juice maker pays opponent's legal fees after soap ruling gets Twitter in a lather. *National Post*. https://nationalpost.com/news/canada/quebec-juice-maker-pays-opponents-legal-fees-after-soap-ruling-gets-twitter-in-a-lather

To her surprise, she received a visit on Easter Sunday from a Lassonde senior executive offering an undisclosed settlement, sufficient to cover all her legal costs.

> *"This settlement is a direct result of the tremendous support of Quebecers. My family and I will be forever grateful. I'm deeply touched by the support I've received."*

> *"I could never in my wildest dreams have imagined the viral aspect of it... I spent seven years fighting this, and within basically 48 hours, because of the outpouring of support, it was resolved."* [380]

For its part, the company also seemed to express surprise. Chief Operating Officer Jean Gattuso told the media next day:

> *"We are entrepreneurs. We are people who react quickly to situations. We are in business to sell products, and we didn't like our consumers to be angry with us. We didn't like the situation at all, and we reacted."* [381]

Predictably there was no public explanation from the company lawyers, and it was left to company spokesperson, Communications VP Stefano Bertolli, to try to put the best possible interpretation on the whole reputational crisis.

> *"We are happy that our recent attempts to arrive at an agreement have been successful and that we now have an amicable settlement... We never intentionally wanted to harm another Quebec business. It is essential that we protect our*

---

[380] Hamilton ibid
[381] Hamilton ibid

trademarks to avoid the creation of any precedents. [382]

Lessons Learned

The first and obvious lesson is, if you don't want your consumers to be angry with you, then don't give them cause. If you don't like the situation, don't let your strategy lead you into it. And if you don't want to harm another business, don't pursue prolonged legal action against them. Perhaps most importantly, remember that you had seven years of largely unreported litigation during which to think about the possible legal and reputational consequences. It was your choice.

Of all the legal outcomes in this chapter, the resolution of Lassonde case is maybe the most baffling. After fighting for seven years, the company won the case, then virtually overnight walked away from the verdict in what they called an "amicable settlement."

It's possible that the company simply wanted to be "proved right" and that they weren't really too concerned about Ms. Kudzman's little soap venture. But it was a costly exercise which seemed certain to damage the reputation of the enterprise. Moreover, I doubt whether the victors would have been so quick to settle if it hadn't been for the online outrage.

Trademark battles are fairly common, and they generally tend to be largely invisible to consumers. What made the outcome of this case unusual was the social media element and the role of a high-profile influencer. While social media intervention in brand disputes is nothing new, there have been few occasions where that intervention was so rapid and so decisive.

---

[382] Agnes, M. (2012, April 19). One Brand's Social Media Crisis is Another Brand's Social Media Salvation. *Melissa Agnes Blog.* https://melissaagnes.com/one-brands-social-media-crisis-is-another-brands-social-media-salvation/

Hopefully, other lawyers and communicators and senior executives will take heed.

Key Takeaways

- The truth sometimes emerges too late to resolve high-profile legal controversies.
- Lawsuits can greatly increase awareness of otherwise little-known issues.
- Prolonged litigation often generates adverse publicity which far outweighs any possible gain.
- Legal persistence in a case must be balanced against potential reputational damage.
- Doggedly pursuing a "point of principle" may be a costly mistake.
- The rise of social media and changed consumer expectations have dramatically changed the perceived balance of power in marathon cases.

Questions for Discussion

1. *What makes companies persist in marathon lawsuits when their reputation is suffering badly?*
2. *How should you manage a combative "warrior lawyer" trying to persuade you to keep fighting in the face of likely failure.*
3. *Is pursuit of "a matter of principle" through litigation ever worth substantial damage to reputation and business?*
4. *How would the existence of social media have changed some of the classic pre-digital era marathon cases?*
5. *Is Professor William Rogers right to conclude from the Exxon Valdez case that "scorched-earth litigation pays?"*

Chapter Ten
Talking to Global Experts

"Wise people understand the need to consult experts; only fools are confident they know everything."

Ken Poirot

You've probably heard the saying "no one person knows as much as all of us" – and that certainly applies in the contentious world of crisis management.

That's why I decided to interview four internationally known crisis experts so they could share their perspectives based on decades of hands-on experience.

The four experts represent best-practice in the United States, England and South Africa, and bring with them genuine thought-leadership in this field.

This chapter will help you to:

- Appreciate the views of leading international experts.
- Learn from first-hand experience of managing crises.
- Understand the similarities and differences from other parts of the world.
- Recognize how legal and communication challenges operate across national borders.

Who are the experts?

There are many self-proclaimed crisis "experts" who simply are not. Some are practitioners who focus solely on what to say to reporters in a crisis, and how to provide information to the media. That's an important part of the job, but it's only one tactical element of a much broader strategic challenge for top management.

I was a speaker at a crisis conference in Asia a few years ago and one of the other participants was the Communications Manager for the local metro train system. His "crisis" case study was about a recent occasion when some high-profile train delays occurred on the same day they had scheduled newspaper advertisements announcing their good record for on-time operation. Certainly embarrassing for the company, and his presentation was professional and well received by the audience. But it surely wasn't a real organizational crisis.

At the other end of the scale are academic experts on different aspects of crisis management who have unmatched theoretical knowledge of the subject and have something valuable to contribute. They are the respected authors of leading textbooks and journal articles and some have become wise personal friends.

However my focus is not on the academic approach and the development and teaching of theory. Instead my aim is to share with you practical, hands-on experience and advice from experts I know who have been at the front line of some major organizational crises.

They are not academics, though they are sometimes invited to speak in an academic context to classes at university. Instead they are all experienced consultants who have spent decades advising top management about crisis preparedness and crisis response, and each one has built an international reputation as an acknowledged expert and thought leader.

They are **Jonathan Bernstein** in California; **Deon Binneman** in Johannesburg; **Jonathan Hemus** in England; and **Richard Levick** in Washington DC. As well as being in-demand consultants, each of them writes and speaks extensively about crisis management for a national and international audience and one – Richard Levick – is further qualified as a graduate from American University's Washington College of Law (Brief biographies of each appear at the end of this chapter).

When I interviewed them, I started each conversation with the same set of questions, and some key themes began to emerge. I will focus on those so you can hear these experts in their own words, working through the issues facing lawyers, communicators, and executives as they prepare for, and respond to, a crisis. While they can't speak on the record about current or very recent clients and crises, this approach will let you learn from the similarities and differences in their global perspectives.

> "Communication advisors and lawyers will give lots of advice but none of it can give you certainty which leaders are sometimes looking for. If crisis management was easy, we wouldn't see so many failures."
>
> Jonathan Hemus

Is it Real?

Given that my experts have each had decades in crisis management, one obvious topic was whether the perceived conflict between lawyers and communicators is perhaps more talked about than real.

There was consensus that the conflict is indeed still very real. Richard Levick told me; "It's real, of course it's real. You're praying to different gods." And Jonathan Hemus agreed that there are still situations where "stereotypical polarization" is largely true.

Yet all the experts believe the situation has improved over time. Hemus went so far as to argue that it has "definitively changed." When he started work in this area 25 years ago it was what he called "an era of greater deference, and an era of greater trust and less questioning." As a result, a legalistic approach was more in keeping with the way the world was in those days. He believes the situation is now "in balance" and that there are significant numbers of organizations listening to their communicators as much as to their lawyers. In fact, he thinks there are now at least as many, if not more, examples where both parties have matured, become more experienced and savvy about evaluating advice in a crisis.

This lack of familiarity by lawyers with communication matters, and desire to be in control, was echoed by Levick, who argues that there was a time when lawyers didn't know what communication was and didn't want communicators "messing up their cases." But he says those days have changed a lot. "Most lawyers are much more familiar with communications and understand how it is both a sword and a shield."

Similarly, Jonathan Bernstein believes it's becoming less common for CEOs to get conflicting advice. He said ten years ago legal dominated the discussion, but the situation is now more equal, with more and more attorneys "reasonably PR savvy" and understanding the need for litigation-related communication support.

However, Deon Binneman reminded me that change has also reemphasized the importance of legal advice and the need to balance it with communication advice. He said we live in a world where compliance has become one of the biggest industries, where companies not only have to comply with the rules of the land where they are based, but also with international best practice. "That's what makes the roles of the lawyers so huge."

Jonathan Bernstein in his own words

"There are times when I have lost the argument to legal. In the US any allegations of sexual wrongdoing by one student to another or against any student are handled under a law called Title Nine, which means the college is obligated to investigate, not an outside agency.

"There is a well-known college in the northeast US where they had kicked a guy off campus a year earlier because they decided he had assaulted a woman. They were now seriously considering letting him back because of pressure from the guy's father and the guy's father's attorney.

"I was saying there is no way this is going to play out well. And they were ignoring that. I was on a conference call and I interrupted in the middle of the call and said 'I hate to say this, but you've got the wrong PR backing.

What you are going to do could hurt people and I will not participate.' That was the end of that account."

Comment: *The experts agreed that conflict between lawyers and communicators is real, and that is it improving. This is in line with an encouraging academic study in 2001 which was based on interviews with lawyers and communicators. However, unlike the international scope of the lawyer and expert interviews in this book, the earlier study was confined to participants only in the United States. It found that lawyers were much more conciliatory and collaborative than communication professionals thought they were, while communicators believed lawyers were more power-grabbing than they are in fact.*

Our experts support the American researchers' conclusion that the relationship between the two groups is "not completely rosy, but at the same time is perhaps not hopeless".[383]

The Rise of Social Media

My expert panel all identified the rise of social media as a key driver of change. Binneman pointed out that social media has "brought real time into the equation" which means looking to make decisions in the instant, and constant monitoring of what is going on. He stressed that with 24-hour media and the news always on, monitoring is vital, and having your crisis plan and your holding statement in place is crucial because of time constraint.

Discussing its rapid evolution, Levick noted that for some years social media was seen by some as "a substitute for polling for politicians or for a sense of brand equity for a company." Now we have realized that social media is the "meanest place on earth" and that it gives space for five or ten percent of the incredibly unhappy to pontificate and inhibit others from participating. "It turns out that social media sounds a lot more like fingernails on the chalkboard than a reasoned democratic discussion."

---

[383] Reber, B. H., Cropp F. and Cameron, G. T. (2001) Mythic Battles: Examining the lawyer-public relations counsellor dynamic. *Journal of Public Relations Research*, 13(3), 187-218

This point was taken up by Bernstein, who argued that many CEOs are of an age where they may or may not be social media savvy. "One of the interesting things I've seen is the gut response on the part of the CEO to overreact to social media." Sometimes it's important to respond, but Bernstein said the CEO may overreact to a single critical post or a single headline or a single negative review online, and won't take the time to assess the risk posed by the particular person who's criticizing them.

He believes that although such critics are sometimes not very credible, with few followers, more and more CEOs now realize that they need someone who's social media savvy – either on staff or an external consultant – particularly during a crisis, when social media may finish up being one of the main ways, perhaps *the* main way, of communicating.

> "There are now a growing number of CEOs who recognize that lawyers are not always the best, and certainly not the only, people who can give you advice which protects reputation."
>
> Jonathan Hemus

Returning to the impact of the speed of social media on crisis management, Bernstein emphasized that the Internet now means everybody is aware of the details of any crisis as it happens. He described his work for an international travel company which runs global tours: he had to help them upgrade their crisis plan to reflect the fact that their first awareness of most of their types of crises happens on social media. He said just one passenger will post angrily about how unhappy they are but, most crucially, they will typically do that quicker than they will call the company and ask for help.

While that reality is increasingly common, Hemus explained that the rise of social media has had a more specific impact on the role of lawyers. He says there is now a recognition that the former legal approach to crisis management was symptomatic of an era in which big business could control to some extent what was said and how a situation played out.

Social media has helped society and business become much more transparent and news – particularly bad news – has become more prevalent, spreading further and faster than ever before. "In that context a purely legal approach is not fit for purpose. It is not the right tool to deal with the current business world in which organizations are operating."

He said the world in which we now communicate – with its lack of trust and deference, and greater challenge, scrutiny and cynicism – "is not a world in which an organization which wields legal muscle is going to succeed."

*Comment. It's pretty much a cliché these days that the rise of social media has dramatically changed the way we work – and that includes crisis management. But as the experts made clear, it's not just the **speed** of social media, but the way in which it has changed the **nature** of communication in a crisis. For example, how it gives a voice to the disaffected and how it can actually trigger a new organizational crisis – think no further than the online campaign which devastated the company making Kryptonite bike locks (see Chapter Three) or the misjudged "April Fools" tweet by Tesla CEO Elon Musk which cost his shareholders seven per cent of the value of their investments (Chapter Five)*

Reputation and the Two Courts

I have written elsewhere in this book that nothing damages reputation faster or deeper than an issue or crisis mismanaged. Another of the key themes from my expert interviews is how the rise of social media has increased this risk to reputation, as well as the divergence between the court of law and the court of public opinion.

> "Money can always be made. Money can always be replaced. But once your good name goes, everything goes."
>
> Deon Binneman

As Binneman emphasized, any CEO or Board of Directors needs to understand they must address both. He always tells his client that there are two issues which have to be addressed. Dealing with the crisis itself – to put the fire out with a fire extinguisher – that's the reality, while the perception created during the crisis is just as important. "So my advice to any person in any situation is cherish your reputation and integrity – the rest will follow."

Levick offered the example of the Martha Stewart insider trading case[384] where the style icon and her outside legal counsel decided to make it about the legal case rather than about settlement and brand. As a result she lost on both grounds – in the court of law and the court of public opinion. He concluded that their strategy was all about the legal case, and it ultimately didn't serve them well.

Similarly, Bernstein outlined a case involving a client, the Del Webb Corporation, which at one time owned a boat maintenance yard on pristine Lake Powell, on the Arizona-Utah border. When the water level dropped due to a drought, it exposed batteries and broken boat parts on the bottom of the lake where they had been dumped by workers instead of being taken up onto the dock. [385] Bernstein said that in the face of threatened prosecution the company attorney was opposed to doing any defensive communication and just wanted to deal with the legal area. But after he met with the CEO and the lawyer it was agreed to do some limited communication "so long as the counsel gets to see it first." The situation finished up being fairly well handled, and he added that the attorney did a complete turnaround in his understanding of the value of communication, becoming one of his best referral sources.

Hemus also acknowledged the need to balance the two courts. His sense is that CEOs have now recognized the importance of reputation and also recognize the fragility of reputation. He added that "legal steps are not the only, and often not the best, way of protecting reputation." Hemus believes we have now got to the point where the "hard business value of reputation" is understood and recognized.

---

[384] Moffatt, M. (2020, January 30). Martha Stewart's Insider Trading Case. *ThoughtCo*. https://www.thoughtco.com/martha-stewarts-insider-trading-case-1146196

[385] Rawson, W. F. (1993, June 27). Firms Fined for Using Lake as a Dump : Environment: A drought revealed that two companies that cleaned houseboats dumped 100 truckloads of debris. They agree to pay $1.3-million penalty, along with $1-million cleanup. *Los Angeles Times*. https://www.latimes.com/archives/la-xpm-1993-06-27-me-7616-story.html

Deon Binneman in his own words

"Some years ago I was asked by Vodafone to write a reputation risk strategy for Vodacom, which is one of the largest mobile phone players in South Africa and Vodafone had become their majority shareholder.

"I went around the company and soon picked up that their Corporate Affairs Director did not serve on the risk committee. So my question was, how can you manage reputational risk when you are only getting to hear about risk emanating from the risk committee 48 hours later?

"She said she didn't want to have to go to more meetings, but they made it compulsory for her to be part of the risk committee, so that she could understand how they thought about risk and understand risk appetite.

"We closed the loop by getting her on the committee so that she could be involved in thinking about risk and understand risk appetite."

Comment. Just about every book on crisis management mentions the disparity between the court of law and the court of public opinion. Our experts underscore that with real-life examples of how it impacts planning for crisis response. Obviously it's a phenomenon that will never go away – and is greatly magnified by social media. But the key is to recognize that the two courts exist side by side and to develop crisis responses which anticipate the outcomes in both arenas.

How to Persuade the CEO

Given that lawyers and communicators will invariably disagree from time to time in their approach to a crisis, I asked my four experts what techniques they use to persuade senior management to help resolve differences.

Hemus explained the first step is to recognize the enormous pressure the CEO is under, to put yourself in their shoes, to empathize with the fact they are facing an extraordinary challenge, with great uncertainty, huge time pressure and severe consequences for those affected.

He said in instances where the CEO was taking advice he did not agree with, he keeps coming back to putting the best interests of the organization to the fore, not trying to win battles versus other advisors, including lawyers.

> "I have always found that the magic words with any attorney are: 'Nothing is going to be finalized without your approval'."
>
> Jonathan Bernstein

Hemus revealed his motto is "backbone and heart." Especially at times of disputed advice, backbone means you have to give the advice you believe is true, and heart is doing it with the best interests of the organization as the priority – "not because of your own ego or wanting to be seen as cleverer than whoever has given the other advice."

> *"The way I do that is – in a diplomatic way – to say, I can see why you have been given that advice, but have you considered X or Y or Z? Or, can I suggest you consider some of the pros and cons of that advice, and describe the upside but also the downside of that advice."*

Most importantly, he added, is to do that with humility, but always staying focused on the client's long-term interests.

Bernstein agreed that an important element of persuasion is to bring a different perspective to the decision-making dilemma, and to draw on personal expertise. He points out to the CEO – "based on my experience and citing examples" – where the other advice would lead. What the consequences would be, based on hard data and actual experience. He finds that anecdotes will sell to the CEO very well. "I worked with this or that company and this is what happened." If you can cite actual cases, particularly in the same industry the CEO gets the message.

"Over and again, I've had the same discussion with CEOs. I say, I understand and respect Counsel's opinion, but understand that you are going to take a lot more damage that way than you need to. And understand there is a way not to damage your legal case and still engage in at least some communication."

Binneman too emphasized the need for different perspectives. He commented that Boards are often made up of people who are influenced by their discipline, even if they don't realize it, and decisions are sometimes made at Board level before the communicator is involved. What's needed, he said, is lateral thinkers who can ask the important questions. How do you think the stakeholders will respond? What will the stockholders think?

He calls it systemic thinking – the ability to connect the dots other people don't see, to be able to be inside the box and yet think outside the box.

"You have to go in with really good intelligence if you want a seat at the table, then tell your clients what's going to happen next. That's how we earn our money."

Richard Levick

In a crisis situation, where a hard decision needs to be made, Binneman invariably puts emphasis on reputation – the reputation of the institution as well as the reputation of the individual concerned. He said there is always a dichotomy between any leader's understanding of their personal role in any situation as well as the company's role, and that needs to be fully explained.

"When I speak to leaders I always quote the famous African-American poet Maya Angelou – 'People will forgive you for making mistakes, but they will never forgive you for not caring'."

Levick sees persuasion not just through bringing different perspectives to the table but also through the ability to bring a big view to the conversation. If all you are going to do is talk PR tactics, then you might as well not be there. He advocates that communicators need to understand more outside their domain and bring intelligence. And by that he means real intelligence, "not just what you find on Google." Who are your adversaries? How are they funded? What's a win for them or third parties? What trends are emerging on social media?

More importantly, when it comes to making key decisions, he says persuasion may depend on being able to fully understand consequences and what follows.

> *"You need to understand fully the facts and the chronology, something that's seldom done. Easy as it is, you don't see a lot of chronology and dating events, what's going to come next. As a result people are responding rather than anticipating. So you need to say, here's all the things that are going to happen next."*

Bernstein reinforced the importance of the persuasive power of facts by summarizing his approach to decision-making under pressure.

> *"Lawyers and doctors may think they know everything, but you come in and give them some facts they might not have known before and show an understanding of what they do and explain how you are going to support them. I'm going to make your job easier. I'm going to make your outcome better."*

Comment. *Our experts' responses about how to persuade the CEO highlight one of the most important messages in this book – namely that lawyers and communicators can advise in a crisis but in the end it's the CEO and executive who have to make the decisions. As one of the lawyers interviewed for Chapter Two told me: "It's important that the client knows my job is to advise. But they don't have to follow my advice and I'm not offended if they don't."*

Who Leads?

Finally, I asked my expert panel two of the same questions we asked lawyers in Chapter Two – namely, who do you think should lead in a crisis? And what do you think should be done to improve the working relationship between lawyers and communicators to reduce and address conflicting advice?

When the lawyers in the international survey were asked who should take the lead in a crisis, most declared it should be them. However, there were several who said it should be the communicator and others felt it should be neither the lawyer nor the communicator, but the Client/CEO who takes the lead.

> "Lawyers are trained to win everything. But in real life there always has to be a sacrifice."
>
> Richard Levick

By contrast, my four global crisis experts were unanimous in their view that communications and legal need to work as a team to help the CEO take the lead and make the right decisions for the organization as a whole.

For example, Bernstein always tells the CEO: "Neither your attorney nor a crisis consultant are the ones ultimately responsible for the reputation of the company. You are." That the CEO's role is to listen to advice and make a decision in the best interests of the organization.

To remind the CEO where to take responsibility, Bernstein added that he creates a list of potential crises which could happen in that industry. He calls it the "oh sh*t" list because that's the reaction when the CEO sees all the issues in one place rather than thinking about them one at a time. As he explained, when you have all the issues – operational and reputational – on one page it's "pretty attention-grabbing."

Jonathan Hemus in his own words

> *"Where I find myself in conflict with legal advice I am driven by wanting to protect not just the organization, but all of the stakeholders affected by the organization.*
>
> *"I will then give my best advice to try and balance the advice which has been given by lawyers. One of the techniques I use is to ask the CEO what is their strategic intent in managing this situation. To get them to define clearly where they want to end up. What success looks like. How they want to be seen in 12 months time or even three years' time. To*

get them to reevaluate their decision-making, their course of action, based on that strategic intent.

"It comes back to understanding that the CEO is under enormous pressure, dealing with a situation they are not dealing with all the time. The legal route is sometimes quite attractive because it frequently requires you to keep your head down, say as little as possible, and that's quite appealing if you are feeling under pressure anyway.

"I believe an overly legalistic approach is rarely likely to take you to the place you want to be in the long term. It may be less painful in the short term, but it's rarely in the best long-term interests of the organization."

Hemus reinforced that some leaders can be overwhelmed with advice, or just as often, paralyzed by too much advice, too much time spent considering it, and unwillingness to make a decision. He said it's important to remember, as advisors, that "99 times out of 100 both parties have got what they perceive to be the best interests of the organization at heart." But it is also important for the advisors to recognize that they are not responsible for the decisions.

And it's crucially important for the CEO to recognize that it's ultimately their decisions, and no advisor is going to give them a cast-iron guarantee that what they are recommending will result in the right outcome.

Levick agreed that it's the advisors' role to help the CEO to make hard calls, but he also emphasized that, when it comes to *functional* leadership, it's not about legal or communication but about where is the greatest liability.

He said that is why – early on – you want to anticipate all of the liabilities and decide where the greatest liability lies, be it the stock price or brand, or if it's litigation or communication. And whatever the greatest liability is, that's the counsel that should lead. Speaking as a qualified lawyer himself, Levick added that lawyers will often assume it's always the legal liability, "but half the time it's not."

Once you know the worst liability, making difficult decisions becomes much easier. "Otherwise you are sitting there playing catch-up. The CEO is drinking from the firehose and having to make a decision and hasn't done the math."

> "In every crisis there comes a situation when you have to do the right thing versus what others might say is legally correct."
>
> Deon Binneman

Comment. *While some of the lawyers interviewed for Chapter Two firmly asserted that communicators should invariably take their cue from legal professionals, our experts were unanimous that neither "side" should lead in a crisis, and that both groups need to work together in a team. But they reinforced that the purpose of the team is not to pre-empt control but to help the decision-makers reach the best judgements in the overall interests of the organization.*

How to Improve

In conclusion, I asked the crisis experts what they think should be done to improve the working relationship among advisors, and their responses were well aligned with the lawyers we surveyed.

Binneman stressed the need for the lawyer and communicator to not only work together but to get in the same room and understand that you need to be able to communicate *and* act swiftly at a time of crisis – always remembering the formula: people first, environment second, money last.

The danger, he warned, is compartmentalization and the breakdown in relationship between, for example, the communicator and the legal counsellor. But this can be prevented "right from the start" if the lawyer and communicator spend more time together.

The same view was expressed by Levick, who agreed the lawyer needs a "strong, solid and trusting relationship" with the communicator. That's really important because in a crisis you are going to have to know and trust your legal counsel and your communications counsel in the middle of the night and make instantaneous decisions before you have enough information.

You are going to have to make what Levick called "Gene Krantz mission control go/no go decisions" without enough facts. In a crisis, so many decisions have to be made with only 51% of the information and you have to base it on experience.

"We're going to zig instead of zag, or we're going to take a hit on our stock price but we're going to do this, or were going to do the right thing even though people won't like it." Levick said you can only do that because the lawyers and communicators know and trust each other. Otherwise it's too hard to achieve.

Richard Levick in his own words

"During the Duke University Lacrosse scandal in 2006, when three team members were accused of rape, ABC news asked me to go on and talk about Duke. This was in the very early days. But something about the facts of the story in the first two days really bothered me.

"Obviously, we didn't know then that she was lying and we didn't know the prosecutor was failing to turn over evidence as required by law. But something wasn't right and Duke's position early on was: we're going to suspend the season, but we are going to examine this before we are willing to say whether the students did anything wrong. So they were taking a cautious but appropriate approach.

"I went on World News Tonight on ABC and said that is why, pragmatically, Duke are doing the right thing.

"A year later, out of the blue, I got a call from the Athletic Director at Duke. They had been exonerated and they were inviting lawyers and others to a big conference on what they had done right and what they had done wrong.

They asked me as the only communications person in America to speak there. I said to him: Why? We weren't involved.

"He said: Because I turn on ABC World News Tonight and you come on and I think Oh no we're going to get clobbered again. Then you talk about taking a reasoned approach, investigate the facts, put away the pitchforks. It may turn out the rape allegations are founded but they might not be. Let the jurisprudential process run its course and in the interim Duke had done what it's supposed to do.

"Most Americans, most people around the world, don't really believe in due process unless they are the defendant. He remembered and appreciated that."

Hemus cautioned that problems occur when advisors become evangelists for their particular area of expertise or craft and forget about the broader business situation they are dealing with. He said it's about "leaving your ego at the door" and recognizing that the situation won't be solved purely though communication or the law. That it's a team effort and we must not be blinkered but be respectful of the advice from all advisors.

He argued that one of the keys is for the CEO or the business to identify who are the likely advisors they will be working with in a crisis and ensure those advisors are part of the planning process – together. Work out in advance what the strategic intent is, and in principle sign it off. If you must, fight the battles before the crisis rather than during it.

The more time the lawyers and communicators spend working together building trust and a relationship, he said, and having a mutual understanding of how things will operate, the smoother it will be during the crisis itself.

> "More than anything else, communicators should come prepared to deal with the natural concerns of everybody in the C-suite, including legal counsel."
>
> Jonathan Bernstein

The theme of mutual understanding to reduce conflict in a crisis was expanded by Bernstein, who described the need for lawyers and communicators to understand each other's job better.

He has spent a lot of time talking to lawyers to understand what they do, what concerns them, and what red flags are for them. He admitted he had been surprised he didn't know some things which are particularly important to lawyers, such as how they would like communicators to work with them, and vice versa. Bernstein said you need to understand that routine matters, and that legal and communication and other components of the crisis response team need to know all about each other's roles and how to intersect with each other.

Speaking as a crisis consultant, he said attorneys need to "understand what we do and understand our value in supporting their litigation." That way makes it more likely they will get a positive legal outcome, which should be the goal for everyone.

Comment. While working as a team is a shared objective, our experts offered their own perspectives on how this can be done. There is no doubt there will always be differences between lawyers and communicators in the face of a crisis. But it is equally clear that the experts here, and the lawyers in Chapter Two, agree that the single most important factor in working better together is better understanding and respect for each other's roles.

Key Takeaways

- Conflict between lawyers and communicators is still very real but is improving.
- Executives need to become more social media savvy.
- Resolving conflicting advice requires diplomacy and understanding the impact on reputation.
- Fresh information and broader perspectives are key contributions to effective decision-making
- While advisors need to advise, the CEO must take the lead and make decisions.
- Better understanding and respect for each other's roles is the single most important factor in working better together.

Questions for Discussion

1. *Does having few followers on social media necessarily mean critics are not very credible?*
2. *While greater co-operation between lawyers and communicators is generally welcome, does it risk unhealthy compromises and weakening of valuable principles?*
3. *Is identifying and addressing the greatest financial or legal liability in a crisis consistent with ethical behavior and the greatest social good?*
4. *What's the best way to resolve conflict between risk to the personal reputation of the CEO and risk to the reputation of the organization?*
5. *Is an unhappy customer who takes taking their complaint straight to social media rather than to the company simply exercising their right to free speech?*

Biographies of the Four International Crisis Experts

Jonathan Bernstein

Jonathan Bernstein is based in California and is chairman and founder of Bernstein Crisis Management. He has more than 35 years of experience meeting clients' needs in all aspects of crisis management. He founded the e-newsletter *Crisis Manager*, currently read in 75 countries, and his article "The 10 Steps of Crisis Communications" has been reprinted in more than 20 languages. He has authored two books and is frequently interviewed by national and international media outlets such *as The Wall Street Journal, Rolling Stone, Bloomberg, CNN, CBC, NY Times and Wired.*

Deon Binneman

Deon Binneman is an internationally recognized keynote speaker specializing in crisis management and its link to reputation. Based in Johannesburg, South Africa, he has appeared on the platform at more than 125 conferences in 17 countries over the last 23 years. He has also advised public and private organizations including across Asia-Pacific and Southern Africa. He is widely published in trade and business publications and his newsletter *Powerlines*, on strategic reputation, has more than 16,000 international and local readers.

Jonathan Hemus

Jonathan Hemus is founder of Insignia, a specialist crisis management consultancy based in the UK. He has more than 25 years experience as a crisis management consultant working with world-leading companies, organizations and brands, coaching, training and rehearsing senior executives in North America, Europe, the Middle East and Asia as well as offering crisis counsel to international clients. He writes and lectures on crisis management and is a regular expert commentator for media including the *BBC, CNN* and *The Wall Street Journal.*

Richard Levick

Richard Levick is Chairman and CEO of LEVICK, working out of Washington DC and New York, which provides strategic communication counsel on the highest-profile public affairs and business matters globally. He has been named four times as one of "The 100 Most Influential People in the Boardroom" and is the co-author of four books and a regular commentator on crisis management. He is a frequent guest on prime time national and international television programs and his extensive media writing includes a regular column in *Forbes* magazine.

Chapter Eleven

What to Do Now

"Can you think of anything more permanently elating than to know that you are on the right road at last?"

Vernon Howard

Lawyers and communicators are usually keen to express their opinions, and some of the chapters here feature and reflect upon their views and actions.

However, the other key participant in crisis management is the CEO or decision-maker, and I have given many examples of CEOs who did the right thing (and sometimes the wrong thing) in the face of a crisis; how they struggle to balance responsibility and liability; and occasionally when they publicly state they are rejecting legal advice.

Yet the crisis decision-maker is central to this book and to effective crisis management. The truth is that an organizational crisis is a crisis *of* the management.

This chapter will help you to:

- Recognize the central role of the CEO in crisis management.
- Identify and address the major factors which build CEO reputation.
- Learn from weaknesses exposed in crisis simulations.
- Turn cases and examples into practical plans to protect your organization from a crisis.

In this book I have variously referred to the leader, or the CEO, or the decision-maker, or the most senior executive. In addition, I acknowledged in Chapter Two that it's sometimes not an individual but a team decision.

In this chapter I will only use the term CEO to identify the person who takes the lead in a crisis, and I want to speak directly to you as the CEO.

CEO Reputation

A central theme so far has been that nothing destroys reputation faster and deeper than a crisis or an issue mismanaged, and in Chapter Six I detailed the well-known data on how reputation accounts for a large, and growing, percentage of a company's market value.

Less well-known is how much your personal reputation as CEO contributes to the market value of your organization, and therefore the importance of your personal reputation when it comes to crisis management.

One of the biggest and most significant research projects in this area was a large international study undertaken for WeberShandwick in 2015.[386] The study surveyed 1,700 C-suite executives (excluding the CEO) across 19 countries in companies with annual revenue over $500 million. On average, the global executives attributed nearly half (45 per cent) of their own company's reputation, and 44 per cent of their value market value, to the reputation of their CEO.

The percentage of market value attributed to the CEO's reputation varied from as high as 68 per cent in Indonesia to as little as 25 per cent in the UK, with the USA coming in at 38 per cent. Even allowing for such variation, the extent of the perceived relationship between CEO reputation and market value was a remarkable finding.

The same survey also asked participants to identify the main benefits from having a positive CEO reputation. Not surprisingly the top benefit was "attracting investors," at 87 per cent, and just behind in second place, at 83 per cent, was "crisis protection," alongside "media attention."

Superficially this data might seem to be encouraging, and an endorsement of strong leadership. But it also highlights just how potentially vulnerable companies are when things go wrong. In terms of crisis management, this relationship is very much a two-edged sword and I have described many case studies of the shocking reputational and financial impact of CEO failure in a crisis.

---

[386] *The CEO reputation premium: Gaining advantage in the engagement era.* (2015). WeberShandwick. https://www.webershandwick.com/news/the-ceo-reputation-premium-a-new-era-of-engagement/

There is a huge library of material about reputation, with global authorities theorizing about how it is formed and how it is maintained.

But for our purposes, I believe that in the context of crisis management, there are three major factors which contribute to perceived CEO reputation – ethical behavior, social media presence and leadership. All three are largely in your hands as CEO.

Trust and Ethical Behavior

In Chapter Seven I discussed the various studies which reinforce the disappointingly and consistently poor reputation of business and business leaders. This continuing erosion of trust is starkly documented each year by the respected Edelman Trust Barometer, which analyzes the level of trust in big business and big government.

As a CEO you might imagine that it's competence which helps justify generous executive salaries. But in 2020, for the first time, the Edelman report broke down how competence and ethics stack up as components of building trust.[387] Ethics (at 76 percent) was three times more important as a driver of company trust than competence (24 percent).

Clearly, ethical failures and erosion of trust are closely related, and both can be cruelly exposed at times of crisis. Moreover, both factors have increased – and are likely to continue increasing – through the rise of social media and through escalating stakeholder and public expectation.

While it might be embarrassing to talk about poor CEO behavior, please don't underestimate its importance when it comes to crisis risk.

For example, a survey by CS&A and PR News in 2019 found that more than half of the 200 senior and middle managers who responded chose "ethics and compliance" as the most likely crisis to affect their industry, ahead of major

---

[387] Kitterman, T. (2020, February 14). Richard Edelman on trust in 2020: 'Make it happen'. *PR Daily*. https://www.prdaily.com/richard-edelman-on-trust-in-2020-make-it-happen/

accidents, product/service quality issues, mismanagement, cyber-attacks and other crisis risks.[388]

Similarly, a 2016 British study of 508 managers found that 40 per cent believed their own higher management was the single biggest risk of a PR crisis. And 30 per cent specifically identified the CEO, and their reputation, as putting the organization at risk of a crisis.[389]

Take the case late in 2019 when the Board of McDonald's sacked their CEO Steven Easterbrook after he had "demonstrated poor judgement" in a consensual but inappropriate relationship with a female employee.[390] The former CEO himself told staff he agreed and that it was time for him to move on.

However, the impact of CEO misbehavior is often a lot more than just temporary embarrassment. There can be very real financial impacts. Think no further than movie producer Harvey Weinstein, whose misbehavior, arrest and subsequent imprisonment led to the virtual destruction of the company he co-founded.[391] Another well-documented case from a few years earlier is when Hewlett Packard CEO Mark Hurd resigned after misusing his expenses to support a relationship

---

[388] Arenstein, S. (2020, February 5). 62% Have Crisis Plans, But Few Update Them or Practice Scenarios. *PR News*. https://www.prnewsonline.com/crisis-survey-CSA-practice

[389] Biggest PR crisis threat comes from higher management, say UK workers (2016, April 12). *Igniyte*. https://www.igniyte.co.uk/blog/biggest-pr-crisis-threat-comes-from-higher-management-say-uk-workers/

[390] Togoh, I. (2019, November 4). McDonald's CEO Steve Easterbrook Fired Over Consensual Relationship With Employee. *Forbes*. https://www.forbes.com/sites/isabeltogoh/2019/11/04/mcdonalds-ceo-steve-easterbrook-fired-over-consensual-relationship-with-employee/#1c727d493eec

[391] Barnes, B. (2018, March 19). Weinstein Company Files for Bankruptcy and Revokes Nondisclosure Agreements. *New York Times*. https://www.nytimes.com/2018/03/19/business/weinstein-company-bankruptcy.html

with a female contractor.[392] The company's shares fell by $10 billion in a day and more than $14 billion over four days.

Such losses are not isolated examples. An American study of 219 cases of arrests, lies or extramarital affairs of CEO and other top executives showed an average share value loss of $226 million in the three days after the revelation.[393] Furthermore, the stock prices of such companies fell in total between 11 and 14 per cent in the subsequent 12 months.

If you still have any doubt about why the issue of CEO ethical behavior is so important to crisis risk, consider the recent rapid rise in executive turnover. Outplacement firm Challenger, Gray and Christmas analyzed a record total of 1,640 American chief executives who left or were ousted in a single year.[394] Fortune magazine dubbed it "the great CEO exodus of 2019."[395]

The firm's report concluded that 15 departed amid "allegations of professional misconduct" and another 20 left "amid scandal." Of course, not all of these departures triggered a public crisis, but the implications for the future reputation of top management is unmistakable. In the report, VP Andrew Challenger spelled it out very clearly:

---

[392] Wood, Z. (2010, August 7). Hewlett-Packard boss Mark Hurd resigns as sexual harassment probe uncovers falsified expense reports. *The Guardian.* https://www.theguardian.com/business/2010/aug/07/hewlett-packard-mark-hurd-resigns

[393] Gianakaris, N. (2015, May 26). Sex, lies and their impact on a corporate reputation. *Drexel University News Blog.* https://newsblog.drexel.edu/2015/05/26/sex-lies-and-their-impact-on-a-corporate-reputation/

[394] Fitzgerald, M. (2020, January 8). 2019 had the most CEO departures on record with more than 1,600, *CNBC News.* https://www.cnbc.com/2020/01/07/2019-had-the-most-ceo-departures-on-record-with-more-than-1600.html

[395] Kelleher, K. (2019, October 2). What's behind the great CEO exodus of 2019? *Fortune.* https://fortune.com/2019/10/02/behind-great-ceo-exodus-2019/

"Following the #MeToo movement, companies were determined to hold CEOs accountable for lapses in judgement pertaining to professional and personal conduct, creating higher ethical standards at the C-level. What may have gone unrecognized or was downplayed in the past was not overlooked by boards, shareholders, or the general public in 2019."[396]

Sadly, despite the profile of #MeToo, this is no recent phenomenon. One long-term study by PWC showed that companies have in fact become more likely to dismiss their CEOs over scandal and improper conduct, such as fraud, bribery, insider trading, inflated resumes and sexual indiscretion.[397] According to the study, reasons for the trend include an increasingly suspicious public; more proactive governance and regulation; risks in emerging markets; the rise of digital communication; the 24/7 news cycle; and media amplification of negative stories.

Little wonder that trust is falling. For you as CEO, what's the bottom line of all these reports and statistics? Hopefully the answer is obvious. Bad executive behavior is a key crisis risk for every organization, and you need to set the culture and lead by example from the top.

"Without a champion nothing significant will occur with regard to any major program in an organization. This is especially true with regard to crisis management."

Ian Mitroff [398]

---

[396] Fitzgerald op cit.

[397] Koehn, E. (2017, June 16). Chief executives who lack ethics should be more afraid of public opinion than ever. *Smart Company.* https://www.smartcompany.com.au/people-human-resources/leadership/chief-executives-who-lack-ethics-should-be-more-afraid-of-public-opinion-than-ever/

[398] Mitroff, I. I. (2000). *Managing Crises Before They Happen: What Every Executive and Manager Needs to Know about Crisis Management.* New York: American Management Association.

Social Media Presence

My second major factor which contributes to perceived CEO reputation might not at first seem obvious, because social media is now so commonplace.

It's all too easy to find well-publicized instances when an ill-advised executive social media post had a disastrous outcome for personal reputation. Take for example PayPal Director of Global Strategy, Rocky Agarwal, who lost his job after abusing colleagues on Twitter.[399] Or AT&T executive Aaron Slator, dismissed for sending a text with a racially offensive photo and caption.[400]

Or my personal favorite, Royal Bank of Scotland Chairman Rory Cullinan who sent Snapchat messages to his daughter about how bored he was at meetings. Snapchat messages are supposed to quickly disappear, but his 18-year-old daughter captured screen grabs and unhelpfully posted them on Instagram with the message "Happy Father's Day to the indisputable king of Snapchat." Shortly afterwards daddy was out of his high-paying job.[401] I can only imagine the ensuing heart-to-heart conversation between the former CEO and a very, very sorry teenager!

Apart from such examples of needless, self-inflicted reputational damage online, social media presence is a substantial positive factor in CEO reputation.

---

[399] Gorman, R. (2014, 5 May). 'No excuses, zero tolerance': PayPal exec fired after bizarre late-night Twitter rant against colleagues he had known for less than two months. *Daily Mail*.
https://www.dailymail.co.uk/news/article-2620526/No-excuses-zero-tolerance-PayPal-exec-FIRED-bizarre-late-night-Twitter-rant-against-colleagues.html

[400] Dillon, N. (2015, 28 April). AT&T fires exec for sending racist texts and images, faces $100m employee discrimination suit. *New York Daily News*.
https://www.nydailynews.com/news/national/t-fires-exec-sending-racist-texts-faces-100m-suit-article-1.2202791

[401] Brinded, L. (2015, 1 April). Royal Bank of Scotland boss out weeks after these Snapchat pictures were put on Instagram by his daughter. *Business Insider*, UK.
https://www.businessinsider.com.au/rbs-boss-rory-cullinan-leaves-just-weeks-after-snapchat-pictures-were-unveiled-on-instagram-2015-3

For instance, the large international WeberShandwick study I referred to earlier reported that of the 1,700 senior executives surveyed across the world, a decisive 81 per cent said it's important for CEOs to have a visible public profile for a company to be highly regarded.[402] The report concluded that executives expect their CEOs to be publicly engaged if they want better corporate reputations.

Specifically, the report found that highly regarded global CEOs have a higher social media participation rate than the average CEO and are about three times as likely as CEOs with a weak reputation to participate on social media.

> "Being a social CEO has gone from reputational advantage to reputational must."
>
> Andy Polanksy, WeberShandwick[403]

The link between social media and CEO reputation was reinforced by a 2017 report issued by Hootsuite, which described how nearly 86 per cent of executives in Australia, New Zealand and Asia believe having a social CEO is positive for a company's reputation, and 76 per cent believe it enhances credibility in the market.[404] Moreover, the vast majority say a social leader has a positive impact on business results.

The word *credibility* is really important here. As a CEO you may have concerns about the rise of celebrity CEOs and how some of them seem more interested in headlines than doing the right thing for the company. However, these days the focus is generally less on celebrity and more on credibility. Which means you need to have greater visibility and greater online presence, but with a purpose and not just pursuit of celebrity.

It's also important to recognize that it's not just business executives who have drawn this conclusion. A public opinion survey by G&S Communications and Harris Poll of more than 2000 American adults reported that over half (54

---

[402] The CEO reputation premium. op cit

[403] *Socializing your CEO IV: The engagement factor.* (2018). WeberShandwick https://www.webershandwick.com/wp-content/uploads/2018/04/SocializingYourCEO_FINAL.pdf

[404] *The social executive: How to influence trust, transparency and the bottom line.* (2017). Hootsuite. https://hootsuite.com/resources/social-executive-apac

percent) say senior leaders who are transparent on social media are most trustworthy.[405] They also found that nearly two-thirds (64 percent) say it's important that senior leaders have a presence on social media.

Likewise, the Hootsuite report disclosed that that three out of four consumers say a CEO's presence on social makes a brand more trustworthy, and companies with CEOs active on social media are perceived 23 per cent more positively than companies with inactive CEOs.

You might ask, if the benefits are so obvious, why do so many CEOs not have a significant presence on social media? Or why do they have a presence and yet fail to actively engage?

The barriers typically cited include lack of time; competing priorities; lack of expertise; uncertainty caused by past failures; lack of evidence of return on investment; or, legal discouragement.

None of these should prevent you from doing the right thing for your personal reputation and the reputation of your organization. Your communicator is there to advise you on how to do it, and your lawyer is there to make sure don't say the wrong thing or breach corporate disclosure laws.

Any concerns can and should be addressed, because compared to the risk of social media participation, the risk of non-participation can be an even greater threat.

---

[405] *Social Media & The CEO*. (2016). G&S Communications and Harris Poll. Cited in Socialising your CEO IV. op cit

Eight Tips for the CEO on Social Engagement

1. **Get online**. Invisible CEOs risk low reputation. Engage online to stay competitive, share messages and help control the narrative.
2. **Own real estate on the company career page**. Help drive recruitment. Research shows many global executives say their CEO's reputation influenced the decision to accept their job.
3. **Aggregate CEO communication**. Centralize CEO communications in one place on the company web page. With attention spans low, aim for easy access.
4. **Take advantage of video**. It humanizes the CEO, allows executives to speak directly to their audiences and is easily shared and reused.
5. **Author content and publish more widely**. Use CEO-written material to help establish thought leadership. Publish on both internal and external media platforms.
6. **Be more than just visible**. Engage and update content on social networks. If someone comments on a post, respond and show you care.
7. **Establish an authentic voice**. Lose corporate jargon. Communicate in a first person, familiar and relatable way.
8. **Be mindful of risks**. Online engagement is not without risks but is worth it. Be ready for the critics and develop a thick skin.

Adapted from *Socializing Your CEO IV*.[406]

The Role of Leadership

The CEO has a range of different roles in crisis management, and many of the examples and case studies in this book focus on what the CEO did – or failed to do – in responding to a crisis. They also focus on how the lawyer and the communicator should support crisis response.

In this respect, I have emphasized how crisis management is much more than simply responding to a crisis when it happens, In addition there is the need to prepare for the crisis in advance; to take actions to prevent or minimize a crisis; and also to recognize the importance of adverse developments after the crisis,

---

[406] Socializing your CEO IV. op cit

which can last for months or years and can be more damaging than the crisis event itself.

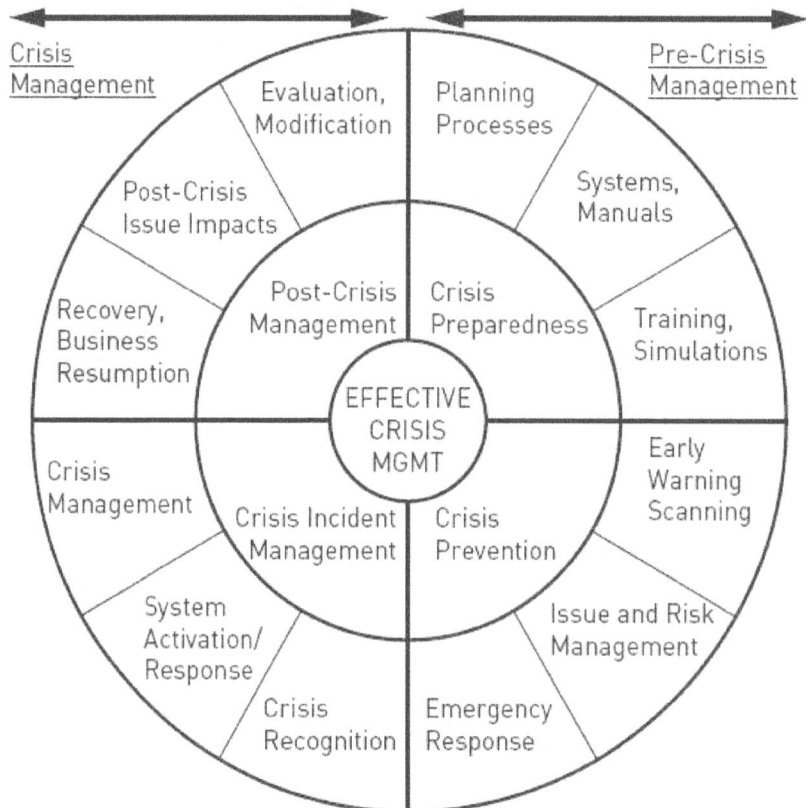

Figure 11-1 The Integrated Non-Linear Crisis Management Model

My original model shows how the main phases of crisis management are integrated and shows the various phases in which the CEO can play a part.[407] It also introduces the idea of pre-crisis management, and its component elements.

---

[407] Jaques, T. (2007). Issue Management and Crisis Management: An Integrated, Non-linear, Relational Construct. *Public Relations Review, 33*(2), 147-157.

The detailed mechanics of how to set up a crisis management team and how to manage a crisis on an hour by hour basis are outside our scope here (and are covered in full in my earlier book *Crisis Proofing: How to save your company from disaster* [408]). Many of these activities are typically assigned to different managers within the organization with relevant technical expertise.

But beyond your role as CEO in overseeing process and implementation, you have a specific leadership role in crisis awareness and preparation, which is the third of my factors linking CEO reputation and crisis effectiveness.

I have often referred to the cost of crises – particularly in Chapter Three – and it seems to me a safe guess that the frequency of crises and their cost can only increase.

For example, a global initiative by Deloitte in 2018 surveyed over 500 senior crisis management executives and found that 60 per cent believe organizations face more crises today than they did 10 years ago.[409] Sadly the same study concluded that while nearly 90 percent of respondents were confident in their organization's ability to deal with a corporate scandal, only 17 per cent of organizations have tested the assumption through simulation.

Similarly, a 2020 survey of senior executives in Australia and New Zealand showed almost 80 percent believe the risks affecting their organization have increased in the past three years, yet only 15 percent in Australia had confidence in their ability to effectively carry out their crisis communication plan.[410]

At a global level, the 2020 annual report of the Institute for Crisis Management, in South Bend, Indiana, tracked more than 760,000 news reports of business crises

---

[408] Jaques, T. (2016). *Crisis Proofing: How to save your company from disaster*. Melbourne: Oxford University Press.

[409] *Despite Rising Crises, Deloitte Study Finds Organizations' Confidence Exceeds Crisis Preparedness.* (2018, June 25). Deloitte. https://www2.deloitte.com/us/en/pages/about-deloitte/articles/press-releases/deloitte-study-finds-organizations-confidence-exceeds-crisis-preparedness.html

[410] Reputation Reality 2020: Getting ahead of the game (2020). Melbourne: SenateSHJ. https://www.senateshj.com.au/assets/files/Reputation-Reality-Report-web.pdf

worldwide, of which 27 per cent involved sudden crisis events and 73 per cent arose from what the ICM calls "smoldering crises" – where the organization concerned could have and should have taken early action to prevent or mitigate what happened.[411]

ICM President and CEO Deborah Hileman warns that management denial remains the most common reason organizations are unprepared for a crisis. "Boards of directors are still disengaged with the potential for crisis," she said, "and executive managers fail to invest in much-needed crisis planning and preparedness efforts."

> "People who behave best in a crisis are not those with the best plan, but those who are value-driven."
>
> John Scanlon[412]

At the same time, cybercrime and IT failure is certainly one of the fastest growing causes of organizational crises. It has been said that there are two sorts of organizations – those which have had a data breach and those which don't yet know they've had a data breach.

The British research company Juniper predicted in 2019 that the cost of cybersecurity breaches would rise by nearly 70 percent over the next five years – increasing by about 11 percent a year from $3 trillion in 2019 to over $5 trillion in 2024.[413] In addition a major global study by management consultancy EY in 2019

---

[411] ICM Annual Crisis Report (2020). South Bend, Indiana: Institute for Crisis Management. www.crisisconsultant.com

[412] Cited in Fitzpatrick, K. R. (1995). Ten Guidelines for Reducing Legal Risks in Crisis Management. *Public Relations Quarterly, 40*(2), 35-38.

[413] Cybersecurity breaches to increase nearly 70% over the next 5 years (2019, August 27). Juniper Research. https://www.juniperresearch.com/press/press-releases/business-losses-cybercrime-data-breaches

reported that CEOs see cybersecurity as the "number one threat to the global economy" over the next five to ten years.[414]

While these reports and predictions are not necessarily a surprise, the really worrisome element is the common theme of lack of preparedness, and lack of capability to identify potential crises. This calls for strong leadership from the CEO.

In Chapter One I quoted the crisis management pioneer Steven Fink:

> *"You should accept almost as a universal truth that when a crisis strikes it will be accompanied by a host of diversionary problems. As a manager, your task is to identify the real crisis."*[415]

This same sentiment was expressed many years later by Harvey L. Pitt, former chairman of the U.S. Securities and Exchange Commission, who warned:

> *"One of the most difficult problems facing executives is confronting the fact that a crisis actually exists."*[416]

Make no mistake. When the CEO fails to properly recognize a crisis there can be a very high cost to pay.

Take the notorious case of former FIFA President Sepp Blatter. When the football governing body was accused of corruption in 2011, he famously responded: "Crisis? What is a crisis? We are not in a crisis, we are only in some difficulties

[414] Taylor, C. (2019, July 9). Cybersecurity is the biggest threat to the world economy over the next decade, CEOs say. *CNBC*. https://www.cnbc.com/2019/07/09/cybersecurity-biggest-threat-to-world-economy-ceos-say.html

[415] Fink, S. (1986). *Crisis Management: Planning for the Inevitable*. New York: American Management Association.

[416] Cited in Levick, R. S. (2010). *The Communicators: Leadership in the age of crisis*. Washington DC: Watershed Press.

and these difficulties will be solved inside our family."[417] Four years later, facing renewed allegations, Blatter was finally forced to resign.

Or consider the infamous Ford–Firestone crisis, when more than 200 deaths were attributed to tire failures, over half of them involving Ford SUVs. Ford CEO Jacques Nasser admitted before a Congressional committee that, despite replacing tires overseas, Ford held off taking action in the United States "…because review of its various databases assured the company there was not a problem here." [418]The databases might have suggested "not a problem here," but the eventual result was one of the largest tire recalls in history.

This same problem was rather more colorfully expressed by Intel boss Andy Grove in the wake of the Pentium Chip crisis, which was explored in Chapter Three:

> *"Most CEOs are in the center of a fortified palace, and news from the outside has to percolate through layers of people from the periphery where the action is. I was one of the last to understand the implications of the Pentium crisis. It took a barrage of relentless criticism to make me realize that something had changed and that we needed to adapt to the new environment."[419]*

I have also experienced this personally. On one occasion, in the course of a research project, I interviewed the CEO of a listed high-reliability organization (HRO), which means it operates in an industry where normal accidents can be expected due to risk factors and complexity. In other words, the risks to people

---

[417] Scott-Elliott, R. (2011, May 31). Crisis? What crisis? Blatter tries to rise above corruption claims. *The Independent.*
https://www.independent.co.uk/sport/football/news-and-comment/crisis-what-crisis-blatter-tries-to-rise-above-corruption-claims-2291083.html

[418] *The Ford-Firestone Case* (2013). New York University. Leonard N. Stern School of Business case study.
http://www.yoest.com/wp-content/uploads/2013/02/ford_firestone_case-study.pdf

[419] Grove, A. S. (1996). O*nly the Paranoid Survive: How to Exploit the Crisis Points That Challenge Every Company and Career.* New York: Currency/Doubleday.

and the environment from a mistake if you are manufacturing woolen socks is far less than the impact of a mistake if you are making commercial aircraft or nuclear power plants.

During our interview it became obvious that the company had no effective crisis management plan, and when we had concluded the formal interview the CEO said: "I really need you to come in and help us get some proper crisis protection in place."

That's what I do, and when I followed up a couple of weeks later he replied: "Yes, we need to talk, but right now we are fully occupied with our end of year close."

I followed up twice more, and on each occasion he had a "reason" not to proceed. It was apparent he had no genuine intention to do anything about it.

A few months later his company was in the news after a process worker was killed in a factory accident which was later shown to have been entirely preventable. Maybe a crisis plan with a thorough risk assessment just might have saved that life.

My British associate Jonathan Hemus (introduced in Chapter Ten) says denial is the enemy of crisis management, and two **separate forces** are at play when senior managers attempt to deny there is a major problem.

The first is a bias towards optimism – the assumption is that nothing can go wrong, and success is sure to continue. The second force at play is willful blindness – when top executives don't or won't hear bad news.

That's the challenge for *you* as CEO.

Lawyers and communicators can play an important role. For lawyers it's particularly in identifying new laws or regulations which may place the organization at risk and advising on any potentially damaging decision which could generate adverse legal consequences. In the case of communicators, they are expected to monitor the environment for potential crises and maintain close relationships with stakeholders to bring warnings and critical perspectives to management. Some people call them the organization's reputation watchdog.

While lawyers and communicators can advise, you will need to ensure processes are in place for vital crisis information to break through "layers of people from the periphery where the action is." And as CEO you need to listen to potentially bad news and to take action.

> "A crisis is like a heart attack. It's not over if
> you don't change your lifestyle."
>
> Eric Bergman[420]

One of the important lessons I have learned from my own work, and from researching crises, is that in just about every case there is someone, either inside or outside the organization, who says after the event; "Oh yes, I knew about that." And oftentimes they go on and say: "I did try to warn someone, but no one listened to me."

Think no further than the case of Smith Dharnasirajo. It's not a name you will know, but in 1998 he was the Chief Meteorologist in Thailand who predicted that a major tsunami would hit the coast of Thailand, and he recommended building a $20 million detection and warning system. But the Thai government was deeply concerned about the possibility of panic and loss of potential tourism. His proposal was ignored, and Smith was fired.

A few years later, in December 2004, came the disastrous Indian Ocean earthquake and tsunami which cost Thailand up to 10,000 lives and billions of dollars. The only good news was that Smith Dharnasirajo was later reinstated.[421]

Or consider the tsunami which struck Japan in 2011 and destroyed the nuclear power plant at Fukushima, triggering one of the world's worst nuclear accidents. Plant engineers warned as long ago as 2008 that the seawall was nowhere near high enough to protect against a tsunami of 10.2 meters high, but management rejected that scenario as "unrealistic." In fact, the tsunami in March 2011 swept in at over 14 meters.

Or think about when the US Emergency Management Agency (FEMA) staged a massive five-day exercise in 2004 based on a fictional Hurricane Pam striking New

---

[420] Bergman. E. (2016, April 13). A crisis is like a heart attack. *Blog At ease with the media.*
http://www.presentwithease.com/aewtm_files/crisis-heart-attack.php
[421] Barta, P. (2005, January 11). Thai Official Once Reviled for Tsunami Prediction Back in Charge. *The San Diego Union-Tribune.*

Orleans and creating a storm surge which topped the levees and flooded much of the city. Some critics argued at the time that the simulated event was far too expensive and unrealistic. But just over a year later – in August 2005 – Hurricane Katrina devastated New Orleans in almost identical fashion and became the costliest natural disaster in American history.

After the real hurricane – and despite the eerie similarities with the crisis exercise – Homeland Security Secretary Michael Chertoff argued that it was "particularly unpredictable" and "exceeded the foresight of planners and maybe anybody's foresight."[422]

It's very telling that the official Congressional report into the response to Hurricane Katrina was titled: "A Failure of Initiative." The report concluded that while there was no failure to predict the inevitability and consequences of a monster hurricane, there was a failure to take action and improve the level of protection.

> *"Too often there were too many cooks in the kitchen, and because of that the response to Katrina was at times overdone, at times underdone. Too often, because everybody was in charge nobody was in charge ... If 9/11 was a failure of imagination, then Katrina was a failure of initiative. It was a failure of leadership."[423]*

---

[422] Lipton, E. and Shane, S. (2005, September 4). Homeland Security Chief Defends Federal Response. *New York Times.* https://www.nytimes.com/2005/09/04/us/nationalspecial/homeland-security-chief-defends-federal-response.html

[423] Select Bipartisan Committee. (2006). *A failure of initiative: Final report of the select bipartisan committee to investigate the preparation for and response to Hurricane Katrina.* Washington, DC: US Government Printing Office. https://www.congress.gov/109/crpt/hrpt377/CRPT-109hrpt377.pdf

Initiative:

Energy or aptitude displayed in initiation of action.

Source: https://www.merriam-webster.com/dictionary/initiative

A similar response played out in 2019 when the US Government staged a series of crisis exercises in Washington DC and 12 states based on a fictional scenario – codenamed "Crimson Contagion" – based on a respiratory virus which began in China and rapidly became a global pandemic.[424]

A draft report on the simulation, obtained by the *New York Times,* revealed just how underfunded, underprepared, and uncoordinated the Government would be, but the newspaper said little was done.

When the real coronavirus struck just a few months later, President Trump said: "Nobody knew there would be a pandemic or epidemic of this proportion... Nobody ever thought of numbers like this."[425] But as the Times pointed out, Crimson Contagion had in fact simulated such numbers and was startlingly similar to the real crisis.

---

[424] Sanger, D. E., Lipton, E., Sullivan, E. and Crowley, M. (2020, March 19). Before Virus Outbreak, a Cascade of Warnings Went Unheeded, *New York Times.* https://www.nytimes.com/2020/03/19/us/politics/trump-coronavirus-outbreak.html.
[425] Sanger et al, ibid.

	12 Tips to Get the Most from Your Crisis Simulation
1	**Avoid repetitious scenarios**. Instead of predictable operational crises such as accidents or disasters, mix it up with management scenarios like a cybersecurity breach or a perceived executive wrongdoing. Research shows these crises are typically high on the list of what's most probable.
2	**Keep it realistic**. If the participants think the scenario is wildly improbable, it becomes an excuse not to take the exercise seriously. You lose both credibility and meaningful learnings.
3	**Have a plan.** The simulation is not just to exercise the team. It's to test your crisis response plan.
4	**Rehearse roles and responsibilities.** Ensure team members know their role and what is expected of them.
5	**Build bench strength**. Involve people beyond just the core team such as designated deputies or alternates. There is always a high chance that key players are absent when a real crisis strikes. Try a simulation with some key managers designated as uncontactable.
6	**Vary the process**. In addition to a traditional tabletop exercise consider a full-scale production with external people playing roles. It can be more expensive but certainly adds realism.
7	**Review a real-life crisis**. To avoid training fatigue, instead of a hypothetical scenario, workshop a recent crisis or near miss which happened to another organization. What can you learn from their experience? Would you have managed it any better?
8	**Simulate media response**. Make the participants develop and practice delivering specific key messages for traditional and social media, and simulate a media conference.
9	**Spring a surprise.** Try not scheduling it weeks in advance. Real crises happen at any time. Will your process work at short notice, at night or at the weekend?

12 Tips to Get the Most from Your Crisis Simulation	
10	**Assess your team performance.** What went well during the exercise? Were any process shortcomings exposed? What needs improvement? Then test again.
11	**Do it regularly.** Hold a full simulation at least once a year and preferably more often. Crisis preparedness is a marathon, not a sprint
12	**Learn from the simulation.** This is not a box-ticking exercise. Use it to honestly identify risks and problems in the plan and in the organization. Commit time and resources to follow up whatever needs attention while there is still time.

Although organized crisis simulations are a staple tool of executive training, and provide a valuable opportunity to test organizational preparedness, they are also a real test for your leadership as CEO.

The communicator or another manager will typically set up the simulation and facilitate the process. But you need to demonstrate you are fully committed, and you need to get buy-in from all participants.

From my experience facilitating scores of crisis simulations, there is nearly always some crisis team member who thinks it's "just an exercise" and wants to send a deputy. It's often the same person who would refuse to evacuate when there is a fire drill and tells the floor warden they're too busy to leave their desk.

You need to remind the recalcitrant that if it was a real crisis, they would drop every other priority for days, weeks, or even months. It's simply not an option to find reasons not to set aside perhaps half a day for a simulation designed to help prevent a crisis happening in the first place.

Without your leadership and commitment – and an understanding of why wholehearted participation is important – the exercise is doomed to fail.

Moreover, even if the simulation exercise is well-attended and enthusiastically executed, there are two potential problems.

The first is the false and dangerous idea that once you've completed a scenario drill, the job of getting ready for a crisis is done. It is not a box-ticking exercise which you can set aside until next time someone thinks crisis management might be important.

The second problem, as shown in my hurricane and pandemic examples, is failing to learn. A simulation should be able to identify gaps and weaknesses in preparedness and prevention which may need to be remedied. And it's you as CEO who must drive change to become fully crisis prepared.

Where to Start?

Every chapter of this book has recommendations and suggestions about how to make the best use of lawyers and communicators to get your organization crisis-prepared and to respond effectively when a crisis strikes.

It doesn't make sense to restate them all here, but I am conscious you may ask: "What are the highlights. Where do I start?"

While the priorities will differ for each organization, depending on the nature of your business and the status of your existing crisis management processes and preparedness, there are some key actions which I believe every organization should implement.

(1) Establish an effective plan
- Appoint a senior-level crisis management team including the lawyer and communicator.
- Document roles, responsibilities and reporting lines.
- Establish and equip a crisis management location.
- Establish processes and enforce expected performance standards.
- Designate and train authorized spokespersons.

(2) Test preparedness
- Objectively assess the full range of risks.
- Commit to regular crisis simulations and other training.
- Monitor and manage the news media, including social media.
- Act on any weaknesses or risks exposed by simulation exercises.

(3) Map and build relationships before the crisis
- Promote open, upward communication.
- Appoint trusted and experienced internal and external advisors.
- Provide a framework for lawyers and communicators to meet regularly.
- Formulate a process to resolve conflicting advice.

Key Takeaways

- Lack of crisis preparedness continues to be a major hurdle.
- Recognizing and responding to crisis warning signs is critical.
- Stakeholder expectations are placing increasing demands on management.
- CEO reputation is crucial in crisis preparedness and management

Questions for Discussion

1. *Why do studies around the world consistently show that crisis awareness is up yet crisis preparedness remains stubbornly inadequate? How would you change that?*
2. *Are ethical breaches really becoming more frequent, or are they now simply more visible and less tolerated?*
3. *Why do organizations so often ignore the lessons which emerge from crisis simulations? How can that risk be reduced?*
4. *What element of an organization's culture, or misalignment with values, could be a warning sign of a potential crisis? How might that be identified and rectified?*
5. *Is it inevitable that trust in big business and big government will always be so low? Do we have to accept as a reality?*

Chapter Twelve

Looking Forward – A Personal Perspective

"Prediction is always difficult, especially about the future."

Niels Bohr

The great Danish physicist Niels Bohr famously warned about the danger of prediction, and so I will avoid any specific forecasts about how legal and communications advice will be given and managed in future crises.

Instead I plan to focus on my experience of the changes which have occurred and, more importantly, where we are going and how I believe crisis management will evolve in a social media savvy, #MeToo-aware and post-COVID-19 world.

Early in my career, I attended an executive meeting assembled to address a particularly knotty crisis strategy question. During the discussion, I very unwisely went far beyond my professional competence and expressed some overconfident opinions about the legal implications of what was being proposed.

The corporate lawyer, very calmly and very politely said; "Remind me Tony, which law school did you graduate from?" It was a well-deserved rebuke and I resolved, there and then, never again to make the same mistake.

Looking back I understand how my embarrassment then characterized an issue today at the heart of how to navigate conflicting crisis counsel – that *lawyers and communicators need to respect each other's expertise and need to work better together in the interests of the whole organization.*

Over my professional career in communication in the ensuing years I have worked with many lawyers, mainly in a corporate environment and most often in relation to high-profile issues and crises. At one stage I led an international issue project with lawyers as members of my team and, as I said in Chapter One, I have found lawyers largely to be cooperative, supportive and respectful.

However, I have also witnessed lawyers and communicators clash over how to proceed in a crisis, placing executives in a position where they need to understand and resolve conflicts.

More recently I have identified a number of trends which have changed our approach to crisis management, and which I think will continue to shape how we manage crises and how we work together in the future.

Professionalization of Communication

The first development is the increasing professionalization of communication. While this should mean executives will be able to secure more professional crisis advice, there will of course always be high profile executive mistakes and crisis management disasters as recounted in this book.

In Chapter Two on lawyers' insights, and Chapter Ten on the opinions of global crisis experts, it is clear both "sides" judge there is improving mutual respect and cooperation between lawyers and communicators. In addition, they see a need for better understanding of each other's roles and of the need to work together.

Although some of the lawyers interviewed in our survey expressed persistent distrust of communicators, I believe increasing professionalization of communication will reduce that distrust and improve the quality of advice to senior management in a crisis.

When I started working in this field, many professional communicators were recruited straight from journalism without any specific training, and many of their bosses also lacked any real depth of strategic and tactical communication skills.

That is now changing, and I am confident it will continue to change. Well-trained young communicators are increasingly taking over management roles in the discipline and providing a new level of professionalism. They are bringing formal education to understanding of crisis management and how to advise top executives – a trend which is evident around the world.

Having taught part-time at universities for more than 20 years, I can see the impetus of this professionalization will be sustained in the future only if we update and expand training for crisis management to meet the environment which is emerging, with new standards and new expectations.

Similar professionalization can be seen in not-for-profit groups and major activist organizations with many senior roles gradually being filled by tertiary-educated managers.

To be clear, I am not suggesting that a tertiary education necessarily makes a good communicator, nor that good communicators necessarily require formal vocational training. It also does not mean bad communication counsel won't sometimes continue to damage organizational response and reputation.

But broadly speaking it's becoming less likely the communication function will be led by a lawyer or an engineer or the HR Director, with a greater prospect that executives facing a crisis in the future will receive more informed and professional communication advice.

Overall, expert communicators (either in-house or at reputable agencies) have a greater understanding of the mechanics of how crises emerge and expand, and have experience or in-depth knowledge of the detail and background to what has worked or failed in the past – and why. They can also offer advice more reflective of the business reality and the experience and expectations of the full range of internal and external stakeholders.

At the same time, lawyers are becoming more aware of the need to protect organizational reputation as well as pursuing legal victory. This is not so much about increasing professionalization, but more about a growing recognition by lawyers of that classic concept that you can "win in the court of law yet lose in the court of public opinion." There is also the continuing reality that the law proclaims a person (or an organization) innocent until proven guilty while the court of public opinion often declares them guilty until proven innocent – and there is no chance of that changing anytime soon.

Functional Encroachment

While increasing cooperation between lawyers and communicators is generally welcomed, somewhat less universally welcome is a growing tendency to blur distinctions between how they contribute to crisis management. Whether you call it encroachment by lawyers into communication, or legitimate professional expansion or integration, depends on your point of view. Some critics have even called it "functional imperialism," though that seems to be going too far. But regardless of the label, it is a clear trend, and is accelerating

My own experience is this distinction between functions is increasingly breaking down and this will continue to influence the interaction between legal and communication advice in future crises.

Encroachment is already becoming more institutionalized, with many larger law firms offering in-house communication capability to provide clients an integrated package including communication. The same applies to some of the big accounting and management consulting companies, now offering programs for crisis planning and response, which may or may not be provided by communication professionals.

This trend goes further than functional encroachment and represents what is effectively a merging between legal and communication services, which is not necessarily for the better.

One of my colleagues was recently approached by a health provider for communication advice on a forthcoming sale and merger with another company.

She said the CEO told her their lawyers had advised them: "Don't worry about communication, we can manage that for you."

Her client's response, of course, should have been: "Yes, but will that be provided by one of your lawyers or by a competent professional communicator?"

There is nothing fundamentally wrong with a law firm offering a "package" of services, including communication, provided that additional service comes from a qualified professional (and some law firms do maintain standing contracts with external communication agencies). In addition, providing communication advice through a law firm may, in some circumstances, extend the umbrella of legal privilege.

Lawyers and communicators basically have different roles and different skills, and my experience is the law firm approach is often rather activity-focused, for example a spread sheet of who needs to be communicated with and when.

It can lack a more nuanced approach and a full understanding of the modern reality of the broader concept of stakeholders, which is often a much wider group than were once recognized.

The modern management consultant model adopted in the "integrated approach" to crisis management often tends to depend on templates, flow charts and systems, and has a strong focus on financial and stock-price impacts rather than broader public and community concerns and reputation. The bottom-line is, a cookie cutter approach when a crisis strikes simply isn't the best, for lawyers or communicators or the CEO.

Another area of encroachment which directly impacts crisis preparedness and response is how risk is managed. Risk assessment is too often focused mainly on financial risk, stock price and security risk.

When I talk to executives about their most probable crisis risks, a common response is: "We have a risk register and that's managed by our financial people". Then, when I ask who's responsible for non-financial risk, like harassment or discrimination in the workplace; or rumors on social media; or bad behavior by executives; or safety violations; or a host of other threats to reputation, there is often a resounding silence as the penny drops that these risks are not being properly addressed.

As I have said before, nothing destroys reputation faster than a crisis mismanaged. Reputation is a responsibility far beyond just the lawyers, governance and financial risk consultants. When a crisis strikes, the focus needs to be on corporate survival and long-term protection of reputation.

What's to Come?

One development which will undoubtedly change the future of crisis management is the continuation of the #MeToo movement. It has already altered the perception of crisis risk arising from behavior which may previously have gone unrecognized or been downplayed by boards, shareholders, or the general public. This change is certainly something we are going to see more of.

The other big event which will help shape the future is the COVID-19 pandemic. It has already changed the way we communicate, such as increased use of remote teleconferencing, and a more agile digital workplace. But in my view there will be two other, less obvious, impacts.

The first is a more sophisticated idea of what a real crisis is. I have previously mentioned the managers who misuse the word crisis to draw attention to their particular problem, and how misunderstanding of the nature of crises can lead organizations to overestimate their capacity to respond. After the coronavirus pandemic, organizations will have a much clearer idea of the real impact of a crisis and will be less prone to mischaracterize adverse events. That in itself would be a very positive outcome.

The second development from COVID-19 will undoubtedly be more organizations taking steps to put crisis management plans in place and to be better prepared. Even as the pandemic raged, organizations around the world were reviewing their crisis preparedness and asking what else they could have done.

My concern is how long this will last. We know from research that after the attacks on New York's World Trade Center and the Pentagon on September 11, 2001, there was a distinct spike in the number of organizations reporting they had a crisis plan in place. Sadly, we also know from research only a year later, that number started to fall back as complacency returned.

Preparedness to deal with a crisis has been one of my central themes and, if the past is any guide to the future, my expectation is many organizations will continue to deny the possibility of a crisis and will continue to suffer the consequences.

For this to change in the future, organizations need to assess their crisis risks with absolute honesty, and CEOs need to listen to the advice of counsellors and provide real leadership.

When I look forward at the changing nature of crises and crisis management, I expect the increasing influence of social media will be the central driving force. #MeToo was a movement whose time had come, but social media was the key facilitator. Similarly, COVID-19 simply accelerated in a very dramatic way how social media will change the way we work and operate.

I have given examples of how social media not only drove perception of selected crises, but in some cases was the triggering cause of a crisis. That will likely continue in the future, which makes it even more important that executives learn how to respond to online crises, and at the same time, that society develops better protocols about who controls and manages online platforms.

In Greek mythology Cassandra was the beautiful daughter of Priam, the last king of Troy, who was loved by the god Apollo. He promised her the power of prophecy if she would comply with his desires. Cassandra accepted the proposal and received the gift, but then refused the god her favors. Apollo revenged himself by ordaining that her prophecies should never be believed.

I make no claim to be gifted with the power of prophecy, but sometimes I feel a bit like Cassandra, knowing that as far ahead as I can see, some companies will never understand the need to be crisis-prepared, despite my efforts and the efforts and warnings of others like me.

I truly hope I'm wrong. One thing I know for sure is the future of crisis management lies in the hands of informed and foresighted executives, and their legal and communication advisors. For the best possible outcome for the organization's success and reputation, they need to navigate conflicting advice and work together.

Tony Jaques

INDEX

Figures are indicated by f following the page numbers.

Bohr, Niels, 339
Boy Scouts of America, 129
BP
    Deepwater Horizon oil spill (2010),
        201, 215, 252, 254
    Huntington Beach oil spill (1990),
        250–254
    reputational value of, 7
    Texas City explosion (2005), 44
Brands. *See also* Product crises; *specific
    brands*
    consumer involvement with, 69–70
    naming considerations, 174
    reputation of, 10, 86, 90
    top ten most profitable, 86
Breast implants, 270–271
Bridging technique, 219–220
British Airways data breach, 138
Brown, Gordon, 128
Buffet, Warren, 65
Burke, Edmund, 10
Burkhardt, Edward, 202–203
Bush, George W., 40, 215

C
Cameron, David, 161
Carnival Cruise lines, 99–103
Carroll, Dave, 107–110
Carson, Ben, 165
Catholic Church, apology for sack of
    Constantinople, 129
CEOs. *See* Chief executive officers
Challenger, Andrew, 320–321
Chaplin, Stewart, 261
Charities. *See* Not-for-profit organizations
Chemical industry, crisis management in,
    1–3
Chertoff, Michael, 333
Chewy Chips Ahoy recall (2019), 83

Chicago Department of Aviation, 111
Chief executive officers (CEOs), 315–337.
    *See also specific names of
    CEOs*
    Boeing 737 MAX crisis and, 71–75
    bonuses distributed to, 7–8
    credibility of, 135–136, 213
    in crisis management, 43, 46–47,
        103, 315
    decision-making by, 40, 44–46, 304–
        307
    denial of crises by, 329–332
    ethical behavior of, 318–321
    in facilitation of crisis simulations,
        336–337
    leadership in crises, 30, 54–55, 55*f,*
        248, 325–329
    message from lawyers to, 58–59
    over-exposure of, 213
    persuasion strategies for, 301–304
    reputation of, 317–324
    social media presence of, 298, 322–
        325
    as spokespersons, 207–209, 211–214,
        238
    trust of, 318–321
    turnover rate for, 320
    visibility during crises, 214–217
Chiha, Jessica, 166
China, business operations in, 89–91, 93–
    94
Christie, Chris, 161
Church of England General Synod, 129
Clair, Judith, 20
Coca-Cola, 168
Cognitive biases, 271–272
Cohen, Jonathan, 262–263
Cohesive voice, 213
Combative attitudes, 37, 272

ABOUT THE AUTHOR

Dr. Tony Jaques has spent much of his working life describing, researching and writing about crisis management, and helping to manage crises in government and in corporations.

As a government ministerial advisor, corporate executive and business consultant he has established an international reputation as an authority on issue and crisis management and risk communication.

In his role as Asia-Pacific Issue and Crisis Manager for The Dow Chemical Company for more than 20 years he was responsible for implementing local issue, crisis and community outreach programs

throughout the region and had a hands-on role in managing a number of high-profile crises.

He continues to serve as a thought leader in those areas with new projects to educate other fellow professionals as a conference speaker.

Dr Jaques is a New Zealander who now lives in Australia, where he runs his own consultancy and lectures post-graduate students at two universities. At an earlier stage of his career he was a journalist in New Zealand and London, and later worked as a management strategic advisor and speechwriter.

He has written very extensively about issue and crisis management.in academic and business publications around the world, and is the author of three previous books in the field – *Don't Just Stand There: the Do-it Plan for Effective Issue Management* (2000); *Issue and crisis Management: Exploring issues, crises, risk and reputation* (2014); and *Crisis Proofing: How to save your company from disaster* (2016). He is also the author of the definitive, three-volume *Dictionary of Battles and Sieges* (2006).

Dr Jaques is a former member of the Board of Directors of the Issue Management Council in Washington DC and received their Howard Chase Award for achievement in the field. He holds a doctoral degree from RMIT University (Melbourne).

Contact the author:

Email: tjaques@issueoutcomes.com.au

Website: www.issueoutcomes.com.au